LATE MODERNIST POETICS

MANCHESTER
1824

Manchester University Press

ANGELAKIHUMANITIES

editors
Charlie Blake
Pelagia Goulimari
Timothy S. Murphy
Robert Smith

general editor
Gerard Greenway

Angelaki Humanities publishes works which address and probe broad and compelling issues in the theoretical humanities. The series favours path-breaking thought, promotes unjustly neglected figures, and grapples with established concerns. It believes in the possibility of blending, without compromise, the rigorous, the well-crafted, and the inventive. The series seeks to host ambitious writing from around the world.

Angelaki Humanities is the associated book series of
Angelaki – journal of the theoretical humanities.

Already published

Evil Spirits: nihilism and the fate of modernity
Gary Banham and *Charlie Blake* (eds)

The question of literature: the place of the literary in contemporary theory
Elizabeth Beaumont Bissell

Absolutely postcolonial: writing between the singular and the specific
Peter Hallward

The new Bergson
John Mullarkey (ed.)

Subversive Spinoza: (un)contemporary variations
Timothy S. Murphy

ANGELAKIHUMANITIES

LATE MODERNIST POETICS

from pound to prynne

anthony mellors

MANCHESTER UNIVERSITY PRESS
MANCHESTER AND NEW YORK

distributed exclusively in the USA by Palgrave

Published by Manchester University Press
Oxford Road, Manchester M13 9NR, UK
and Room 400, 175 Fifth Avenue, New York, NY 10010, USA
www.manchesteruniversitypress.co.uk

Distributed exclusively in the USA by
Palgrave, 175 Fifth Avenue, New York,
NY 10010, USA

Distributed exclusively in Canada by
UBC Press, University of British Columbia, 2029 West Mall,
Vancouver, BC, Canada V6T 1Z2

British Library Cataloguing-in-Publication Data
A catalogue record for this book is available from the British Library

Library of Congress Cataloging-in-Publication Data applied for

ISBN   0 7190 5885 6 *hardback*
EAN   978 0 7190 5885 1

First published 2005

13 12 11 10 09 08 07 06 05   10 9 8 7 6 5 4 3 2 1

Typeset by Northern Phototypesetting Co Ltd, Bolton
Printed in Great Britain
by Bell & Bain Limited, Glasgow

'Sandhoppers' is an inadequate word for this Order, as comparatively few of them live in sand and fewer still hop. However a large number of individuals live between the tide marks, chiefly under stones and in the rotting seaweed at the top of the beach. (John H. Barrett and C. M. Yonge, *Collins Pocket Guide to the Sea Shore*)

CONTENTS

ACKNOWLEDGEMENTS

Late modernist poetics could not have been written without the generosity and critical acumen of Ann Wordsworth, Fiona Robertson, Tim Clark and Robert Smith.

I would like to thank the staff of the Bodleian Library; Jan Martin at the Library of Trinity College, Oxford; Simon Smith and everyone at The Poetry Library, South Bank Centre, London; and Professor Victoria Fromkin and the staff of the Research Library, University of California Los Angeles. Thanks also to Matthew Frost and Kate Fox at Manchester University Press and Pelagia Goulimari and Gerard Greenway of Angelaki Humanities.

The following people have been of immense help, both directly and indirectly, in forming this book: Don Mackenzie, Allen Fisher, Andrew Benjamin, Christina Britzolakis, Peter Larkin, D. S. Marriott, Andrew Duncan, Esther Leslie, Peter Riley, Iain Sinclair, Gareth Reeves, Terry Eagleton, Barry MacSweeney, J. C. C. Mays, Stephen Rodefer, Marjorie Perloff, Peter Middleton, David Chaloner, Wolfgang Gört-schacher, Sabine Coelsch-Foisner, Nate Dorward, Tom Raworth, Steve McCaffery, Karen MacCormack, Gavin Selerie, Frances Presley, Simon Glickman, Naomi Wolf, Andrew Lawson, Anthony Barnett, Rod Mengham, Antony Easthope, Ric Caddel, John Wilkinson, John Welch, Alan Halsey, Romana Huk, Robert Young, Geoff Ward, Mike Inwood and Sarah Wood, I am grateful to them.

Finally, I would like to dedicate this book to my mother, Pauline, and, in memoriam, to my father, Henry: teach us to care and not to care.

INTRODUCTION

This book explores the uses of obscurity in the poetry of the Pound tradition. As a literary theorist, I initially approached the subject of obscurity in formal terms as a question of how we might reassess the epistemological and ontological bases of modernist poetics in the light of later phenomenological, psychoanalytic and deconstructive criticism. But as I went deeper into research on the origins of modernism, I realised that one of its most important aspects – myth – seemingly done to death by criticism, was the subject of massive historical and theoretical confusion. Myth is such a familiar feature of the literary landscape that it has become almost invisible, an essential but intellectually banal item on the checklist of modernist 'themes', yet its handiness for competing schools of textual interpretation has obscured a fundamental problem of reception.

Critics remain divided as to whether modernists, and Pound in particular, treat myth as a metaphor for sceptical inquiry or as a spiritual reality. Put in terms of a misleading but still influential opposition: if modernism is a 'classical' reaction to 'romanticism', if it values the clean edge of intellect, imagistic precision, and masculine objectivity over mystical mumbo-jumbo, woolly rhetoric, and subjectivist *o altitudos*, how does one account for the modernists' obsessive interest in mythic symbolism, esoteric doctrines and mystery cults? The standard response to this question is to divorce myth from the occult by pointing to the influence on modernist writing of the relativist, anthropological discipline of comparative mythology, exemplifed by Sir James Frazer's *The Golden Bough*, which explains ritual practices as ways of ordering irrational phenomena. For this new 'science', myths are real only insofar as they can be seen as 'supreme fictions', intuitive representations of social and cosmic unity. Following this principle, the modernists latched on to any and every form of 'primitive' religious expression as part of a revolutionary strategy to shake the foundations of established patterns of thought and perception. While this sceptical and relativist approach might be true of the political avant-gardes, it hardly accounts for Anglo-American modernism's deeply reactionary belief in a secret tradition of divinely inspired wisdom, grounded in ancient fertility rites and destined for a new age of racial purity. Because this chthonic faith does not square with Pound's luminous, 'scientific' pronouncements on the nature of poetry, history and culture, it tends to be dismissed as little more than a flirtation with the spiritualist *Zeitgeist* of the late nineteenth century, just as Yeats's dabblings with the 'lunatic fringe' of Madame Blavatsky and the Golden Dawn is seen as tangential to his poetic identity. Yet Pound never rejected the theurgic ideas he formed during his time spent with Yeats at Stone Cottage, and came to regard them as fully compatible with his later objectives: 'I know . . . one man who understands Persephone and Demeter, and one who understands the Laurel, and another who has, I should say, met Artemis. These things are for them *real*.'[1] The conflation of mysticism with material 'evidence' is a characteristic of both Pound's poetics and occult speculation, and it is a central tenet of the twentieth-century preoccupation with alternative religious experience. Until recently, however, historians of modernism have been loath to make the connection between esoteric thought and positivist methodologies, possibly because their (well-founded) association of the occult with charlatanism threatens both the cultural value of modernism and their own academic legitimacy. Similarly, almost no critical attention has been given to the impact of the modernist occult on the 'late modernism' of mid-century American poetry and British poetry of the 1960s and 1970s. Again, this is because esoteric enthusiasm has been read in the same allegorical light applied to modernism as a metaphor for aesthetic experimentation and political idealism.

My research, however, finds that Pound treats the mythic method not as metaphor but as fact, and that understanding how this is the case entails a fundamental reassessment of the rôle played by mythic and esoteric thought in the poetics of obscurity and the political ideology of modernism and its offshoots. In extending modernism into a theory of 'late modernism', I am primarily interested in the work of those poets who, like Pound, have a problematic, ambiguous and at times even tenuous relationship with the occult, rather than with overtly mystical writers such as Robert Duncan, Robert Kelly and Allen Ginsberg.

The book begins by attempting to define the theoretical and ideological factors contributing to what I call 'late modernism' (schematically, occupying the period 1945–1975). Late modernist texts remain true to the modernist imperative that eclecticism and difficulty form a hermeneutic basis for cultural renewal, but their belatedness involves a disavowal of the unifying and totalising gestures of modernist aesthetics. At issue here is the distinction between 'modernism' and 'postmodernism': late modernism helps to identify a poetics which is neither a simple continuation of modernist practice nor a decisive break with modernism's various idealisations of the aesthetic. For all the recent critical energy expended on it, postmodernism remains a nebulous category, constantly falling back onto the modernist tenets against which it is defined. My purpose in creating a mediating category is to avoid the epistemological confusion surrounding postmodernism while offering a way of clarifying the historical issues. The term I use for this category has been used differently by others. In fact, its use in recent literary criticism has brought distinctive new problems of historicism. Tyrus Miller's recent book *Late Modernism* lays claim to 'a reemergence of innovative writing after modernism' and argues that 'the double life of this significant body of writing – its linkage forward into postmodernism and backward into modernism – has not, by and large, been accounted for by critics of this period.'[2] But the title is a misnomer, since the study is limited to what Miller calls the 'dissolution of modernism' in the 1920s and 1930s. In that case, modernism was dissolving almost before it had begun. I argue against this common misconception that modernism ended with the onset of World War Two; on the contrary, it continued to be the driving force of innovative art and literature in the post-war context. How can one describe modernist poetry of the 1930s as 'late', when American modernist epics such as Pound's *Cantos*, William Carlos Williams's *Paterson*, Louis Zukofsky's *A*, and Charles Olson's *The Maximus Poems* were either not completed until the 1970s or not even begun until the 1940s and 1950s? Moreover, British poetry did not get the modernist 'idea' in any real sense until the 1960s, when significant works such as Basil Bunting's *Briggflatts* and J. H. Prynne's *The White Stones* were published. And what is one to make of the rise of international trends in image- and sound-based poetry, or the emergence of one of Europe's greatest modernist poets, Paul Celan, whose major work was written between 1950 and 1970?

This book defines late modernism primarily by exploring the 'hermetic' poetry of Pound, Olson and Prynne. The first, preparatory, chapter sets out the historical bases of my argument, and the second chapter reexamines Pound's use of hermetic sources in the light of recent scholarship on the modernist occult. The hermetic in poetry is generally associated with forms of modernist writing deriving from romantic and symbolist models. Primarily, it describes works encoded with highly individualised symbolic meanings – two notable examples being Novalis's quest for the 'blue flower' and Mallarmé's nexus of 'white' attributes – but it can also be applied to the

Symbolists' efforts to purify language of base, commercial, and everyday meanings, an alchemical principle of the transubstantiation of matter designed to elevate poetry to the condition of music. Therefore, 'hermetic' refers to both the forging of private, enigmatic iconologies and the subordination of sense to sound, creating an interplay of deeply obscure significance and numinous vacancies. Occult symbolism derived from gnostic, Neoplatonic, and theosophical sources is used impressionistically rather than systematically, contributing to an aura of mystery and transcendence. The poetry of Valéry, Yeats, Rilke, Apollinaire, Ungaretti, Montale, and Stevens has been described as hermetic or as including hermetic elements.

Yet Pound, the poet who engages most seriously with the hermetic tradition, also denounces the Symbolist aesthetic for its lack of conceptual and presentational clarity. Pound's poetry is frequently described as obscurantist, but since his poetic theory from the invention of Imagism onward calls for the 'direct treatment of the thing', it would appear to be anything *but* hermetic. Pound's desire to have the objective world inform the imaginative space of the poem rather than allow subjective fancy to dictate reality is based on the classical virtues of clarity and the 'clean edge' of intellect, not on an occult rhetoric of impenetrable mystery. Moreover, he believed that 'the most pernicious literary and intellectual habits of Westerners derive from Jewish allegory, metaphor, hermeticism, and interpretation.'[3] The *Cantos*, however, are filled with mystical, pagan, Neoplatonic and alchemical references, and Pound's 'mythic method' inaugurated a modernist tradition which presents the poet as a shamanic figure spelling out the archetypal, spiritual values allegedly lost to rational technocratic society.

How is it that Pound demands a poetry stripped of obscurity and ambiguity but also cloaked in the dark light of arcane knowledge? The answer is political as much as poetic, and this conjunction is essential to modernism. For Pound, the Symbolists' artificial paradise is a travesty of 'real' symbolism which retreats from nature into lyric reverie. By contrast, symbolism in its profounder sense lays claim to a *Paideuma*, or 'culture-instinct', which stands against the enervated lifeworld of modern societies driven by an international conspiracy of Jewish financiers, emasculated by Judaeo-Christian religion, and stymied by dependence on mass opinion. The hermetic ideal in the *Cantos* is exemplified by a counter-conspiracy or secret tradition of what Pound calls 'intelligence' stemming from archaic mystery cults and presided over by Kore, goddess of redeemed nature, and Hermes, the phallic god of fertility who, in Eleusinian myth, guides Kore back from the underworld. For Pound, Hermeticism is a religious principle of light and love heralding the rise of Renaissance *intelletto* and justifying his own erotic theory of male vitality. The hermetic intellect combines reason and aesthetic intuition to form symbols of illumination against the 'tyranny of the syllogism, blinding and obscurantist'.[4] As a supposedly instinctual and holistic form of knowledge it is distinguished from modern rationalism, which divorces science from its roots in natural philosophy and privileges impotent analysis over vitalist faith. Thus Pound aligns wisdom, sensuality, science, masculine strength, myth, occult religion, and what he comes to call 'totalitarian faith' against logic, technocracy, feminine weakness, anality, ascetic religion, and democracy. He invests charismatic individuals such as Thomas Jefferson, John Quincy Adams and, ultimately, Mussolini, with redemptive historical power because their instinctual faith allows them to act virtuously rather than become mired in self-reflection and analysis. Mussolini becomes an occult magi or 'artifex' distilling political and economic order from the chaos of world history. His wisdom is guided by a force of destiny unacknowledged by those too ignorant to see it or too corrupt to allow it. Similarly, the *Cantos* are obscure because they are meant to contain wisdom which, although clear in essence, can only be imparted to the 'present knowers' committed to the act of intellection required to penetrate its *secretum*. Pound identifies the poet less with the figure of the magus than with the adept of occult scholarship, whose interminable commentaries on esoteric documents and supernatural 'evidence' make him (or her, in the case of Madame Blavatsky, Dion Fortune, et al.) the conduit of the divine mysteries.

The first, introductory, chapter explores the origins of hermetic poetry with the aim of theorising and historicising Pound's arcana and developing the theory of late modernism by comparing Olson's poetics of nature with that of Pound. Olson's best-known poem, 'The Kingfishers', is in part a riposte to Canto LXXIV, which elegises Mussolini by associating his execution at the hands of the Partisans with the flaying of Manes, another marytr to orthodoxy. Where Pound laments the death of Italian Fascism, sinking into historical pessimism, Olson sees the birth of a new redemptive era in the form of the Maoist revolution. Yet the poem's equation of praxis with the reclamation of a primordial sense of oneness with nature means that it cannot make an ethical distinction between productive and destructive kinds of revolutionary action. Its highly paratactic, 'open' form enacts an *aporia* of the call to act and the need to reflect on the consequences of action so that its Heraclitean mantra 'What does not change / is the will to change' becomes the central problem of history, not its solution. Olson tries to tough his way out of the negative influence of what he calls Eliot's 'symbology', which limits poems to being acts of comparative thought rather than allowing them to become actions themselves. But his faith in Pound's principle of *intelletto* as a viagra for Eliot's Christian impotence compromises his 'post-modern' rejection of Pound's reactionary politics.

Chapter 2 gives a more detailed account of modernism's reception of occult history, concentrating on Pound's use of hermetic ideas. Pound's essay on the Duocento poet Guido Cavalcanti complements Eliot's 'The Metaphysical Poets' in arguing that modern thought is abstract and dissociated, unlike the medieval and Renaissance intellect that posits reality as a network of identities and correspondences giving concrete form to what is abstract to the senses. Pound's main example is the 'modern scientist', who fails to extend his discovery of 'shapeless' phenomena to the totality of the natural world. Insisting on a division between literal and figurative truth, the scientist cannot bring imaginative substance to empirical observation: 'The rose that his magnet makes in the iron filings, does not lead him to think of the force in botanic terms, or wish to visualize that force as floral and extant.' By contrast, the medieval 'natural philosopher' 'would find this modern world full of enchantments, not only the light in the electric bulb, but the thought of the current hidden in air and in wire would give him a mind full of forms.'[5] In the context of Cavalcanti's *Canzone d'Amore*, this becomes an hermetic fusion of imperceptible spiritual realities with the perceptible images that correspond to them. Yet Pound's use of scientific paradigms suggests that he wants the correspondence between the visible and the invisible realms to be rendered in as objective a way as possible. He is attracted to the *Canzone d'Amore* because it offers a 'scientific' psychology of love which unites erotic energy with a Neoplatonic metaphysics of light. For Pound, the conjunction of desire and spiritual illumination in Cavalcanti's poem crystallises a vitalist tradition extending from the cult of Eleusis into Troubadour verse and the *Dolce stil nuovo*. The canzone's subversion of the medieval church's ascetic theology accounts for its textual obscurity, since any period in which Church and State combine forces to suppress natural wisdom makes it necessary to express radical ideas in language understood only by the cognoscenti.

The notion of a secret tradition veiling its heresies in symbolic texts is fundamental to the conspiratorial bent of occult history. While Pound rejects the theory that poetry of the Provencal *Trobar clus* (which means 'enclosed') and the Tuscan *stilnovisti* is based on allegorical codes and ciphers, he embraces the occultists' hostility to 'revealed' religions such as Christianity, believing that divine wisdom can only be the domain of inspired individuals and an elect group of 'knowers'. Hence the idea that Cavalcanti's 'message' is hidden because, as it were, it cannot speak its name, is beside the point; since reality can only be grasped by the intuitive intellect, its gnosis must involve obscurity: 'Verbal manifestation is of very limited use to the candidate. Any intelligent man has understood a great deal more than he has ever read or ever written or ever pushed into verbal manifestation even in his own mind.' What Pound calls 'the polytheistic anschauung', unlike Christianity, 'never caused the assertion that everyone was fit for initiation'.[6] Therefore, he can attest to the 'clarity and precision' of the canzone while admitting its textual obscurity.

However, the problem with self-evident but secreted truth is that it requires a commentator to tell the world that it *is* truth. Pound is too attracted by the authority of scholarly exegesis not to glean certainties from a poem that is radically uncertain. His translations and commentary on the 'clarity and precision of the text where it is clear' are not always clear themselves, and their attempts to express Cavalcanti's 'eclectic' meaning 'with the suavity of a song, with the neatness of scalpel-cut' suture gaps in the body of the text.[7] Crucially, Pound elides the 'dark' side of Cavalcanti's poetic in order to establish the 'whole' poem as 'a metaphor on the generation of light' derived from the Neoplatonic philosopher Robert Grosseteste.[8] Pound makes this idea a central structuring principle of the *Cantos*, bringing together the worlds of Confucius, Plotinus, John Heydon, the Scholastics, the *Paradiso*, John Adams, Mussolini and the troubadours: 'in midst of darkness light light giveth forth / Beyond all falsity, worthy of faith.'

Chapter 3 moves on from Pound's use of the psychology of the Amor tradition to Charles Olson's incorporation of Jung's occultist 'analytic psychology' into *The Maximus Poems*. Jung rejected Freud's view of the artist as a neurotic phantasist, arguing instead that art gives expression to archetypal images of the collective unconscious. He therefore considered the personality of the artist to be of less importance than the creative process made manifest in the work of art. Yet, if art is imbued with autonomy and universality in its use of archaic symbols, Jung's stress on its power to symbolise the creative development of the self heroises the artist in 'his' quest for spiritual unity. Jung bought heavily into the romantic cult of the artist as visionary, treating art as comparable with (if subordinate to) religious experience in its movement towards an ideal totality. Jung's concept of the Self is theorised as an holistic condition in which the (male) subject reconciles the imaginary coherence of the ego with the 'real' coherence of collective archetypes, nurtured by the desire to restore lost unity with the mother but extending to the apprehension of God.

Jung's belief that the conscious ego may be superseded by the unification of conscious and unconscious elements into a total personality lies at the heart of Olson's theory of poetic 'objectism'. Olson's prime figure of 'Maximus' (the 'Archeus' of Hermetic tradition) represents a shift from the isolated lyric ego to a universal poetic Self which embraces both the specific facts of history and the archetypes that supposedly underlie and give spiritual meaning to those facts. Olson regards the gathering of this knowledge as an esoteric process through which the individual poet achieves an organic reintegration of body, place, nature and history. I argue that although Olson's rejection of ego is coherent in terms of its critique of North American 'confessional' poetry, it nevertheless evades the problematic relation of the ego to the self in Jung's theory (as does Jung). Not only does the ego return to haunt the alleged 'completeness' of selfhood, notably in phallic imagery, but the ideology of totality informing the concept of the Self is always already undermined by its own rhetoric of transcendence and exclusion. Both Jung and Olson achieve their figures of identity by reifying stereotypical oppositions of race and gender rather than – as they claim to be doing – by overcoming them.

Pound's artifex and Olson's Maximus are versions of the artist as shamanic healer. They are not merely personae, but represent the central organising principle of a redemptive aesthetic. The Anglo-American avant-garde (including late modernism) finds in pagan religion the model for a unified, spiritual culture which offers an alternative to the perceived disorder of advanced captitalist society. Clearly, this is a continuation of the nostalgic tribalism familiar from the pronouncements of Eliot and Pound. But little critical attention has been given to the fact that, although the modernists' identification of the 'mystic man' of so-called primitive cultures has long been discredited as politically reactionary, its influence on the left-leaning, liberationist movements in mid-century poetry has been profound, and it is largely taken for granted today that the 'metaphor' of the poet as arcane magician affirms the revolutionary potential of the neo-romantic visionary. The poet Iain Sinclair, for example, lays claim to a vital link between the tribal healer's 'sickness-vocation' and countercultural politics. 'The health of the city,' he writes in *The Shamanism of Intent* (1991), 'and perhaps of the culture itself, seemed to depend on the flights of redemption . . . artists could summon and sustain. Icarus-bloody, they were twinned with all the other avatars of unwisdom: scavengers, antiquarians, bagpeople, outpatients, muggers, victims, millenial babblers.'[9] Sinclair's poets are modern alchemists who seek to transform the dross of urban life into spiritual sustenance – no coincidence, perhaps, that this tract is published by Goldmark – but whereas Pound's artifex disavows abjection, these traumatised visionaries meet it head-on, always running the risk that the chaos on which they 'improvise' will swallow them up. Sinclair defines this condition as 'deregulated shamanism', distancing his pull-quote apocalypse from the ritual order of the modernists. Yet his intention to fuse the 'heavenly and mundane' is close to Pound's *virtu*: despite the overtures to multiculturalism, the ideal remains one of purifying the language of the tribe, and the wish for 'health' is couched in the reified, monocultural rhetoric of *the* city and *the* culture.

As Sinclair's references to the work of the occult historian Mircea
Eliade indicate, his poetic revises the mythic anthropology associated with
Jung's theory of the collective unconscious. I argue in Chapter 3 that the
archetypal theory of self and community converts the racist, *volkisch*
theurgy of the Central European right into a liberal humanist ideology
centred on heroic self-transcendence. Its impact on post-war Western
culture has been vast, especially in the United States, where Jungian psychology and its offshoots have been a driving force behind (to give only
a few examples) Abstract Expressionism, the Beat movement, the redemptive narratives of Hollywood cinema, New Age spiritualism, and masculine wilderness cults. Olson's *Maximus* represents the most sustained
poetic engagement with this tendency in American culture, and his interpretation of Pound's artifex as shaman goes some way in accounting for
how the poetics of authoritarianism comes to be read as a poetics of anti-
authoritarianism.

Chapter 4 introduces the work of J. H. Prynne, which is the primary
focus for the chapters that follow. Compared with Pound and Olson,
Prynne is not widely known, and until very recently has received little
attention outside a small group of poets and literary critics dedicated to his
writings. A major influence on the revival of British modernist poetics
since the 1960s, his notoriously difficult poetry extends Pound's attention
to form into a highly reflexive hermetic medium. To examine Prynne's
poetry in the context of the late modernist poetics defined in my first three
chapters is to reappraise Prynne's importance as a key figure in assimilating and departing from modernist ideology. The chapter, therefore, turns
to the significance of the shaman-figure for late modernist British poetry,
taking Prynne's early collections *Kitchen Poems* (1968) and *The White
Stones* (1969) as its key texts. Prynne's work fields all the issues of aesthetic
mysticism exemplified by Pound, Olson and Sinclair, subjecting them to
dialectical scrutiny. A belated modernist, Prynne embraces Pound's and
Olson's historical eclecticism and mythic ontology (e.g. 'the spirit
demanded the orphic metaphor / *as fact*'), but he does not sustain what he
calls their 'fantasy of control' over the past.[10] For Prynne, the mythic
method reconstitutes history as an eternal present by refusing to mourn
the past as a lost object. Pound and Olson achieve mythic identity only by
spiriting away the contingency of historical representations (hence Pound
wants to 'present' not 'represent' the past as if its meaning were self-
illuminating). Their 'objectivism' reinforces the sovereign Self and its
phallic appropriation of the real. Prynne, however, sees the recognition of
self-loss as a necessary condition for any 'divine sense' of being in the
world, and he treats the history of mythic determinations as a dialectic
in which the desire to return to a timeless, organic state of self-identity

cannot be separated from the experience of temporal distance. The only hope of returning 'home' is, paradoxically, to keep on the move, understanding that the nostalgia for origins is always already a temporal dislocation. Prynne's shaman is a wanderer who can only find himself by becoming displaced. Like Heidegger, he interprets the division between the natal and the nomadic as an uncanny relationship: awareness of mortality necessitates the recognition that the not-at-home-to-itself is a condition of becoming at-home. *The White Stones* fuses Poundian epiphanies with complex rhetorical displacements of self-identity, drawing out the irony in Eliade's *The Myth of Eternal Return*: 'the desire felt by the man of traditional societies to refuse history, and to confine himself to an indefinite repetition of archetypes, testifies to his thirst for the real and his terror of 'losing' himself by letting himself be overwhelmed by the meaninglessness of profane existence'.[11]

While Chapter 4 focuses on Prynne's use of the shaman as a figure mediating between crude archetypal theories of the historical subject and a sophisticated temporal dialectic, Chapter 5 moves on to explore Heidegger's influence on late modernist poetics in more detail. Heidegger is a highly problematic figure in modern critical theory because he is at once the modernist thinker par excellence and the architect of postmodernism. On the one hand, his philosophy evokes a world alienated from spiritual values by scientific rationality, and which can only be redeemed by returning to the utopian idealism he associates with the origins of Greek and Teutonic culture. His onto-theological notion of culture is deeply nostalgic, uniting pagan mysticism with *volkisch* sentimentality and distaste for the 'idle, public talk of *das Man*'. His aesthetic is Hermetic and Orphic, investing art with a 'saving power' which both illuminates and creates reality. His belief in 'presence' has clear affinities with Pound, and involves similar contradictions: 'What is striking in Heidegger's re-configuration of the Hölderlinian hymns is that, notwithstanding his blanket rejection of allegory, symbol, simile . . . as attesting to representational thinking, his own reading tacitly avails itself of these interpretive structures.'[12] On the other hand, Heidegger is credited with the deconstruction of Western metaphysics by way of positing an 'ontological difference' (for poststructuralists the site of Being under erasure), and he is regarded as a key thinker of radical alterity, the theorist of the uncanny Other and the non-identical subject. The question of the 'two Heideggers' has a crucial bearing on how modernist texts are read, and this chapter examines the issue with special attention to Heidegger's use of the terms 'spirit', *'Geschlecht'* ('race', 'sex', 'type') and *'Gestalt'* ('form'). As Avital Ronell asks, 'how does the experience of fascination and originary disappropriation turn itself into an experience of appropriation and individuation? Heidegger gives no answers to these questions.'[13] I argue that these questions must be focused, once again, on the aesthetic sublimation of racist myths, and in order to examine their relevance for Heidegger's readings of Hölderlin, Trakl and Rilke, and for Prynne's poetic, I discuss Derrida's writings on 'spirit' and Lacoue-Labarthe and Nancy's work on the politics and poetics of National Socialism. A conclusion which may be drawn at this point is that, in a very general sense, late modernist poetics are an amalgam of the onto-theological Heidegger and Jungianism, and what we call postmodernism is the introduction of ontological difference into this originary scheme.

Chapter 6 draws together the strands of the previous chapters to provide an account of late modernism's revision of the fundamental romantic and modernist tropes of obscurity and fragmentation. It theorises the dialectical grounds of the relationship between hermetic poetry and philosophical commentary. The survival of romantic aesthetics in modernism is considered, leading into preliminary remarks on the deconstruction of the romantic fragment and Heidegger's theory of the *Unheimliche*. I discuss the paradox of poetic uncanniness, which both presupposes and denies subjective investment, and this leads to a Lacanian reformulation of Heidegger. A comment on Objectivism, phenomenology and subjectivity prefaces a description of Derrida's analysis of identity and genre. The questions of identity and dispersal, meaning and non-meaning, return to the uncanny by way of the Lacanian problematic of translation and the dream-work, involving the position of the subject 'called' by the otherness of the obscure text. My theory of the uncanny is applied to readings of Prynne and Paul Celan, clarifying the questions of obscurity and fragmentation in terms of the politics of desire, radical loss, and subjective and aesthetic autonomy.

The features of obscurity and fragmentation must be carefully theorised in order to avoid their assimilation into mysticising explanations of the 'meaning' of highly tendentious texts, which would lead to a simplified acceptance of hermetic poetry as autonomous and self-revealing. I argue that Prynne's poetry is most challenging in this respect, since it continually displaces the ground on which sense, reference and value are based, even as it gestures toward a transcendent reality inhering beyond all temporal determinations. While it can be seen to be complicit with the modernist belief in obscurity and fragmentation as the 'surface' signs of a hidden order of aesthetic unity, it radically questions this tradition of determining the indeterminate and unifying the fragmentary. Prynne's poetry complicates notions of order and determination to the extent that the figural metaphysic of an art intended to reveal presence in absence must be rethought. As the final chapter of the book argues most explicitly, the condition of modernist poetry can be theorised in terms of the hermeneutic gap between its intention towards a fundamental ontology and a textual practice which radically suspends any determination of essence. Any literary criticism which attempts to reveal the meaning of a modernist poem by appealing to either the author's designs or to its own coherence inevitably constructs meaningfulness for critical discourse alone and not for the poem. This much is axiomatic in poststructuralist readings of literary texts. But my interest is in the ways in which critical commentaries on modernist 'reflexivity' and 'unreadability' in turn revert to the condition of essences that define the autonomy of the poem 'itself'. If the modernist poem radically suspends meaning, it must do so at a reflexive level entirely beyond the positive attribution of its own effect, autonomy or presence. This means that we cannot go on reading modernist literary texts as if they are particular instances of a single critical principle: they can only be read dialectically in terms of the categories, frames of reading, and institutions through which, and against which, they function.

Because so much recent critical theory has its roots in modernist practice (a fact often overlooked by those academics who use it as a master-discourse applicable to all 'literary' texts), it proves an important source of critique, especially as Prynne's work developed concurrently with the shift in theoretical attention from paradigms based on phenomenology to those based on the 'linguistic turn'. For this reason, I have been concerned with mapping the modernist background of psychoanalysis and deconstruction as much as attempting to understand the paradigm shifts in Prynne's poetic. A complicating factor here is that, because Prynne's poetry works increasingly to 'lure' the reader's investigations into hermeneutic possibility, constantly inaugurating yet suspending the desire for unifying interpretations, the critical project must turn to reflection on its own presuppositions and validity rather than simply describing its poetic 'object'. Just as the New Critics found aesthetic significance in images of symbolic unity, literary critics who depend on arguments based on post-phenomenological and poststructuralist theory too often end up by positively evaluating modernist texts in terms of 'rupture', dislocation and 'disunity', as if forms of non-unity possess value in and of themselves. In fact, modernist writing only falls into one side of this binary opposition or another when it is least successful: if the gesture to symbolic coherence is too blatant or if its metonymy results in an indifferent word-salad, the poem becomes an object that is always already read and fails to offer significance beyond the self-enclosed space of the text.

Prynne's poetry engages with both of these formal dangers to varying degrees of success, but when fully achieved it pushes the reader's attention toward forms of inquiry which are not limited to aesthetic enclosure. This is why to begin to understand his work it is necessary to think through the variety of other disciplines it incorporates, including anthropology, geomorphology and physics. However, it is arguable that in opening the space of poetry to those forms of inquiry which seem at the furthest remove from it, Prynne is merely following in the footsteps of Pound and Olson, who treat poetry as a distilling vessel for the transformation of 'base' discourses into myth. If the historical avant-garde sought to destroy the aura of art by projecting the aesthetic into a politics of contingency and difference, modernism attempted to renew aesthetic autonomy as the privileged site for representing cultural totality. Reading Prynne's poetry of the 1960s and 1970s in the context of his own polemics places it firmly in the modernist camp, and I argue that it is based on, as Angela Moorjani puts it, a 'repetition of loss that helps to explain the powerful appeal of aesthetic mysticism'.[14] Nevertheless, the heuristic strength of Prynne's poetry makes it available to larger frames of reference, and it needs to be considered in terms of the similarities and differences between the avant-garde and modernism, which lie at the heart of all debates about the ideological significance of modern literary form, including its relationship to romanticism and postmodernism.

Notes

1 Ezra Pound, *The Spirit of Romance* (New York: New Directions, 1952), 92.

2 Tyrus Miller, *Late Modernism: Politics, Fiction, and the Arts Between the World Wars* (Berkeley: University of California Press, 1999), 7.

3 Ezra Pound, 'Idee Fondamentali' (1942), translated by Peter Nicholls in 'Lost Object(s): Ezra Pound and the Idea of Italy', in Richard Taylor and Claus Melchior, eds, *Ezra Pound and Europe* (Amsterdam: Rodopi, 1993), 171–2.

4 Ezra Pound, 'Cavalcanti', in David Anderson, ed., *Pound's Cavalcanti: An Edition of the Translations, Notes, and Essays* (Princeton: Princeton University Press, 1983), 211.

5 Pound, 'Cavalcanti', 209.

6 Ezra Pound, 'Terra Italica' (1931–32), in *Selected Prose: 1909–1965*. Ed. with an introduction by William Cookson (New York: New Directions, 1973), 56.

7 Pound, 'Cavalcanti', 211.

8 Pound, 'Cavalcanti', 214.

9 Iain Sinclair, *The Shamanism of Intent: Some Flights of Redemption* (Uppingham, Rutland: Goldmark, 1991), 7.

10 J. H. Prynne, 'Aristeas, in Seven Years', in *The White Stones* (Lincoln: Grosseteste Press, 1969), 64.

11 Mircea Eliade, *The Myth of the Eternal Return: Cosmos and History*. Trans. Willard R. Trask (London: Arkana, 1989), 91–2.

12 Veronique M. Fóti, *Heidegger and the Poets: Poiesis / Sophia / Techne* (New Jersey: Humanities Press, 1992), 53–4.

13 Avital Ronell, *The Telephone Book: Technology, Schizophrenia, Electric Speech* (Lincoln and London: University of Nebraska Press, 1989), 58.

14 Angela Moorjani, *The Aesthetics of Loss and Lessness* (London: Macmillan, 1992), 80.

HERMETIC POETRY
AND LATE MODERNISM

Enough has been said to suggest that the style of the Delphic responses is a somewhat unstable amalgam of varied and dissonant elements. (H. W. Parke and D. E. W. Wormell, *The Delphic Oracle*)

Summer, 2000: in rural Sussex, not far from the cottage where, from 1913 to 1916, Yeats and Pound worked together to forge their aristocracy of the arts, Emerson College hosts 'A Summer Gathering of Poets & Lovers of Poetry'. This residential week of creative writing, 'emphasising both the schooling of imaginative perception and crafting of the written and spoken word', offers workshops on topics such as 'The Sacred Space of the Word', 'Down from the Ivory Tower', 'Writing and the Search for Self', and 'The Heart of Things'. Sunday suppers, woodland walks and evening concerts ('the music of Earthwards and Phoenix') set the scene for exploring poetry's 'healing, social and literary aspects', and the spiritual dimension of the creative process is nurtured in the quest to unify the writer's solitary ways with interpersonal growth: *'The great religions are ships . . . poets and storytellers the lifeboats.'*[1]

This adult education programme sets out from a widely held set of beliefs about the value of poetry at the end of the twentieth century. That is to say, it views poetry as essentially romantic in the sense of the term set out by Rene Wellek in 1949: 'imagination for the view of poetry, nature for the view of the world, and symbol and myth for poetic style.'[2] Poetry bespeaks the essence of 'the world' as a flight from urban noise. Taking their 'pens into the woods and garden', members of the Gathering aim to turn their 'senses toward the language of nature'. Discovering nature leads to self-discovery, a 'living process' that knits solitary wanderings with group activities and the exercise of perception. The poet's hypostasy of

Selfhood is both sensual and spiritual – art is never far from the religious impulse – but in case budding poets are tempted to see their calling as high faluting, they are reminded of the need to come down from the 'Ivory Tower' which reduces imagination to elitism and obscurity. The summer school capitalises on its geographical associations with Yeats and Pound, yet it is at pains to distance itself from the lofty hermetism associated with these modernist inheritors of the romantic–symbolist tradition. Just as the spiritual life of the late twentieth century turns from theosophy's cabals to the democratic cure-alls of New Age mysticism, poetry modulates from an aesthetic purism designed to preserve it from the secular realm of mass consumption to an expressive medium which voices an ineffable but egalitarian language of the soul. Where Yeats, Rilke, Robinson Jeffers and C. G. Jung found in their towers sanctuary from the public and the symbol of transcendence, the summer school rejects such private monumenta in favour of a democratic version of the country-house idyll.

For the modernists, poetry is linked with occult religion, disclosed only to those initiated into its formal rules and arcane associations. In the New Age parlance of the summer school, poetry is a mystical offering revealed to all comers. Before going on to define the modernist strain in contemporary poetry, it is important to understand how the 'alternative' spirituality of the summer school differs from modernism by tempering its occult origins with the notion of universal revelation. Emerson College bases its programmes on the teachings of Rudolf Steiner, a key figure in the Spiritualist movement whose theories of personal growth combine occult speculation with Christianity and Green agriculture. His work was also a major influence on the pioneer of early twentieth-century Italian hermetic poetry, Arturo Onofri (1885–1928). From the 1890s to 1912, Steiner's beliefs were close enough to those of Yeats's mentor Madame Blavatsky to allow him to become leader of the German Theosophical Society. But he broke with the theosophists by privileging Christian ideals over the melting-pot of arcane knowledge favoured by Blavatsky's 'Secret Doctrine'. The 'god-wisdom' of theosophical or occult discourse holds that the established world religions are the weakened, ossified forms of an original, unifying wisdom, knowledge of which is encrypted in the sacred texts and communicated only to a few inspired – and almost exclusively male – individuals. The guru, magus or artifex who claims to be a diviner of gnosis or secret wisdom conveys its 'message' in ways that become clear to those adepts willing to apprehend the truth behind the obscure (or occulted) language of revelation. Hermetic revelation, therefore, is a closed hermeneutic system, its prophecies self-fulfilling since its truths are available only to those who already know the truth. As Leon Surette argues in *The Birth of Modernism*,

> The incommunicable nature of the enlightenment justifies the label 'occult' and distinguishes occultism from other postclassical Western religions which, although they have mysteries or incomprehensible dogmas, do not have *secrets* – teachings revealed only to a select group of initiates. The touchstone for the occult is neither mysticism (which it shares with most world religions) nor, of course, a belief in the divine (which it shares with all religions) but rather a belief that throughout human history certain individuals have had intimate contact with the divine and from this contact have gained special knowledge . . . which they have preserved in a form comprehensible only to the already enlightened and which is passed on in texts whose esoteric interpretation is preserved by secret societies.[3]

The varieties of occult experience converge at one, crucial, point. Incommunicable though the divine mysteries may be (the basic meaning of the word occult is 'something that cannot be apprehended by the mind'), they all derive from the idea of recovering a primal awareness of godly power in 'man'. Unlike Christianity, which regards human beings as subject to an omnipotent deity, occult religion sees man created in the image of god and containing god within man: 'The essence of God is "wisdom", his energy "intellect and soul".'[4] God, then, becomes a principle rather than a deity, and in this sense occult religion is better classified as 'hyper-humanism' than as theology. The task of those seeking enlightenment is to realise the hidden power within themselves which will enable them to overcome the human, all too human, condition of passive, everyday consciousness. As with the alchemical search for the philosopher's stone, earthly dross has the potential to be transmuted into heavenly gold, not in the Christian sense of salvation after death, but as a sublimation of individual being. The popularised version of the occult, the dodgy world of 'phenomena', all the paraphenalia of spiritualism, astrology, astral projection, parapsychology and the like derives from Hermetic religion in that it is an extension of the principle of divine capabilities in the human suppressed by centuries of subjection to religions which debase man before God. Steiner's Christianity was seen by his critics in the Theosophical Society 'as a competing revelation, a corrupt or imperfect version of the true revelation of which the occultists are the custodians.'[5]

Nevertheless, from an orthodox Christian perspective, Steiner's attempt to reconcile Western monotheism with the esoteric tradition is typically occultist. He claims that in antiquity human beings had clairvoyant access to the spiritual world but that increasing attachment to materialist values have formed a barrier between the physical and the spiritual realms. The barrier can only be removed by kinds of psychic training. The network of Steiner Waldorf schools and further-education institutions such as Emerson College are designed to address this problem by developing intuitive and imaginative skills thought to aid spiritual development; they therefore place emphasis on the arts, mythology, and practical activities such as biodynamic farming, which seek to restore a balance between nature and technology. According to Steiner, this balance is lost to modern cultures, which teach the individual merely to reflect the material needs of the State. Much of the appeal of Steiner schools is due to their celebration of free individualism opposed to a repressive state apparatus. This gives opting out of state education a radical allure, but seemingly without the bogey of 'indoctrination'. The schools themselves play down the doctrinal content of their curriculum by promising a holistic approach to learning based on 'Christian ideals as articulated by Rudolf Steiner'.[6] Even here, Christianity is relegated to the status of a benign principle aiding creative development; Steiner's heretical interpretations of scripture (for instance that Christ is not a redemptive figure but a sun god maintaining equilibrium between the Zoroastrian forces of light and darkness) do not feature in any brochure. The schools' quest for pedagogic legitimacy means that wherever possible they avoid reference to the secret wisdom on which their teaching practice is based.

None of Steiner's theories find their way into the Emerson College flyer, probably because, here too, any mention of the arcane beyond the blithely animistic harks back to the ivory towers and secret societies from which the College is at pains to distance itself. Myth and mysticism are key elements in what the flyer calls 'Shaping a Language for the New Millennium', but where for the modernists they belong to the high realms of embodied enigma, here they have become comfortable features in the landscape of the collective unconscious. Just as Steiner's less palatable theories are elided by the institutions based on his teachings, the New Age romantics of the 'Poetry Otherwise' summer school appeal to a democratic, universalist view of myth which ignores the elitist origins of twentieth-century occultism.

This banal recreation of romantic conceptions of self-expression and communion with nature forms one of two distinctly *anti*-modernist strains in late twentieth-century poetry. The other, generally associated with the New Lines verse of the 1950s and its legacy but extending far beyond the formal conservatism of 'The Movement', assumes that poetry took an interesting if mistaken detour through modernism and the avant-garde, then returned to its wellsprings in a multicultural revision of the Wordsworthian ideal of 'a man speaking to men'. This view of poetry is sometimes classed as 'empirical' due to its premise that perception validates both the self and its objects. The 'I' that stands at the centre of this writing may be transformed by epiphany and chastened by irony, yet it is always a stable, controlling presence. *In absentia*, it personifies landscapes and animals, and claims inside knowledge of other human beings, reducing them to similitudes or exposing their 'real' identity, as for example when Thom Gunn describes Californian bikers: 'They strap in doubt – by hiding it, robust – / And almost hear a meaning in their noise.'[7] The assumption that the bikers strap in their doubt is pure projection on Gunn's part, modulating with 'almost' into condescending knowingness. In less Augustan form, such conceits have become the stock-in-trade of aspiring and established poets across Britain and the United States who see themselves as heirs to Hardy and Frost, Larkin and Lowell, Hughes and Plath.

This does not mean that all poems using personal pronouns are anti-modernist. Frank O'Hara's work, for instance, drives personalism to camp extremes where the lyric ego is revealed as staged, equivocal and contingent. And the wandering I of Denise Riley's poetry becomes part of the social structures it strives to discern, its thetic moments disturbed by shifting tenses and syntactical elisions which threaten any easy distinction between subject and object:

> When I'm unloaded and stood in dread
> at home encircled by my life, whose
> edges do show – then I so want it to run
> and run again, the solitary travelling perception.
> Road movie: Protectedness, or, Gets through time.[8]

A passenger returning from fervent yet aimless motor car journeys, the subject of this poem is unloaded from, and unloaded like, the vehicle which has contained her and the automobiles she sees 'repeating / themselves fast and fast as if they were one'. She is at one and the same time disburdened and 'stood in dread' ('stood' instead of 'standing', as if fixed by some outside force), caught between the demand to be 'held' and the desire to keep moving ('to have that held sense of looking out / from a container'). The pararphernalia of her own life surrounds her, perhaps like the 'ring-road' on which she travels round the city. She wants to be both container and contained, half-aware that to keep running is not escape but repetition, as a movie is run and re-run; that, paradoxically, to stay on the move may be a fantasy of endlessness which has to end at some arbitrary point, just as in Road Movie convention there is no end to the road except sudden death (or when, in the case of *Two Lane Blacktop* (1969), the film itself burns up). Where Gunn's 'On the Move' projects the beliefs of its omniscient narrator onto the motorcyclists who represent a 'division' between blind action and knowing perception, the I of Riley's poem discloses the splitting of the acting/perceiving subject as a projection founded on metaphors of movement and stasis. Riley's work traces the complex manoeuvres of the subject as it builds and confounds itself; it deconstructs the lyric ego, yet remains deeply personal.

For reasons that should become clear during the course of this study, Riley's lyrical deconstruction of the lyric is an example of 'post-modernism'; that is to say, a thoroughly reflexive, demystifying approach to modernist form. What I call 'late modernism', however, is contemporary with the emergence of anti-modernist tendencies after 1939, the date used by most academic commentaries to mark the end of the modernist period. In a basic sense, albeit one that has been consistently overlooked by literary historians, late modernism can be said to refer to the continuation of modernist writing into the war years and until at least the end of the 1970s. This was a period of consolidation, when substantial parts of long poems begun before 1939 were composed and published, and new ones were written: *The Cantos, Four Quartets*, Louis Zukofsky's *A*, David Jones's *The Anathemata*, William Carlos Williams's *Paterson*, Charles Olson's *The Maximus Poems*, Basil Bunting's *Briggflatts*, Charles Reznikoff's *Testimony: The United States*. Many poets whose modernist aesthetic was formed earlier in the century developed it beyond the 1930s; some, like Marianne Moore, found a wide audience in later years; others, such as Lorine Niedecker, Nelly Sachs and Bunting, did not publish major work until long afterwards. More significantly, new conceptual, concrete and performance-based poetries inspired by the avant-garde gained international recognition, and younger poets working within modernist traditions appeared, among them Olson, Jack Spicer, Edmond Jabes, Robert Duncan, Anne-Marie Albiach, Paul Celan, Andrea Zanzotto, Charles Tomlinson, Rosemary Tonks and J. H. Prynne. A curiosity of periodisation is the general acceptance almost to the point of hegemony of post-1945 modernism in the plastic arts, music, and architecture. Paintings by, say, Roger Hilton and Gillian Ayres, or compositions by Pierre Boulez and Iannis Xenakis, are seen as unquestionably modernist even though they were made in the 1950s and 1960s. This does not apply to poetry, where late modernist writing is commonly regarded by academic critics and metropolitan reviewers alike as anachronistic. Arguing the case in 1959 for Charles Tomlinson as the 'most profound and original of all our postwar poets', Donald Davie noted that 'he refuses to join the silent conspiracy which now unites all the English poets from Robert Graves down to Philip Larkin, and all the critics, editors, and publishers too, the conspiracy to pretend that Eliot and Pound never happened'.[9]

Identifying the lineage in this general way is fine as far as it goes, since the newer poets and poetics mentioned here are clearly not antimodernist.

But why not simply call them 'postmodernist'? Confining late modernism to the tail-end of the 1920s and the 1930s, Tyrus Miller argues that

> At first glance, late modernist writing appears a distinctly self-conscious manifestation of the ageing and decline of modernism, in both its institutional and ideological dimensions. More surprising, however, such writing also strongly anticipates future developments, so that without forcing, it might easily fit into a narrative of emergent postmodernism . . . It is as if the phosphorescence of decay had illumined the passageway to a reemergence of innovative writing after modernism . . . the double life of this significant body of writing – its linkage forward into postmodernism and backward into modernism – has not, by and large, been accounted for by critics of this period.[10]

According to this version of events, modernism – Miller means Anglo-American modernism – was moribund shortly after peaking in 1922, rallied for a brief time in parodic form, then expired with the onset of World War Two; its reemergence as innovative writing is therefore best described as postmodern. While there are precedents for this account in the work of postwar poets – Charles Olson, for example, saw himself as a 'postmodernist' reclaiming the negative landscape of *The Waste Land* for a positive mythos[11] – the thesis begs serious questions. First, Miller's sophisticated analysis of the cultural factors contributing to the 'end' of modernism shows that World War One was a crucial turning-point in the development of high modernist aesthetics, but it says next to nothing about its imputed demise by 1939. According to Miller, the modernists' emphasis on autonomy and formal originality was compromised by the arrival of the political avant-gardes, which threw into crisis any belief in the separation of art from its political context, and was made archaic by the highly technologised dissemination of mass culture, so that 'By the immediate postwar years, the movement had already begun to show signs of drift, neoclassical reaction, and nationalist or provincialist obstacles to new ideas. A cunning dialectic had seized the process of stylistic innovation, confronting the writer with historical limits and threatening to exhaust modernism's dynamic from within.'[12] What Miller reductively terms *the movement* appears to have been over almost before it had begun. His contention that modernism's already fragile self-image was eroded by the forces of modernity (history, trauma, technocracy, metropolitanism, commodification, the 'loss of a stable, authentic social ground'[13]) inverts the relatonship of modernism to modernity. While it is fair to say that the onward march of modernity put increasing ideological pressure on an aesthetic dedicated to preserving cultural aristocracy, it can hardly account for the decline of modernism since modernism is nothing if not a response *to* modernity and is therefore an effect *of* modernity. Furthermore, Anglo-American modernism was not simply reactionary; as Lawrence Rainey argues, writers colluded with the commodification process by turning their works into

> a commodity of a special sort, one that is temporarily exempted from the exigencies of immediate consumption prevalent within the larger cultural economy, and instead is integrated into a different economic circuit of patronage, collecting, speculation, and investment – activities that precisely in this period begin to encroach upon and merge into one another in unexpected ways. Modernism marks neither a straightforward resistance nor an outright capitulation to commodification but a momentary equivocation that incorporates elements of both in a brief, necessarily unstable synthesis.[14]

The circuit of patronage, subscriptions, private presses and limited editions which floated many of the early modernists show these writers negotiating with capitalist society in a 'creative' fashion. A world in which the literary work escapes mechanical reproduction only by becoming that economically ambiguous entity the 'priceless' artefact is already the world of modernity, and the modernists' hostility to exchange value did not prevent them from trading themselves and their products as elite goods. While such niche marketing was a way of maintaining the value of traditional art in an increasingly popularised cultural marketplace, the modernists were painting themselves into a corner, and Miller argues that the period *entre deux guerres* left them struggling with a 'lack of credible options' for self-justification.[15] This explains the turn to bitter caricature, parody and satire in the fiction of Wyndham Lewis, Mina Loy, and Djuna Barnes, which Miller sees as definitively late modernist, but by making these baroque tirades stand for the decline of modernism in general he ignores the fact that key figures like Pound and Eliot were carried beyond the 1930s by the success of imprints such as James Laughlin's New Directions and Faber & Faber, and a new phase of modernist writing came into being after 1945 with the transformation of elite support for the arts into the more liberal circuit of universities and colleges, public endowments, and the rise of influential 'little' magazines and presses (now published by artists themselves instead of wealthy benefactors). Modernism carved out a vital, if still marginal, space within mass culture, a space that was to coincide for a brief period with popular counterculture.

Secondly, limiting late modernism to the inter-war period means that Miller has to use the term postmodernism to define all 'innovative writing after modernism'. For all his caveats about assigning periods and commonalities, he is sure that modernism 'peaked much earlier' in literature than in the other arts, and that its 'undeniable historical "decline"' (the scare quotes are not applied to this word elsewhere) led to a variety of aesthetic positions united only by their abandonment of any belief in the transcendent power of art.[16] The modern world finally rushed in, leaving a heap of broken images that could not be restored by a higher symbolism. Late modernism toyed with the fragments for a while before giving way to postmodernism, which registers 'the disenchantment of modernism's redemptive myth', deconstructing its desire for unity and totality.[17] However, Miller concurs with Fredric Jameson and Alan Wilde in seeing the need for late modernism as an intermediate concept that would finesse the period of transition between modernism and postmodernism. According to Jameson, it is exemplified by Nabokov, Beckett, Olson and Zukofsky, who prolonged 'unseasonable forms' through an exilic period spanning the 'two eras'; Wilde argues that it is a weakened form of modernist irony that fails to offer any 'embracing vision' or 'symbolic compensation for the chaos and impoverishment of modern life'.[18] Rather than complicating the relationship between modernism and postmodernism, late modernism reifies Jameson's assumption that there are indeed two separate eras, and Wilde seems convinced that modern life is chaotic and impoverished without pausing to consider that this narrative of disorder and decline may itself be a modernist fiction. These difficulties apart, the fixing of a 'transitional' moment remains problematic. Miller has already taken issue with Charles Jencks's periodisation of late modernism (an architectural style, in coexistence with postmodernism, emerging in the 1960s) by arguing that its literary form occurs between 1926 and 1939; but Miller ought not to subscribe to Jameson's literary periodisation either, since it includes Charles Olson, a poet of the 1950s and 1960s. (And Samuel Beckett, included by Jameson and also one of Miller's examples, wrote his major work after 1945, though because his formative years were the 1930s he can be safely included in Miller's late modernist canon). The point, however, is not that Miller should not be able to revise the time-line, but that periodisation becomes increasingly difficult to contain. If late modernism presages the end of modernism, why does it seem so interminable? And if postmodernism is the condition of art after modernism, how is it that poets such as Olson can be seen as belonging to both the late modernist and postmodernist camps? The simple answer is that Miller's periodisation is more flexible than it appears; as he states, late modernist writing 'might easily fit into a narrative of emergent postmodernism'. But then why bother with the between-the-wars apparatus and the death of modernism thesis in the first place? My own view is that Miller is right to see the emergence of a troubled, belated version of Anglo-American modernism, but wrong to confine it to the period before World War Two, and wrong to define it as essentially negative in character:

> Late modernist writers were divested, by political and economic forces, of
> the cultural 'cosmos' – the modernist 'myth' in its most encompassing sense
> – in which the singular works of high modernism seemed components of

an aesthetically transfigured world. In the empty spaces left by modernism's dissolution, late modernists reassembled fragments into disfigured likenesses of modernist masterpieces: the unlovely allegories of a world's end.[19]

If modernism dissolved, its solution was more modernism. If it died, it had an afterlife, not an empty space. Its survival is still a powerful force in aesthetic practice and cultural ideals today. I argue that although late modernists were disenchanted by the political consequences of high modernist culture, they continued to uphold its mythic values against perceived threats to selfhood and community. Late modernism is therefore antithetical to postmodernism, which discloses myth as ideology and treats the 'self' as a construct, not as an organic unity. A complicating factor here is that, when presented in the context of mid-century American poetics, postmodernism is sometimes defined as an organic theory of culture based on the rejection of modernist values. Charles Altieri has argued that the turn to postmodernism in American poetry – under which heading he includes poets as diverse as Robert Lowell, Denise Levertov, Gary Snyder, Robert Bly, Richard Wilbur, Theodore Roethke and John Ashbery, but which coalesces in the 'immanent' poetics of Charles Olson and Robert Duncan – is a fundamental rejection of modernism's humanist drive to order and comprehend experience through the aesthetic appropriation of myth.[20] By contrast with modernism, the postmodernists use myth as a way of intensifying experience, with or without order. Mythic consciousness attests to cosmic powers that allow 'man' to recover and participate in natural processes rather than symbolising the division between human significance and a chaotic universe. The shift is towards an ecological theory of artistic enactment: man is created by his environment, therefore he must learn to express himself through it, to permit himself to be expressed by it, instead of trying to beat it into shape. Hence the value placed on 'primitive' ways of seeing by Olson, Duncan, Snyder, Jerome Rothenberg and other key figures in the development of ethnopoetics; while these poets take it as read that native peoples are more in touch with the rhythms of the natural world than modern man, they insist that their interest in the primitive is not 'directed backward toward a past viewed with feelings of decontextualized nostalgia' but reflects

> a concern over the last two centuries with new communalistic and anti-authoritarian forms of social life and with alternatives to the environmental disasters accompanying an increasingly abstract relation to what was once a living universe. Our belief in this regard is that a re-viewing of 'primitive' ideas of the 'sacred' represents an attempt – by poets and others – to preserve and enhance primary human values against a mindless mechanization that has run past any uses it may once have had.[21]

The scare-quotes around the words 'primitive' and 'sacred' evince a cautious approach to subject-matter swamped in romantic and modernist cliché. The new 'totality' of which Robert Duncan speaks (again in inverted commas) runs counter to modernism in seeking to include 'all the old excluded orders . . . the female, the proletariat, the foreign; the animal and vegetative; the unconscious and the unknown; the criminal and failure – all that has been outcast and vagabond must return to be admitted in the creation of what we are.'[22] Even so, the enterprise is belatedly modernist and somewhat disingenuous, since it is firmly attached to atavistic beliefs about the decline of an organic, whole, concrete, centred, religious mode of being into the fragmented, alienated, abstract and mechanised culture of modernity. Far from being 'antihumanist', as Altieri claims, this postmodernism continues to set denatured consciousness against 'primary human values' which approximate religious experience (and which are essentially masculine: it is always modern man who is in search of a soul, even when soul is placed under the sign of woman). In order to distance this divine ecology from modernism, Altieri talks up the latter's subjective investment in the poetic act, eliding its classicist, antihumanist strain. The real difference is political: an inclusive, liberal humanist and/or revolutionary project versus an exclusive, conservative and/or fascistic one; yet both orientations are problematically ordered by the ideological figure of 'totality'.[23] This retention of the totality and its sublimation into the religious is what I would call the condition of late modernism. Postmodernism, for better or worse, destroys immanence. Altieri's definition, for all its sophistication and its reservations concerning the plausibility of a sacramental poetic in an age that no longer believes in ritual absolution, is inadequate because symptomatic of the very condition it claims to analyse. If it is the case that 'While incarnation for the moderns exemplified the union of form and significant value on an otherwise empty and chaotic natural world, God for the contemporaries manifests himself as energy, as the intense expression of immanent power', Altieri's postmoderns remain adepts of the Hermetic order that Surette identifies as a key element in the birth of modernism.[24]

Robert Duncan's praise for Olson's poetry as 'magic' and 'alchemy' seems out of key with Olson's antipathy towards what he calls the modernist 'suck of symbol' and his emphasis on historical fact until we see that the polarity is sutured by an act of faith in natural supernaturalism.[25] Olson's 'Anti-Wasteland' means the foundation of a revolutionary poetic based on verbal force and conceptual immediacy, which would replace symbolism with documentary evidence, galvanised by the poet's associative powers. He wants to reinvest poetry with the cultural energy he finds in Mayan civilisation: 'O, they were hot for the world they lived in, these Maya, hot to get it down the way it was – the way it is, my fellow citizens.'[26] What reads here like the Beat mantra of 'first thought best thought' is in practice something else entirely. Telling it like it is, the cool preserve of 'a people who are more or less directly the descendents of a culture and civilization which was a contrary of that which we have known and of which we are the natural children', is theorised in a passage in 'Human Universe' (1951) which claims that value is both inherent in the thing itself and in its 'human' significance. Olson begins by exposing '*comparison*, or, its bigger name, *symbology*':

> These are the false faces, too much seen, which hide and keep from use the active intellectual states, metaphor and performance. All that comparison ever does is set up a series of *reference* points: to compare is to take one thing and try to understand it by marking its similarities to or differences from another thing. Right here is the trouble, that each thing is not so much like or different from another thing (these likenesses and differences are apparent) but that such an analysis only accomplishes a *description*, does not come to grips with what really matters: that a thing, any thing, impinges on us by a more important fact, its self-existence, without reference to any other thing, in short, the very character of it which calls our attention to it, which wants us to know more about it, its particularity. This is what we are confronted by, not the thing's 'class,' any hierarchy, of quality or quantity, but the thing itself, and its *relevance* to ourselves who are the experience of it (whatever it may mean to someone else, or whatever other relations it may have).[27]

The thing has a self-identity that demands attention from the perceiving subject, yet it is not without relative value, since its meaning depends on variable experience. This conflation of realism and empiricism cancels itself unless resolved by a transcendental argument. Olson's appears to be located in the specious distinction between 'ourselves' and 'someone else': *we* experience the relevance of the thing, *others* imbue it with meaning not derived from experience. The big question is, who are 'we'? Olson defines 'human values' as deriving from an energy located in natural processes, which in modern society becomes dissipated. The only way to restore the 'human house' is to realise that 'The meeting edge of man and the world is also his cutting edge. If man is active, it is exactly here where experience comes in that it is delivered back, and if he stays fresh at the coming in he will be fresh at his going out. If he does not, all that he does inside his house is stale, more and more stale as he is less and less acute at the door.'[28] There is a right way and a wrong way to experience experience. Staleness, the wrong way, equals 'pejorocracy' (a term Olson takes from Pound), the decline into a system of 'worse-rule' that is the antithesis of the natural οικονομοσ and lies at the farthest remove from the thing itself. 'Relevance', in the end, is not subjectively variable but what distinguishes human energy from the de-humanised condition of stasis. Olson's model for the active, energised community he calls the 'pure place' is the ancient Greek concept of the city or 'polis'. The polis is a microcosm of 'the very whole world' based on the homogeneity of the Greek city which, though a totality, allows us 'to invert totality – to oppose it – by discovering the totality of any – every – single one of us.'[29] Once again, the spectre of authoritarian totality is disavowed by converting it into a universal, holistic resource which nevertheless remains under the sign of totality. The classical polis was indeed a microcosm dedicated to self-sufficiency; it was, as M. I. Finley describes it, composed of 'people acting in concert' who 'must be able to assemble and deal with problems face to face'. But its power was total, 'the source of all rights and obligations, and its authority reached into every sphere of human behaviour without exception'. Action was opposed to stasis as order is opposed to anarchy; the Greeks equated *stasis* with sedition, and the 'classic description of extreme stasis is Thucydides' account of the singularly brutal outbreak in Corcyra in 427, treated by the historian explicitly as a model of this chronic evil in Greek society ... It was Aristotle who tied it more closely, and very simply, to the nature and idea of the polis. "Speaking generally," he said in the *Politics* (V 1301b), "men turn to *stasis* out of a desire for equality."'[30] For all its rhetoric of inclusiveness, Olson's 'Human Universe' is founded on an exclusive 'natural' epistemology and on idealised historical paradigms.

Olson's separation of metaphor from symbolism is equally problematic. It cannot mean, in practice, a rejection of symbolism *tout court*, since symbol and metaphor are closely linked, but it does amount to an attack on explicit analogy, metaphor reduced to simile. Metaphor, for Olson, is an active intellectual state because it prefers the concrete image to the abstract idea; simile merely compares an image with an idea, dulling the relationship between subject and analogy by making it prosaic. Simile is low-energy metaphor. Yet this does not explain Olson's impatience with 'likenesses and differences', set against the 'thing itself'. As we have seen, the 'self-existence' of the thing is of interest in its 'particularity' and when it has '*relevance*'; in other words, the thing functions both as an entity and as symbolic value. The nature of the thing might be said to 'carry over' into human significance. This is, in a basic sense, metaphorical, less concerned with comparison than with transport or transferral. But it is also symbolic, in that a material object is made to represent an immaterial quality; the thing is, so to speak, 'raised up', made relevant. So why does Olson bother with the distinction between metaphor and symbol at all? The answer may be located in his appropriation of Pound's view that 'constation of fact' should replace symbolism in modern poetry. 'Unless a term is left meaning one particular thing,' Pound writes, 'and unless all attempt to unify different things, however small the difference, is clearly abandoned, all metaphysical thought degenerates into a soup.'[31] In his discussion of Canto LXXXI, D. S. Carne-Ross argues that

> What is difficult about Pound's poetry is its 'simplicity' . . . the whole reverberating dimension of inwardness is missing. There is no murmurous echo chamber where deeps supposedly answer to deeps. Not merely does the thing, in Pound's best verse, not point beyond itself: *it doesn't point to us*. The green tip that pushes through the earth in spring does not stand for or symbolize man's power of spiritual renewal . . . Pound's whole effort is *not* to be polysemous but to give back to the literal first level its full significance, its old significance . . . The green thrust is itself the divine event, the fruit of the marriage at Eleusis. Persephone is in that thrusting tip, and if man matters it is because he too has a share in that same power, he too is a part of the seasonal, sacred life of nature. But only a part.[32]

Carne-Ross's double evaluation follows a similar logic to 'Human Universe': the thing is self-sufficient, it is a natural fact, not a comparative value; at the same time, it is the 'divine event' relevant for human beings. Its message is that nature's relation to man is metonymic, not symbolic. Crucially, the thing is equated with a 'literal first level', which is both 'old' and 'full'. Polysemous, figurative language is a mystification of ancient truths which must be given back their original significance. In the Canto, the eating of bread (cereal) is 'not just symbolic as in the Christian sacrament but a *real* part of the Eleusinian mystery'.[33] Paradise is not artificial. The word 'cereal' derives from Ceres, the corn goddess, thus the breaking of bread in the ancient mystery cult has an elemental function, underlined by its etymology, which is not available to the Eucharist, where the token wafer symbolises the body of Christ.

Why the use of bread in one ritual rather than another should be more 'real' is, to say the least, questionable. The distinction is presented as ontological but is in fact purely rhetorical. The 'green thrust' that Carne-Ross describes as the thing itself might not be a symbol in the same way as the communion wafer, but it does work as a synecdoche of a natural process that is never merely Nature 'itself'. On one hand, nature is treated *ipso facto* as if it were prior to all representation; on the other, it bespeaks a religious unity, the divine marriage of earth and sky ('Zeus lies in Ceres' bosom'). For many Christians, the communion bread *is* the body of Christ, just as for Carne-Ross and Pound spring 'is itself the divine event'; the Eucharist is arguably no more or less a symbol than the seven pomegranate seeds that represent 'the seven phases of the moon during which farmers wait for the green corn-shoots to appear'.[34] Pound is simply justifying his belief in natural sacrament and his hostility to Christianity by appealing to occulted fact or, to call it by its more traditional name, myth: myth being, according to C. Kerényi, a narrative which 'expresses in a primary and direct fashion precisely what it relates – something that happened in primordial times' but which, like Frobenius's concept of *Paideuma* ('cultural instinct'; 'active culture'), is so profound and universal that it transcends explanation and theory[35]

Olson's push is likewise to return metaphor to its supposedly literal, ety-mological origins. This means, in the first instance, rejecting the rationalist, comparative view of metaphor. Both metaphor and simile are based on resemblance, but metaphor is the more complex figure because it implies an ontological connection between one idea, image or symbol and another. Simply stated, this means that X is not *like* Y, X *is* Y. The relationship between X and Y presupposes identity rather than similarity, yet it must also entail difference, otherwise there could be no X and Y on which to base the metaphorical relationship. From a logical point of view, then, metaphor is a symbolic, abbreviated version of simile; by condensing the proposi-tional form of the simile it offers what Aristotle calls the intuitive percep-tion of the similarity in dissimilars. Olson, however, seeks a pure identity not clouded by the abstractions of 'like' or 'is'. He quotes Fenollosa's remark that '"is" comes from the Aryan root, *as*, to breathe. "Be" is from *bhu*, to grow.' 'Breath' is the literal, guiding presence of Olson's theory of Projec-tive Verse: 'Because breath allows all the speech-force of language back in (speech is the "solid" of verse, is the secret of a poem's energy), because, now, a poem has, by speech, solidity, everything in it can now be treated as solids, objects, things'.[36] Like Nietzsche's reduction of 'Being' to 'respira-tion', Fenollosa's 'war on the copula' (as Hugh Kenner calls it) is an example of what Jacques Derrida terms etymological empiricism, 'thinking *by* metaphor without thinking the metaphor *as such*'.[37] While Pound was aware that Fenollosa's picture theory of the Chinese ideogram was mistaken, this did not prevent him from endorsing its ideal of a language of direct communication, based on primitive metaphor, in touch with the verbal energy of natural processes, and unsullied by decadent alphabetical writing, which divides signifier from signified. Fenollosa described the ideogram in terms that are identical to the vitalistic monism of Hermetic thought:

> The whole delicate substance of speech is built upon substrata of metaphor. Abstract terms, pressed by etymology, reveal their ancient roots still embed-ded in direct action. But the primitive metaphors do not spring from arbi-trary *subjective* processes. They are possible only because they follow objective lines of relations in nature herself. Relations are more real and more important than the things which they relate. The forces which produce the branch-angles of an oak lay potent in the acorn . . . This is more than analogy, it is identity of structure. Nature furnishes her own clues. Had the world not been full of homologies, sympathies, and identities, thought

would have been starved and language chained to the obvious. There would have been no bridge whereby to cross from the minor truth of the seen to the major truth of the unseen.[38]

The world full of 'homologies, sympathies, and identities' points to a universe 'alive with myth', essentially poetic and archaic yet allied with natural philosophy. Fenollosa alludes to the shamanic tradition of antiquity, ancient Greek and Chinese alchemy, the theurgy of Iamblichus, Plotinus and Porphyry, and their reemergence in the Renaissance *spiritus mundi* of Cornelius Agrippa, of Paracelsus and Bruno, Pico and Ficino, Dee and Heydon. This is the episteme of radiating correspondences, divine signatures and natural magic elegised by Michel Foucault in *The Order of Things*, an era prior to the taxonomic imagination of scientific rationality which consists 'in *drawing things together*, in setting out on a quest for everything that might reveal some sort of kinship, attraction, or secretly shared nature within them' and which persists today only in the 'counter-discourse' of modern literature, with its memory of a 'raw being . . . forgotten since the sixteenth century'.[39] Its perspective is one of *divination*, where earthly phenomena mirror the divine *mens* and can be known only through interpretation, where words and things are unified in the sign.

There is, however, an important difference between Hermetic discourse and its appropriation by Fenollosa, Pound, and Olson, a crack in continuity papered over by the moderns' embracing term 'myth'. Occult language is essentially symbolic, it discovers meaning not in things 'themselves' but in resemblances, and its way of representing the material world has little to do with 'conceptual clarity'. In the Hermetic cosmogony, things exist in an infinitely complex system of relationships; the significance of a natural object consists in a secret sympathy with something beyond itself and is governed by celestial virtues. For Paracelsus, a walnut may cure brain disorders because its kernal resembles the structure of the brain; for Plotinus and Grosseteste, the generation of light becomes identified with divine truth and goodness. Literal and metaphorical levels are confused, analogies are collapsed into identities, and arbitrary correspondences are treated as logical arguments. Of course, the whole point is that for occultists the correspondences are not arbitrary, but organic; the doctrine of the arbitrary nature of the sign is a rationalist imposition on a belief-structure which posits a causal relationship between words and things. The audacious, speculative nature of alchemy paved the way for experimental science, but in turn experiment disproved alchemical analogies. Paracelsus defines a fever variously as a microcosmic earthquake, as the product of burnt or smoking mercury, and as a disease of sulphur and nitre

– sympathetic equations rubbished by later medical discoveries.[40] Fenollosa embraces the idea that relations are more real than the things which they relate, and Pound remarks that 'A medieval "natural philosopher" would find this modern world full of enchantments, not only the light in the electric bulb, but the thought of the current hidden in air and in wire would give him a mind full of forms'.[41] Both Fenollosa and Pound believe in the ritual value or *praxis* of Hermetic symbolism, but they see its mystical philology as continuous with scientific notions of directness and clarity: 'Thought deals with no bloodless concepts but watches *things move* under its microscope.'[42] Paradoxically, what Pound calls 'real symbolism' or 'symbolism in its profounder sense', as opposed to the 'mushy technique' of the French *Symbolistes*, is defined by an essential obscurity. Like esoteric discourse, the modernist poem should be an embodied enigma, impervious to rational analysis but able to mystify the rabble while acting as a visionary text for the initiated few.[43]

The poetics of this super-natural language underwrites the ideological force of the ideogram. Pound regards the Symbolists' artificial paradise as false alchemy, a retreat from decadence into an hermetically sealed aesthetic realm, contrasting with his own project to transform Western culture from the base matter or 'tawdry cheapness' of liberal democracies driven by commerce and sustained by usury into enlightened, hierarchical city-states run by virtuous dictatorship. The hermetic ideal in the *Cantos* is exemplified by the Eleusinian Mysteries, symbolising the chthonic overcome by the metaphysics of light, and Pound's models for the ideal state and statesman derive from classical and arcane sources: the agrarian idyll personified by Hermes, phallic god of fertility, the walled, temple-centred heavenly city, the dictator as theurgist. Pound sees the heavenly cities of Ecbatana and Nineveh as archetypes of the cultural potential of Rome under Fascism, insisting that Mussolini be recognised as an 'artifex' whose 'actions are comprehensible not by logical analysis but only through the synthetic and sensuous immediacy of aesthetic intuition'.[44] The poet and the dictator share this ability to distil the rational into the sensuously immediate; both promote instinct and faith over analysis, and both subordinate history to myth because they believe that myth cultivates the desire to act (*praxis* as ritual), whereas historical analysis causes men to become bogged-down in impotent reflection. Pound's authoritarian poetic is consonant with the Fascist appeal to faith and praxis in that it invokes myth as the ground of racial identity and as an instinctual force for cultural renewal. The *Cantos* are 'impenetrable' because they condense raw historical data, esoteric speculation, demotic satire and personal epiphany without logical progression. Their paratactic arrangement reflects Pound's intuitive approach to gathering evidence. Coherence is a matter of having faith in the unity of the speaking subject, the poet's ability to combine disparate elements. Guy Davenport notes approvingly that 'Pound cancelled in his own mind the dissociations that have been isolating fact from fact for four centuries'.[45] To re-associate these 'facts' is to restore a form of archaic consciousness by which history is translated into a gnosis of mythic archetypes. Since this secret wisdom is based on interpretation and assertion, it should need no recourse to the empiricist terminology of fact, yet Pound justifies his *eidos* by relating it to scientific truth. By the early 1940s, when his Fascist sympathies are most pronounced and his anti-Semitism is at its most virulent, he gives up the appeal to clarity altogether: 'The sacred symbols are totalitarian ... That fatal inclination to want to understand logically and syllogistically what is incomprehensible is Hebrew and Protestant.'[46]

Fenollosa and Pound use scientific analogies that have only a tenuous connection with their fundamentally arcane, typological understanding of knowledge. According to Leon Surette, '[t]o men like Yeats and Pound, who were scientifically illiterate, occult physical theories – which were essentially just ancient pre-Aristotelian monism – probably seemed no more mystical than Mme Curie's radiation, Einsteinian relativity, Planck's quantum theory, Freud's subconscious, or Bergson's *élan vital*. Indeed, in many cases they seem to have thought that all of these descriptions of the nature of reality were interchangeable.'[47] Olson, too, was convinced of the need to reconcile modern scientific paradigms with the older wisdom of poetry. Inspired by the holistic reasoning of Eddington, Bohr and Whitehead, which invested physics with quasi-mystical importance – still seen today in the 'mind of God' speculations of Stephen Hawking and others – his writings are peppered with references to non-Euclidean geometry, Heisenberg's uncertainty principle, and other versions of 'process' seen as building on the foundations provided by Heraclitus. Yet, here too, as Michael Bernstein points out, 'Olson's analogies are usually more metaphoric than logical, his appropriation of scientific terminology dependent more upon parallels of resonance than upon any objectively defined reference. For Olson, science seemed to affirm both the interdependence and the permanently changing nature of reality, and he was eager to draw upon its authority, as a confirmation, not a source, of his own instinctive attitudes towards the world.'[48] Similarly, Olson's privileging of metaphor over symbol has less to do with analysis of figural language than with a desire to assimilate Poundian poetics to his own metaphysics of praxis.

> What has been lost
> is the secret of secrecy, is
> the value, viz., that the work get done, and quickly,
> without the loss of due and profound respect for
> the materials[49]

Olson's call to action, carried through his kinetic theories of 'projective verse', 'composition by field', and the faux artisanal 'objectism' ('a word to be taken to stand for the kind of relation of man to experience which a poet might state as the necessity of a line or a work to be as wood is, to be as clean as wood is as it issues from the hand of nature, to be as shaped as wood can be when a man has had his hand to it'[50]), emerges as a hard-hat revision of Imagism, maintaining the principle of direct treatment while discarding the tendency to focus on static moments. The danger is that a poetics of action will revert to what Pound and Lewis criticised as a mechanistic immersion in the present: 'No man can reflect or create, in the intellectual sense, while he is acting'.[51] But Olson follows the later Pound's development of a narrative poetic, evolving from his research on the Noh theatre, the ideogram, and his theory of phanopoeia, which reconciles the 'fixed image' with 'praxis or action' by dramatising it.[51] From 1919, Pound was formulating a historical method based on the paratactical juxtaposition of particulars: 'Any historical concept and any sociological deduction from history must assemble a great number of such violently contrasted facts if it is to be valid. It must not be a paradox, or a simple exposition of two terms.'[53] In 'Projective Verse', Olson asserts that *The Cantos* are more dramatic than Eliot's plays, and that in general Eliot's 'root is the mind alone, and a scholastic mind at that (no high *intelletto* despite his apparent clarities)'.[54] Eliot's works, therefore, are products of 'symbology', acts of comparative thought rather than acts themselves. Olson sees the poetic *act* stemming from an intellectual energy that is figuratively higher than the reflecting mind and literally lower than it ('breath'); he accuses Eliot of failing both to aspire to Renaissance *intelletto* and to respire 'down through the workings of his own throat to that place where breath comes from, where breath has its beginnings, where drama has to come from, where, the coincidence is, all act springs.'[55] There is good reason to suppose that 'symbol' in this context works as a synonym for Christianity. We have seen that for Pound true religion is occult, an *ur*-text of secret symbolism, whereas the orthodox religions he despises seek enlightenment through explanation. Pound therefore vilifies the Hebraic and protestant traditions for their use of arbitrary symbols and logical thought and attacks Jewish allegory and interpretation. Olson's ire was reserved for Catholicism, the 'filthy faith' in which he was brought up. Although not without a residual affection for Church ritual, just before beginning work on the 'Projective Verse' essay he laid claim to a poetic that would be 'truly hermetique, / Nothing catholique'.[56] As an ardent Anglo-Catholic, Eliot was bound to become the whipping-boy in Olson's campaign for organic renewal. Eliotic symbolism, therefore, stands for all that is most enervated in modernist poetry. Olson's hostility betrays a certain anxiety of influence, since his early poetry was dismissed by Edward Dahlberg as an example of the dried-up intellectualism he wished to overcome, abstract medita- tions based on 'private symbolism' that 'could be comprehended only by a reader armed with the right kind of attention'.[57] Olson never escapes this problem other than by attesting to the 'real', collective nature of symbols as Jungian archetypes, reconciling, at least in theory, *muthos* with *logos* or fact. Myth always remains as the horizon of meaning, the point at which historical facts *should* cohere. But this will to coherence is at odds with poetry that gets its energy from the symbolic irresolution of violently contrasting elements. Formally, the poem, as a field of energy, circulates an eclectic array of documentary evidence from any and every kind of research, along with personal anecdotes, snatches of overheard conversa- tion, literary quotations and allusions, and translations. Whatever its sym- bolic origins, private or public, its *objective* condition is to remain fragmentary, unstable, and unresolved; energy derives from the act of reading (the reader's desire to piece together fragments) as much as from the paratactic nature of the text itself – otherwise the poem would be nothing more than a message. Olson's commentators and biographers have tended to elide this tension between an essentially typological poetic, which assumes a matrix of symbolic unity, and a poetic of *bricolage,* in which competing fragments resist textual closure. Tom Clark, for example, describes Olson's poetry as 'based not on abstract ideas but on solid build- ing blocks of fact and document. The process of change would involve less an innovation of technique than a return to archaic means, with document taking over the onetime role of magic in the human mystery, fact that of religious ritual.'[58] The 'fact' remains, however, that documentary evidence only accedes to magical status if we buy into the symbolic determination of 'the human mystery'.

This formal problem has crucial implications for Olson's concept of action, which supposedly distances the 'post-modern' poem from modernism's lethargic symbology. The difference is ethical and political as well as aes- thetic. Ralph Maud warns against identifying Olson's project too closely with that of Pound on the grounds that Olson was 'a long-time Roosevelt Democrat and publicly declared anti-fascist' who had considered joining the war against Franco and was sympathetic to the Cultural Revolution in China.[59] Olson clearly associated the complex of ideas centred on his theory of action with revolutionary politics, as is well known from 'The Kingfishers' (1949), his most famous poem and one he saw as representing an 'Anti-Wasteland' in opposition to both Eliot's cultural negativity and Pound's nostalgic (and recently voided) political agenda.[60] The poem begins with a Heraclitean tag that 'was to become a rallying cry for a generation of poets' and was generally received as the poem's 'cultural force': 'What does not change / is the will to change'.[61] Taken as the poem's guiding principle, the maxim finds a topical example in Mao's revolution, which in 1949 was entering its final stages. Interspersed with reflections on Delphic inscriptions and the Christian mythology of the kingfisher, Olson quotes a passage from Mao's 1948 report to the Chinese Communist Party, as read to him in French by the emigré businessman and advocate of the Revolution Jean Riboud:

> I thought of the E on the stone, and what Mao said
> la lumière"
> > but the kingfisher
> de l'aurore"
> > but the kingfisher flew west
> est devant nous!
> > he got the color of his breast
> > from the heat of the setting sun!

Paraphrased later in the poem, this becomes 'The light is in the east. Yes. And we must rise, act.'

In medieval tradition, the kingfisher's yearly renewal of its feathers symbolises the Resurrection of Christ. Here, it becomes little more than an obsolete fiction ('The legends are / legends') associated with the decline of the West. The Western sun is setting, yielding to the rising light of Asia. The emphatic 'Yes' suggests we accept this call to renewal as a metanarrative within the field of the text, uniting its array of seemingly disparate allusions. Yet the poem is not so easily resolved. Guy Davenport notes its thematic correspondence with the *Pisan Cantos*: Pound and Olson see the imminent rise of Communist China as a momentous event, but both 'are equally uncertain as to its meaning', Pound because he regards Mao as a 'snotty barbarian ignorant of T'ang history', Olson because he plays Mao's call to action against 'ancient considerations that seem to have nothing to do with his revolution'.[62] In fact, Olson appears to be much more uncertain than Pound about the worth of the Cultural Revolution in that his poem sets Mao's actions in the context of other bloody historical 'changes'; as well as the Hellenic empire in the time of Plutarch and the Khmer dynasty of Cambodia, these 'considerations' include the destruction of Mexican civilisation by the conquistadores, an event that was to become close to Olson's heart following researches in the Yucatan which led him to mourn the loss of what he saw as the ancient Mayans' direct contact with nature and the cosmos. The Mayan hieroglyphs share with other archaic inscriptions, such as the mysterious E carved on the omphalos at Delphi, an occult vitality, their signs 'so clearly and densely chosen that, cut in stone, they retain the power of the objects of which they are the images'.[63] The exact significance of these inscriptions which now function as symbols of ancient wisdom, is lost to the modern world, – Olson's term is 'use' – waiting to be reclaimed. But while this communicative power fits neatly with his revision of the Poundian image, Olson recognises that the historical gap between signifier and signified may never be closed; as Davenport writes in 'The Symbol of the Archaic':

> At the heart of Olson's poem is 'the E on that oldest stone', meaning the epsilon on the omphalos stone at Delphi, which Plutarch puzzled over at the behest of Nero. We are still not certain whether it is part of the word, *Gea*, Earth, or part of a Greek citizen's name; Plutarch, always willing to be Pythagorean, gives many symbolic explanations, but for Olson the import of that conical, ancient stone was precisely that it is so ancient that we have lost the meaning of the writing upon it. When we discover what it means, we will still be dissociated forever from the complex of ideas in which it occurs. And that is the center of Olson's concern in this poem, that culture is both historically and geographically discrete. 'We are alien', Olson said, 'from everything that was most familiar.'[64]

The signifier (which might not even be an epsilon) has no signified. It therefore becomes a symbol, radically overdetermined but offering, like the ideogram itself, the potential for new meanings and connections between discrete facts. Where, in all this, the objects (as Nature or *phusis*) so integral to Olson's poetic manifest themselves remains a mystery. All the poet knows is that there was once a different way of being, in tune with natural processes, before Western pejorocracy stuck the boot in:

> When the attentions change / the jungle
> leaps in
>   even the stones are split
>   they rive
>
> Or,
> enter
> that other conqueror we more naturally recognize
> he so resembles ourselves
>
> But the E
> cut so rudely on that oldest stone
> sounded otherwise,
> was differently heard
>
> as, in another time, were treasures used

Attentions change, civilisations come to the end of their natural life and return to the chaos from which they emerged. More often than not, however, they are conquered and ruined by other civilisations. Sometimes demise results from the combined forces of natural catastrophe and cultural incursion, as is thought to be the case with the ending of the Classic Maya period in the tenth century AD. The collapse of the later period of Mayan settlement, however, is not so ambiguous: it was caused by Spanish conquest. Modern man finds destruction by 'acts of God' a more alien concept than destruction by war; the poem distinguishes invasion by the jungle from that *other* conqueror, e.g. Cortes, whose acts resemble our own inclination to rapaciousness. Whether the poem employs the term 'naturally' as an ironic comment on civilised barbarity or to say that warlike behaviour is an essential constituent of the human universe is one of its many complications. There is constant equivocation between a view of history as the fall from natural grace into pejorocracy and an account of the will to change as inevitably and naturally involving human cruelty. The section quoted above, however, suggests the former; other again to the 'other conqueror', the Delphic E 'was differently heard' just as, once, treasures were used for ceremonial, sacrificial purposes rather than as commodities. War, here, is an acquisitive, expansionist folly, the antithesis of culture as natural cultivation:

> And now all is war
> where lately there was peace
> and the sweet brotherhood, the use
> of tilled fields.

Cortes committed genocide in the name of Christianity. His violence, therefore, is linked with Western decadence as manifested in the false symbolism of the kingfisher. By presenting the bird's genesis and behaviour as cold scientific facts (culled largely from the *Encyclopaedia Britannica*), Olson repudiates the Christian legend of Resurrection. In Nature, there is no upward path to transubstantiation; the kingfisher's eggs are laid on regurgitated bones:

> On these rejectamenta
> (as they accumulate they form a cup-shaped structure) the young are born.
> And, as they are fed and grow, this nest of excrement and decayed fish
> becomes
> a dripping, fetid mass.

The precise, visceral image works against a whole tradition of romanticised bird symbolism; the effect of the real produced by documentary evidence is at the farthest remove from apparitions of poetic imagination such as Yeats's 'great peacock', made 'With the pride of his eye', and parodies the quaint 'water-dripping song' of *The Waste Land*.[65] But this does not mean that it escapes symbolism altogether. The kingfisher stands for cyclical against linear history, change as recurrence as opposed to the redemptive stasis it evinces in *Burnt Norton*: 'After the kingfisher's wing / Has answered light to light, and is silent, the light is still / At the still point of the turning world'.[66] By contrast, the principle of changingness, its paradoxical constancy

is the birth of air, is
the birth of water, is
a state between
the origin and
the end, between
birth and the beginning of
another fetid nest.

This passage, too, as Sherman Paul notes, though marked by Olson's rhythm, is also a parody of *Four Quartets*.[67] As 'revolution', the turning world has as its axis not 'light' but an agency 'no more than itself' which cannot prevent re-turn to foulness (excuse the pun). The proximity of birth and decay resonates through the poem as an emblem of historical paradox (already violating Pound's injunction that the historical image must not be a paradox): new life is born from the corpse of one civilisation, yet eventually returns to 'another fetid nest'. The question is, how to stop the will to change from revolving as the same 'old appetite' for power and destruction. Despair seeps through the cracks in the poem's fractured rhetoric, and Olson's trust in volition is at best a condition of hopefulness. Read symbolically, the kingfisher should reconcile the finite with the infinite, the tragedy of human casualty elegised by Neruda's 'Not one death but many' with the ecological awareness of Heraclitean process: 'For not only is it true, as Heraclitus used to say, that the death of heat is birth for steam, and the death of steam is birth for water, but the case is even more clearly to be seen in our own selves . . . Dead is the man of yesterday, for he is passed into the man of today; and the man of today is dying as he passes into the man of tomorrow'.[68] But because Olson has reduced the symbol to biological fact, it is doubtful whether the kingfisher can represent anything more than the closed temporality of animal behaviour and the unchanging, unwilled replication of natural forms. The thing itself allows for no redemption by *coincidentia oppositorum*. Hence the poem's final line, 'I hunt among stones', sees the poet asserting potential use-value in these remains of archaic civilisations, yet uncertain of their significance beyond the inert.

At the same time, the poem is too terse, too fraught with the questions of will and action, for it to settle into the meditation on ruins Davenport takes it to be. Olson struggles to find a revolutionary alternative to Western conquest, both in the metaphysics of process and in the recognition of contraries, which might justify the Maoist model of necessary cultural upheaval:

> with what violence benevolence is bought
> what cost in gesture justice brings
> what wrongs domestic rights involve

The danger of underlying rottenness is never far from disturbing any com-placent acceptance of such a *realpolitik*, though even here Olson's moral disgust ('what pudor pejorocracy affronts . . . what breeds where dirtiness is law') contends with the naturalised image of the 'fetid nest'. Is dirtiness a man-made law against nature or a law of nature? If the law of change involves the inevitable decline into filth, how are we to read the plea for transfiguration 'Shall you uncover honey / where maggots are?' ? Like much of the poem, this line is a riposte to Canto LXXIV, which laments the execution in 1945 of Mussolini and his mistress Claretta Petacci by the Partisans:

> The enormous tragedy of the dream in the peasant's
> bent shoulders
> Manes! Manes was tanned and stuffed,
> Thus Ben and la Clara *a Milano*
>   by the heels at Milano
> That maggots shd/ eat the dead bullock[69]

Mussolini, the dead bullock devoured by maggots (Pound's name for the anti-Fascists), becomes, like Manes, spiritual father of the Cathars, another martyred defender of the true (occult) religion. The question as set out by Olson is not his own, but flung back at an addressee who might be Pound or an imputed general audience seeking redemption within the Western tradition that led to Fascism: 'I pose you your question'. In this case, the answer is negative: honey, being one of only two foods (the other is milk) not requiring the destruction of animal or plant life, cannot be found where maggots are, therefore no redemption is possible. But the question may also be seen as directed toward spiritual transubstantiation, counter-ing Pound's historical pessimism with the possibility that sweetness may come forth from the death of Fascism. While the poem's bitterness and concluding sense of resignation suggests the former reading, its hope for renewed value in the light of non-Western alternatives implies the latter. For Pound, the fight against orthodox Christianity went hand-in-hand with Fascist neo-paganism, whereas Olson takes the opposite view; his history of persecution associates pagan cultures, such as that of the Maya, destroyed in the name of Christianity, with Maoist communism, struggling to consolidate a China which 'had been attacked, defeated, partitioned and exploited by every foreign state within reach since the middle of the nine-teenth century'.[70] As Sherman Paul argues, Davenport's liberal humanist reading of 'The Kingfishers', which tars Mao with the same brush as the destructive Cortés, ignores the fact that 'Mao is an example of the very thing Olson advises: he does not (necessarily or wholly) destroy civilization, as Davenport claims, but renews it by going outside its traditions, in this instance by bringing western thought (Marxism) to bear on the East ... this does not mean that Olson is a Marxist or sanguine about revolution, though he thought, as he later told Creeley, that "Mao makes Mexico certain." '[71] Olson distinguishes regenerative violence from wars of conquest, the maintenance of the organic community from the acquisitive society. Respect for the ancient Mayans includes accepting the blood sacrifice believed to restore order to the cosmos. The temple walls, 'black with human gore', allowed what the poem calls 'the excuser' (William H. Prescott, in his *History of the Conquest of Mexico* (1843), which Olson read in 1941) to justify massacre by the Spanish; but Olson sees the Mayan way, now reduced by centuries of colonialism to 'pitiful cultural inertia', as 'a mythic consciousness operating through energized organs of perception to produce a keen attention to the totality of the cosmos'.[72] This romanticised account of archaic consciousness, set against the alienation of commodified Western values, feeds directly into the countercultural sentiments of the 1960s and 1970s:

And the women all were beautiful
And the men stood straight and strong
They offered life in sacrifice
So that others could go on.

Hate was just a legend
And war was never known
The people worked together
And they lifted many stones

They carried them to the flatlands
And they died along the way
But they built up with their bare hands
What we still can't do today.[73]

While Olson might have objected to the glibness of Neil Young's lyric, its ecological and political heresy in the context of US imperialism is consonant with his own ideals. The inversion of colonialist representation shows 'primitives' to be more physically, mentally and technically advanced than their 'saviours'. Yet this reflection of colonialism is made in its image. Montezuma's sovereign nation is composed of peaceful, radiant subjects who gather round their king 'like the leaves around a tree', happy to be sacrificed for the good of the community. A fervent anti-war stance comes to endorse human cruelty when seen as part of the natural order, as if Mesoamerican culture were an organism precluding dissent or division.

What appears as respect for the 'otherness' of so-called primitive peoples becomes a typically colonialist reduction of complex societies to species-being, having no need for such appurtenances as civil rights since they are of one mind or *Paideuma*. In reality Mayan civilisation, for all its sophistication, was built on war, slavery, and the maintenance of order by the fear of death; causes for the decline of the Classic period include agricultural collapse, disease, foreign invasion and social revolution.[74] Where cultural nostalgists reject contemporary Western racial and national mythologies as ideological props, they prefer to treat the myths of the ancients as indexes of social unity and spiritual necessity. Olson's emphasis on the facts of locality appears to run against the grain of such atavism, yet he seeks to resurrect the polis on 'new' foundations imbued with archaic myth, and to rebuild requires destructive force. When he endorses destructiveness, as in the poem 'La Torre' (1950), it is as an organic, rejuvenating power, the apotheosis of 'breath' and mythic virility:

> To destroy
> is to start again, is a factor of
> sun, fire is
> when the sun is out, dowsed

> (to cause the jaws to grind
> before the nostrils flare
> to let breath in[75]

The modernist tower must be brought down if a new one is to be raised on the solid foundations that allow breath in: 'It will take new stone, new tufa, to finish off this rising tower.' Applied to 'The Kingfishers', this late-modernist symbol supports a reading of the poem as a rallying cry for revolutionary praxis.

As Davenport shows, for all its thetic insistence the fragmentary text of 'The Kingfishers' cannot be reassembled to form a single message. Like an ideogram, it is a mobile structure comprising numerous perspectives, a quality that has made it 'rich material for classes in schools. Its seeming inarticulateness is not a failure to articulate, but a declining to articulate images and events which can be left in free collision.'[76] By remaining open to debate, creating a dynamic field which stirs readers not only to try to make sense of formally and conceptually difficult material but also to question their own investment in the process of meaning, the poem achieves a political reflexivity lacking in works that appeal to emotive directness. Otherwise, as Jack Spicer says, what you have is not a poem but 'a letter to the editor'.[77] But like all definitions of the open text which negotiate a political dimension, Davenport's claim for the irreducible nature of the poem collides with his desire to *give meaning* to it. The critical gesture that invests the poem with an essential freedom also 'tags' freedom with a message: 'the unwilled change of war. And do not miss, out of ideological blindness, the fact that Mao, like Cortés, was exterminating a civilization, with comparable cruelty.'[78] As we have seen, the problem posed by the poem is not that readers may be ideologically blind to universal cruelty but that they cannot be sure of any insight they think they might have into the 'nature' of that cruelty. Because the poem can be read as both a cautionary meditation on the futility of war and an incitement to revolution, it cannot be resolved into support for either option. Davenport's preference for the humanist interpretation, which makes the poem a romantic elegy on ruins, disavows the possibility that Olson admires Mao and therefore promotes ideological blindness. Sherman Paul, by contrast, accepts the contextual evidence that Olson *does* support Mao, but strives to resolve the poem's oppositions by uniting its call for action with historical reserve. What the poem declares, Paul concludes, is 'that civilizations decline when there is no will to change; that the decline of civilization is not necessarily followed by the rise of another – only the agency of "actual willful men" opens that possibility; and that there is ground for hope and reason to act because all history is present and what linear history and restricted traditon have denied us is still there to be used.' What has been denied is the 'lesson' of the Maya, 'that there were people who were not estranged from the familiar, who lived in the physical world and knew how to attend to it closely, to make it a "human universe".'[79] This is all very tidy but owes more to Olson's theoretical pronouncements than to the poem itself, which, like the Delphic omphalos, cannot answer the questions raised by its glyphs. Reflexively, Paul reminds us that meaning should be sought in the formal terms of the ideogram rather than as an unequivocal message, for 'the poem, above all is an action, as most of those who have exegeted it forget, and what matters is the movement of thought that makes it a "starter", that moves Olson to further action.'[80] But if the poem is itself an action, what it enacts is the *impasse* of praxis and meditation on praxis, acts of comparative thought and acts themselves, symbology and self-identity. As Paul admits, Olson is enjoined to act but '*ponders* the difficulties of taking action in the West'.[81] 'The Kingfishers' looks to move beyond the revolutionary failure of modernism into a new world of recovered use-value and volition, yet its redemptive aesthetic is intellectually, aesthetically – and even politically – governed by the modernist *symbolon* it disavows.

Late modernism, then, identifies a specific, belated appropriation of high modernist culture which distinguishes it from neo avant-garde tendencies and postmodernism. Postmodern facture is based on the assumption that art is always already enmeshed in ideology, 'its deconstructive thrust . . .

aimed not only against the contemporary myths that furnish its subject matter, but also against the symbolic, totalizing impulse which characterizes modernist art.'[82] Responding to this account, Tyrus Miller argues that postmodernism's radical cultural scepticism 'may be more melancholy than liberating', in that to 'lose faith in the modernist myth was to recognize that art no longer had an essential function; that it could offer no comprehensive answers to spiritual, sexual, or social problems. It was to realize that the arcadia of the text or painting was not significantly different from anywhere else. Art offered no secure position from which to oppose oneself to the rest of the social world.'[83] While Miller's jeremiad may be prone to the belated modernist thinking it seeks to explain, it does highlight a very real crisis in the arts today, and nowhere more so than in the world of poetry, which offsets its often debilitating sense of irrelevance by retreating into identity politics and tribal warfare. The cultic nature of aesthetic mysticism arguably causes rather than transcends sectarian conflict, and the turn to postmodernism represents a general movement away from the belief in art as religion by other means. For many poets and critics, however, the identification of art with one form of redemptive power or another is so complete that any attempt to think otherwise negates the very essence of poetry. The late modernist poets whose work forms the basis of this study write on the brink of the postmodern abyss. Distinct, if not entirely separate, from mid- to late twentieth-century poetries which are indebted to modernism but which return to highly individualised, bardic modes of expression, such as the neo-romantics of the 1940s, the Beats of the 1950s, and the countercultural visionaries of the 1960s, they continue to affirm a redemptive aesthetic that links *poesis* with occult power while disowning the reactionary politics of high modernists such as Yeats, Eliot and Pound. Art remains the alternative order to rationalising and inevitably compromised political systems. But precisely by being posited as alternative to the political, art becomes the political alternative, albeit in the guise of 'culture'. Upholding culture, the province of the organic community, over the institutionalised collectivity, late modernism misrecognises its own temporal investment in the political. As with high modernism, its aesthetic ideology is its equation of culture with nature. Late Modernism is belated because it maintains this ideology while dissociating it from Anglo-American modernism's complicity with authoritarian regimes.

Not surprisingly, the experience of World War Two testified to the political consequences of literature that regularly attacked women, Jews and the poor, and represented dictators as cultural saviours; after this, few poets of any political tendency were about to fly the modernist flag as if nothing had muddied the pitch.

The chastening effect of the war years did not, however, bring an end to aesthetic practice predicated on the belief that modernism remains in essence a vital force which bespeaks cultural redemption. Sara Blair points out that understanding the commitment to modernism 'as necessarily linked with conservative, fascist, or right-wing political ideals is to miss the contestatory nature of Modernism's investment in form, technique, and literary value. If the landscape of modernity reads to Eliot and company as a symbolic wasteland, it appears for other writers to be a Mecca, a metropolis of multivalent possibilities.'[84] Significantly, this plea for the heterogeneity of international modernism finds its retort to the reactionary 'men of 1914' (Hulme, Eliot, Pound, Lewis) in the progressive *mêlée* of literary life in contemporary New York, with its preference for the 'American now' over the nostalgic quest for pre-modern values in the Cradle of Civilisation. The division is a little simplistic; it would be complicated by, for example, the more wide-ranging approach taken by Peter Nicholls's *Modernisms*.[85] Even so, Blair is right to see in the United States a positive reception of modernity disinclined to equate formal innovation with aesthetic autonomy.[86] Late modernism owes much of its impetus to the American scene, which maintained an avant-garde trajectory long after the taste for experimentation in Britain had soured. Charles Olson and the poets associated with Black Mountain College tended towards liberalism and the left, as did the San Franciscan coterie of Robert Duncan, Jack Spicer and Robin Blaser, and therefore appear less in tune with with the Anglo-Americans Eliot and Pound than with Williams, Zukofsky, Niedecker and Oppen, who all rejected Pound's Eurocentrism, had no truck with his fascist politics, and produced work devoid of any occult or mythic investment. And when British poetry rediscovered modernism in the 1960s, notably through J. H. Prynne and what is erroneously known as the 'Cambridge School', its primary inspiration was the United States, with its seemingly unbroken tradition of artistic experimentation. Contributors to the fugitive journal *The English Intelligencer* looked forward to a time when the British Isles would no longer be separated from America, symbolically reinstating their 'union' before continental drift fragmented the great land mass of Pangaea. Yet Pound remains the crucial influence on these poets, ostensibly because his work remained the galvanising force it was for the early modernists; the *Cantos* were an ongoing project, demanding endless exegesis in the tradition of great occult texts, and the disturbing relationship between his luminous teachings on poetic form and his postwar status as a deluded Nazi propagandist represented a huge challenge to reconcile aesthetic mysticism with contemporary ethics and politics. Until recent (postmodern?) times, liberal and left-wing poets were reluctant to equate the mythic sources of modernist tradition with the rise of fascism, even though such links were latent in the mystery cults – such as that of the *Georgekreis* – rampant in Central Europe in the late nineteenth and early twentieth centuries.[87] As Robert Casillo argues,

> Many Poundian values which critics do not consider fascistic – among them his anti-monotheism, his agrarian paganism, his solar worship, his phallocentrism, his anti-feminism, his attacks on abstraction, his anti-usury, his longing for mythical rather than historical time, his demand for a ritualized and hierarchical society – are characteristics of many versions of fascist ideology.[88]

Olson, a regular visitor to St Elizabeth's, the mental hospital where Pound was held from 1946 to 1958, deplored the ravings of 'this filthy apologist and mouther of slogans which serve men of power', whose belief in the degenerateness of Semitic cultures was 'the same god damned kind of medical nonsense Hitler and the gang used with the same seriousness, the same sick conviction'.[89] Yet he kept faith with Poundian tradition, embracing the occult, archetypal, and diffusionist cultural theories of such figures as Spengler and Jung and their mentor Frobenius, described by Janheinz Jahn as 'a pacesetter of fascism'.[90] Pound's preferred word for 'culture' is Frobenius's term *Paideuma*, used throughout his writings after 1930 to distinguish between sick and healthy racial, linguistic, aesthetic and economic 'symptoms'.[91] Olson's distinction between the moribund West and the potential resurgence of archaic consciousness is similarly indebted to Frobenius's *Kultursymptome*. An entire (late modernist) tradition of poetry and scholarship has dissociated aetiological theories of history and anthropology from their racist origins, seeing them as benignly pluralist and relativist alternatives to rational thought. That the two academic journals devoted to Pound studies are called respectively *Paideuma* and *Sagetrieb* ('myth-drive') testifies to the esteem in which these key concepts are held.

Eva Hesse's remark that although 'Pound is known to have expressed . . . some of the most purblind and even vicious notions of his generation, it is no less true that his fundamental instincts and sympathies have generally been sound' is both revealing and symptomatic of wider trends in the interpretation of modernism.[92] Hesse's assumption that humanist 'instincts and sympathies' outlast superficial political 'notions' fails to address Pound's identification of moral goodness, aesthetic beauty, and intellectual clarity with masculine power and blind faith in charismatic leadership. Neither does it comprehend the extent to which Pound's phallic, racist and authoritarian beliefs follow from his theories of instinct, nature and secret wisdom. The separation of Pound's fascist ideas from his 'fundamental instincts' has long been recognised as an inadequate response to the complex relationship between modernist aesthetics and ideology. However, the persistence of his aesthetic mysticism into later modernist poetry has never been fully acknowledged. In order to approach this issue, we need to understand how an apparently retrograde mysticism was seized as a progressive creative device in the twentieth century. That is the subject of the next chapter.

Notes

1 Flyer for *Poetry Otherwise: Shaping a Language for the New Millennium*, Emerson College, Sussex, 16–22 July 2000.
2 Quoted in Jerome J. McGann, *The Romantic Ideology: A Critical Investigation* (Chicago: University of Chicago Press, 1983), 18.
3 Leon Surette, *The Birth of Modernism: Ezra Pound, T. S. Eliot, W. B. Yeats, and the Occult* (Montreal: McGill-Queen's University Press, 1993), 13.
4 Peter French, *John Dee: The Life of an Elizabethan Magus* (London: Ark, 1984), 74.
5 Surette, *The Birth of Modernism*, 94.
6 Quoted from the website of Camphill School, Aberdeen (www.camphillschools. org.uk). See also the Steiner Waldorf Schools Fellowship website (www.steinerwaldorf. org.uk).
7 Thom Gunn, 'On the Move', in *Selected Poems 1950–1975* (London: Faber & Faber, 1979), 15.
8 Denise Riley, 'A Set of Seven' in *fragmente: a magazine of contemporary poetics*, 4 (autumn/winter 1991), pp. 14–17.
9 Donald Davie, *The Poet in the Imaginary Museum: Essays of Two Decades*. Ed. Barry Alpert (Manchester: Carcanet, 1977), 66–7. The situation can't have been quite that bad, otherwise Tomlinson, Bunting and Roy Fisher would never have been published by Oxford University Press. Until *very* recently, however, J. H. Prynne's poetry was regularly invoked by reviewers in *The Times Literary Supplement* wishing to dismiss what they saw as the crazy and irrelevant world of British modernism.
10 Miller, *Late Modernism*, 7.
11 See George Butterick, *A Guide to* The Maximus Poems *of Charles Olson* (Berkeley: University of California Press, 1980), xxii–xxv.
12 Miller, *Late Modernism*, 29.
13 Miller, *Late Modernism*, 43.
14 Lawrence Rainey, *Institutions of Modernism: Literary Elites and Public Culture* (New Haven: Yale University Press, 1998), 3.
15 Miller, *Late Modernism*, 32.
16 Miller, *Late Modernism*, 9; 24.
17 Miller, *Late Modernism*, 125.
18 Quoted in Miller, *Late Modernism*, 10–11. The texts referred to are Jameson's *Postmodernism, or, The Cultural Logic of Late Capitalism* (Durham: University of North Carolina Press, 1991) and Wilde's *Horizons of Assent: Modernism, Postmodernism, and the Ironic Imagination* (Baltimore: Johns Hopkins University Press, 1981).
19 Miller, *Late Modernism*, 14.
20 Charles Altieri, 'From Symbolist Thought to Immanence: The Ground of Postmodern American Poetics', in Paul A. Bové, ed., *Early Postmodernism: Foundational Essays* (Durham, NC: Duke University Press, 1995). 'Early Postmodernism' is yet another variation on the theme. In submitting a revisionary theory of late

modernism, I hope I am providing a critique of conceptual and periodic vagueness rather than merely adding to the proliferation of jargon. On a recent BBC Radio 4 programme, John Cage was described as 'a pre-post-modern ironist'.

21 Jerome Rothenberg and Diane Rothenberg, *Symposium of the Whole: A Range of Discourse Towards an Ethnopoetics* (Berkeley: University of California Press, 1983), vii.

22 Quoted in Rothenberg and Rothenberg, *Symposium of the Whole*, xii.

23 In a later survey of poetry from after World War Two, Rothenberg writes that 'There was a breakdown, first, of the more tyrannical aspects of the earlier literary and art movements, and a turning away with that from totalizing/authoritarian ideologies and individuals', which led to 'an alliance for some with previously suppressed religions and cultural forms: shamanism, tantrism, sufism, kabbala, peyotism, etc.' Introduction to Jerome Rothenberg and Pierre Joris, *Poems for the Millennium: The University of California Book of Modern and Postmodern Poetry. Vol. 2: From Postwar to Millennium* (Berkeley: University of California Press, 1998), 5; 7. 'Totality' is now linked with modernist authoritarianism instead of being a synonym for 'holism'. Late modernists struggle constantly to redefine terminology, either to prise themselves free of reactionary language or to make their own atavism more acceptable to public scepticism.

24 Altieri, 'From Symbolist Thought to Immanence', 106.

25 Robert Duncan, quoted in Catherine R. Stimpson, 'Charles Olson: Preliminary Images', in Bové, ed., *Early Postmodernism*, 161; Charles Olson, 'Human Universe', in *Collected Prose*. Ed. Donald Allen and Benjamin Friedlander (Berkeley University of California Press, 1997), 161. Altieri notes that 'arguments for value based on nature, or for that matter on any prereflective qualities of experience, require an act of faith. And faith does not come easily today, a factor which may help explain why poetry plays such a small role in contemporary intellectual life.' ('From Symbolist Thought to Immanence', 134.)

26 Olson, 'Human Universe', 166.

27 Olson, 'Human Universe', 157–8.

28 Olson, 'Human Universe', 158–9; 162.

29 Quoted in Butterick, *A Guide to* The Maximus Poems, 24–5.

30 M. I. Finley, *The Ancient Greeks* (Harmondsworth: Penguin Books, 1966), 58; 60.

31 Ezra Pound, 'Cavalcanti', in *Literary Essays of Ezra Pound*. Ed. T. S. Eliot (London: Faber & Faber, 1968), 185.

32 Quoted in Marjorie Perloff, 'Pound/Stevens: Whose Era', in *The Dance of the Intellect: Studies in the Poetry of the Pound Tradition* (Cambridge: Cambridge University Press, 1987), 9–10.

33 D. S.Carne-Ross, quoted in Perloff, *The Dance of the Intellect*, 9.

34 Robert Graves, *The Greek Myths: Volume One* (London: Penguin Books, 1960), 95. Carne-Ross assumes, moreover, that the meaning of a myth is cut and dried: 'Persephone is in that green tip'. Yet the equation of Persephone's reappearance from the underworld with spring has been contested: 'Many cultures have a myth in which the earth goddess, or goddess of reproduction, hides for part of the year – an obvious explanation for agricultural seasons. However, in the Greek myth two goddesses disappear, and only Demeter [Ceres] is the earth goddess proper. So what are we to make of Persephone's disappearance? The clue is in the pomegranate, a fruit which gives a blood-red juice and which is always associated with Persephone and the underworld. My interpretation is that Persephone's arrival at the menarche, symbolized by the pomegranate, and her disappearance articulates the confinement

connected with menstrual taboos. She cannot possibly be connected with agricultural "seasons" since the narcissus, which effects her disappearance, is a spring flower.' (Barbara Smith, 'Greece', in Carolyne Larrington, ed., *The Feminist Companion to Mythology* (London: Pandora Press, 1992), 89.)

35 C. Kerényi, 'Prolegomena', in C. G. Jung and C. Kerényi, *Essays on a Science of Mythology: The Myth of the Divine Child and the Mysteries of Eleusis*. Trans. R. F. C. Hull (Princeton: Princeton University Press, 1969 [1949]), 5–6. Jung and Kerényi repeat the classic modernist contradictions, testifying to the ineffable nature of myth while classifying, psychologising, anthropologising and typologising it – in short, explaining it. Like Fenollosa and Pound, they seek to preserve Nature from its denigration by modern scientific rationalism but want 'the freedom from falsehood that true science confers upon us' (1). They describe myth as primary and direct yet rich and many-sided, resisting symbolism even though it is manifest in 'budlike' symbolic forms. Interpretations of these symbols may be erroneous, yet the 'ground' of myth retains a timeless reality. Thus, while we do not know what the rituals at Eleusis actually mean, we can be sure of the redemptive, primordial value of their δραμα μνστιχον. Myth is ultimately mysticism. And, in case anyone were to object to the validity of this *coincidentia oppositorum* (which is, in effect, a romantic notion of the symbol, the unification of opposites), Jung offers a get-out clause: 'as soon as one tries to abstract the "real essence" of the picture, the whole thing becomes cloudy and indistinct. In order to understand its living function, we must let it remain an organic thing in all its complexity and not try to examine the anatomy of its corpse in the manner of the scientist, or the archaeology of its ruins in the manner of the historian.' ('The Psychological Aspects of the Kore', in *Essays on a Science of Mythology*, 156.)

36 Olson, 'Projective Verse' (1950), in *Collected Prose*, 242.

37 Jacques Derrida, 'Violence and Metaphysics: An Essay on the thought of Emmanuel Levinas', in *Writing and Difference*. Trans. Alan Bass (London: Routledge and Kegan Paul, 1978), 139. Derrida argues, via Heidegger, that philological accounts of Being always emerge as ontic metaphors for an ontological category that theoretically resists '*every metaphor*' (138). 'Every philology which allegedly reduces the *meaning* of Being to the metaphorical origin of the *word* "Being", whatever the historical (scientific) value of its hypotheses, misses the history of the meaning of Being', because it will not 'be able to account for the thought for which "respiration" (or any other determined thing) becomes a determination of Being among others' – such as 'grow' (138–9). Kerényi and Jung's science of myth follows a similar *Schlitterlogik*. As the ultimate ground of culture, myth precedes even the 'monads', which Frobenius describes as the structural principles of the various views of the world in various cultures; yet its mystery is always made available to archetypal thought: 'Proclaimed, it were but a word; kept silent, it is *being*.' (Kerényi and Jung, *Essays on a Science of Mythology*, 19; 183.) Once again, the history of the meaning of being is missed. Kenner's discussion of the copula is in his *The Pound Era* (Berkeley: University of California Press, 1971), 224–5.

38 Ernest Fenollosa, *The Chinese Written Character as a Medium for Poetry*. Ed. Ezra Pound (San Francisco: City Lights Books, 1964), 22–3. On conceptual problems with the ideogram, see Jean-Michel Rabaté, *Language, Sexuality, and Ideology in Ezra Pound's* Cantos (London: Macmillan, 1986), 78–81; Paul Smith, *Pound Revised* (London: Croom Helm, 1983), 62–4.

39 Michel Foucault, *The Order of Things: An Archaeology of the Human Sciences* (London: Tavistock, 1974), 55; 44. The philosophers of late antiquity preferred to call themselves theurgists (*theurgy*, 'higher magic') because the title dissociated them

from common jugglers and charlatans, the *magoi* and *goetes*. E. R. Dodds uses the term *shaman* in the context of Greek studies because it is more neutral than *magus* or *thaumaturge* ('miracle-worker'): 'Empedocles represents . . . a very old type of personality, the shaman who combines the still undifferentiated functions of magician and naturalist, poet and philosopher, preacher, healer, and public counsellor.' (*The Greeks and the Irrational* (Berkeley: University of California Press, 1951), 146.) See George Luck, *Arcana Mundi: Magic and the Occult in the Greek and Roman Worlds* (UK: Crucible, 1987), 11; 21; 25.

40 See Brian Vickers, 'Analogy versus Identity: The Rejection of Occult Symbolism, 1580–1680', in Brian Vickers, ed., *Occult and Scientific Mentalities in the Renaissance* (Cambridge: Cambridge University Press, 1984).

41 Pound, 'Cavalcanti', in *Literary Essays*, 154–5.

42 Fenollosa, *The Chinese Written Character*, 12.

43 See *Ezra Pound and Dorothy Shakespear: Their Letters 1909–1914*. Ed. Omar Pound and A Walton Litz (New York: New Directions, 1984), 302; Ezra Pound, *Gaudier-Brzeska: A Memoir* (New York: New Directions, 1970), 89; 84–5; James Longenbach, *Stone Cottage: Pound, Yeats and Modernism* (New York: Oxford University Press, 1988), Chapter 3; Boris de Rachewiltz, 'Pagan and Magic Elements in Ezra Pound's Works', in Eva Hesse, ed., *New Approaches to Ezra Pound: A Co-ordinated Investigation of Pound's Poetry and Ideas* (London: Faber & Faber, 1969), 174. For Surette, literary modernism 'retained the obscurity of the *Symbolistes* but justified it on the grounds of philosophical relativism, or philosophical perspectivism, rather than on the esoteric grounds of ineffability as *Symbolisme* had done.' (*The Birth of Modernism*, 81.)

44 Robert Casillo, *The Genealogy of Demons: Anti-Semitism, Fascism, and the Myths of Ezra Pound* (Chicago: Northwestern University Press, 1988), 110.

45 Guy Davenport, 'Persephone's Ezra', in Hesse, ed., *New Approaches to Ezra Pound*, 157.

46 Pound, 'Idee Fondamentali', in *Meridiano di Roma* (10 May, 1942), translated and quoted by Peter Nicholls in his 'Lost Object(s): Ezra Pound and the Idea of Italy', in Taylor and Melchior, eds, *Ezra Pound and Europe*, 171–2.

47 Surette, *The Birth of Modernism*, 150.

48 Michael Bernstein, *The Tale of the Tribe: Ezra Pound and the Modern Verse Epic* (Princeton: Princeton University Press, 1980), 242.

49 Olson, 'The Praises', in *The Collected Poems of Charles Olson*. Ed. George Butterick (Berkeley: University of California Press, 1987), 100.

50 Olson, *Collected Prose*, 247.

51 Wyndham Lewis, 'Essay on the Objective of Plastic Art in our Time', in Walter Michel and C. J. Fox, eds., *Wyndham Lewis on Art: Collected Writings 1913–1956* (London: Thames and Hudson, 1969), 213.

52 Ezra Pound, *ABC of Reading* (London: Faber & Faber, 1961), 52.

53 Ezra Pound, 'Pastiche. The Regional', in *The New Age*, Vol. XXV, No. 17 (21 August, 1919), p. 284.

54 Olson, 'Projective Verse', in *Collected Prose*, 248–9.

55 Olson, 'Projective Verse', in *Collected Prose*, 249.

56 Olson, 'The Morning News', in *The Collected Poems*, 118. At the same time, Olson had become intensely preoccupied with D. H. Lawrence's pagan physicalism, the theory of breath emerging as a version of the 'sacral ganglion' of Lawrence's *Psychoanalysis and the Unconscious*. See Tom Clark, *Charles Olson: The Allegory of a Poet's Life* (New York: Norton, 1991), 161.

57 Clark, *Charles Olson*, 145.

58 Clark, *Charles Olson*, 124. This literary ideal harks back to modernism's original fusion of opposites: 'if, finally, one were to seek the precisely defining event, the supremely symbolic point, one would surely turn back to the nineties; and to, for instance, Strindberg's complete, desperate and protracted attention to alchemy, that unique fusion of reason and unreason, science and magic'. (Malcolm Bradbury and James McFarlane, eds, *Modernism: 1890–1930* (Harmondsworth: Penguin, 1976) 49.)

59 Ralph Maud, *Charles Olson's Reading: A Biography* (Carbondale: Southern Illinois University Press, 1996), 63.

60 See Butterick, *A Guide to* The Maximus Poems, xxiv; Maud, *Charles Olson's Reading*, 59–60; Sherman Paul, *Olson's Push: Origin, Black Mountain, and Recent American Poetry* (Baton Rouge: Louisiana State University Press, 1978), 10–11.

61 Clark, *Charles Olson*, 147. All quotations from 'The Kingsfishers' refer to the text in Charles Olson, *The Distances* (New York: Grove Press, 1960), 5–11.

62 Guy Davenport, 'Olson', in *The Geography of the Imagination: Forty Essays* (San Francisco: North Point Press, 1981), 88.

63 Olson, 'Human Universe', in *Collected Prose*, 159.

64 Davenport, *The Geography of the Imagination*, 18.

65 W. B. Yeats, 'The Peacock', in *Collected Poems* (London: Macmillan, 1950), 135–6. James Longenbach notes that this paean to imaginative richness 'was a justification for a kind of poetry that excluded "the mob," who were interested in accumulating different sorts of riches.' (*Stone Cottage*, 51.) The peacock's splendour was obviously not enough to prevent Yeats tucking into the bird served up at Wilfred Blunt's poets' banquet; Pound told his mother that the peacock 'went very well with the iron-studded barricades on the stairway and other mediaeval relics and Burne-Jones tapestry.' (*Stone Cottage*, 67.) In any case, the link between ingestion and acquisitive power is mythic: 'There are many ways in which man could participate in bird-*mana*. He could, and also ruthlessly did, eat the bird.' (Jane Harrison, *Themis: A Study of the Social Origins of Greek Religion* (London: Merlin Press, 1963), 110.)
The relevant line of *The Waste Land* is 357: 'Drip drop drip drop drop drop drop', glossed in a note at the end of the poem on the hermit thrush *Turdus aonalaschkae pallasii*: 'Chapman says (*Handbook of Birds of Eastern North America*) "it is most at home in secluded woodland and thickety retreats . . . Its notes are not remarkable for variety or volume, but in purity and sweetness of tone and exquisite modulation they are unequalled". Its "water-dripping song" is justly celebrated.' (T. S. Eliot, *Selected Poems* (London: Faber & Faber, 1961), 65; 72–3.)

66 T. S. Eliot, *Four Quartets* (London: Faber & Faber, 1964), 12.

67 Paul, *Olson's Push*, 21–2.

68 Plutarch, 'The E at Delphi', quoted in Davenport, *The Geography of the Imagination*, 93.

69 *The Cantos of Ezra Pound* (London: Faber & Faber, 1964), 451.

70 Eric Hobsbawm, *Age of Extremes: The Short Twentieth Century 1914–1991* (London: Michael Joseph, 1994), 463.

71 Paul, *Olson's Push*, 16.

72 Clark, *Charles Olson*, 192; 199.

73 Neil Young with Crazy Horse, 'Cortez the Killer', on *Zuma* (Warner Brothers Records, 1975).

74 See Michael D. Coe, *The Maya* (Harmondsworth: Penguin, 1971); Elizabeth Bone, ed., *Ritual Human Sacrifice in MesoAmerica: A Conference at Dumbarton Oaks, Octo-*

ber 13th and 14th, 1979 (Washington, DC: Dumbarton Oaks Research Library, 1984).

75 Olson, *Collected Poems*, 189–90.

76 Davenport, *The Geography of the Imagination*, 99.

77 Jack Spicer, *The House that Jack Built: The Collected Lectures of Jack Spicer*. Ed. Peter Gizzi (Hanover: Wesleyan University Press / University Press of New England, 1998), 14.

78 Davenport, *The Geography of the Imagination*, 92.

79 Paul, *Olson's Push*, 28–9.

80 Paul, *Olson's Push*, 11.

81 Paul, *Olson's Push*, 23 (my italics). 'For, as Aristotle saith, it is not γνφσισ but πραξισ must be the fruit. And how πραξισ can be, without being moved to practise, it is no hard matter to consider.' (Sidney, *A Defence of Poetry*. Ed. Jan van Dorsten (Oxford: Oxford University Press, 1986), 39.)

82 Craig Owens, 'The Allegorical Impulse: Towards a Theory of Postmodernism', in Brian Wallis, ed., *Art After Modernism: Rethinking Representation* (New York: New Museum of Contemporary Art, 1984), 235.

83 Miller, *Late Modernism*, 125.

84 Sara Blair, 'Modernism and the Politics of Culture', in Michael Levenson, ed., *The Cambridge Companion to Modernism* (Cambridge: Cambridge University Press, 1999), 166. Blair's essay shows the difficulty of containing the modernist 'period'. One of her key texts is William Carlos Williams's epic poem *Paterson* (1946–58); like most academic surveys of modernism, the *Cambridge Companion* makes 1939 its cut-off point.

85 Peter Nicholls, *Modernisms: A Literary Guide* (London: Macmillan, 1995). Nicholls's history of literary international relations complements Bradbury and McFarlane's *Modernism* in emphasising the plurality of artistic responses to the condition of modernity. Even so, the 'men of 1914' are seen as standing for the 'hegemonic' definition of modernism as a critique of modernity, in contrast to the expressionistic and revolutionary tendencies of the European avant-gardes. The 'tangential' writings of women modernists such as H. D., Stein and Loy 'seem to stand outside "modernism"' because they disrupt both the phallic classicism of the Anglo-American tradition and 'the gendered aesthetics of the various avant-gardes' (222). The modernism in scare quotes continues to act as what, in her paean to H. D.'s marginalism, Susan Stanford Friedman calls 'the reactionary center' from which revised definitions of modernism radiate, even if the tag is a contradiction in terms. (Friedman, 'Modernism of the "Scattered Remnant": Race and Politics in the Development of H. D.'s Modernist Fiction', quoted in Rainey, *Institutions of Modernism*, 148.) H. D. may be described as marginal for current critical purposes, yet it is hard not to recall her centrality to early modernist polemics. (Rainey derides her aesthetic as a thin assimilation of mainstream modernism: 'a mix of bland notions from popular occultism and generalizations that denounce contemporary humanity in the abstract and yet promise everyone that he or she is assured of becoming a god.' *Institutions*, 164.)

86 By contrast, Vorticism and Imagism, often described as the British avant-garde, asserted autonomy. Again, see Rainey, *Institutions*, 30: 'Imagism, in short, was a movement to end all movements: informal, antitheoretical, absorbed in matters of writerly technique, and averse to more global programs that linked poetry to contemporary social transformations or posed questions about the status and functions of art. Though Imagism is commonly treated as the first avant-garde in Anglo-American literature, it was really something quite different – the first anti-avant-garde.'

87 Hindsight is, of course, all too easy. Many adepts of vitalist cults did not know where

their cultural experiments were leading. Stefan George himself was horrified by the emergence of Nazism and anti-Semitism, and fled from Germany in 1933. Another member of the *Kreis*, Ernst Kantorowicz, was a Jew and Polish aristocrat who emigrated to California, where he became a professor of medieval history. At Berkeley, where his pupils included Spicer and Blaser, Kantorowicz was a flamboyant and somewhat anti-authoritarian figure who nevertheless (like Olson) 'discouraged women from attending his classes; his male students thought of him as a god'. (Lewis Ellingham and Kevin Killian, *Poet Be Like God: Jack Spicer and the San Francisco Renaissance* (Hanover: Wesleyan University Press / University Press of New England, 1998), 20–1.) The influence of Central European scholars with a background in 'secret wisdom' on the intellectual and artistic life of the United States cannot be overestimated, the pervasive presence being that of C. G. Jung.

88 Casillo, *The Genealogy of Demons*, 22.

89 Olson, quoted in E. Fuller Torrey, *The Roots of Treason: Ezra Pound and the Secrets of St Elizabeth's* (London: Sidgwick and Jackson, 1984), 226–7. Pound is the only US poet to be convicted of treason. His incarceration in St Elizabeth's was the result of a successful campaign by members of the American literary establishment (including Archibald MacLeish, Dudley Fitts, James Laughlin, T. S. Eliot, H. D., and Robert Frost) to save him from trial and execution by pleading insanity. According to Torrey, Dr Winfred Overholser, the presiding government psychiatrist in the case, 'had exaggerated Pound's symptoms and disabilities; when exaggeration under oath crosses an indefinable line it can be perjury. Some of Dr Overholser's colleagues think he may have crossed the line but say such perjury was carried out with the best of intentions. As one of them succinctly summarized it: "Of course Dr Overholser committed perjury. Pound was a great artist, a national treasure. If necessary I would have committed perjury too – gladly"' (218).

90 Janheinz Jahn, *Leo Frobenius: The Demonic Child* (Austin: University of Texas African and Afro-American Studies and Research Center, 1974), 13–17. On Frobenius and diffusionist theories of history see Surette, *The Birth of Modernism*, 60–73.

91 In a letter to T. S. Eliot of 1 February 1940, Pound writes 'I know you jib at China and Frobenius cause they ain't pie church, and neither of us likes sabages, black habits, etc. . . . I shd. claim to get on from where Frobenius left off, in that his Morphology was applied to savages and my interest is in civilizations at their *most*.' (*The Selected Letters of Ezra Pound 1907–1941*. Ed. D. D. Paige (London: Faber & Faber, 1950), 336.) See Casillo, *The Genealogy of Demons*, 76: 'Pound uses the term Paideuma in a racial sense, as when he tells the supposedly pro-Semitic English that they are at the end of their "paideuma", that is their "race conviction", their "race consciousness".' See also Rabaté's discussion of 'organic symptoms' in *Language, Sexuality and Ideology*, 47–51.

92 Eva Hesse, Introduction to *New Approaches to Ezra Pound*, 49.

2

CUNNING MAN: EZRA POUND AND SECRET WISDOM

> To be, Guido,
> a simple and elegant province all by myself
>
> like you, would mean that a toss of my head,
> a wink, a lurch against the nearest brick
>
> had captured painful felicity and all its opaque
> nourishment in a near and cosmic stanza, ah!
>
> (Frank O'Hara, 'A Poem in Envy of Cavalcanti')

> For a moment she rested against me
> Like a swallow half blown to the wall,
> And they talk of Swinburne's women,
> And the shepherdess meeting with Guido.
> And the harlots of Baudelaire.
>
> (Ezra Pound, 'Shop Girl')

> Kore! O visage as of sun-glare, thunderous
> awakener, light-treader!
> will you not wake us again? shake the earth under us?
>
> (Robert Duncan, 'Evocation')

The essence of occult gnosis is its deification of the human. It is not a form of secular humanism, but a belief in the power of the human to become god-like. A ready-made for romantic individualism, it posits exceptional souls as strangers in a strange land awaiting the moment when their privileged access to supernatural wisdom will usher in a new age of expanded consciousness, reuniting humanity with the organic forces suppressed by technocracies and world-renouncing religions alike. From a Christian perspective, of course, any emphasis on the self-deifying power of man is idolatrous. But it would be too simplistic to view the post-classical tradition of occult religion as fundamentally opposed to Christianity. During the fifteenth and sixteenth centuries, Hermetic philosophy was largely a reactionary movement which tried to preserve a medieval episteme based on universal analogy and sympathetic magic against the new scientific cosmology of Galileo, Kepler and Copernicus. Its discovery of the *Corpus Hermeticum*, a set of mystical writings attributed to the ancient Egyptian magus Hermes Trismegistus and thought to be the *ur*text of revealed wisdom, appeared to validate an intuitive and eclectic approach to the divine which fused the astro-magical universe of paganism with Christian mysticism. While the enthusiasm for speculation based on ritual magic was bound to fall foul of the Church, which associated such practices with demonism, and regarded the equation of God with the *intellectus* of man as heretical, Renaissance magi such as Marsilio Ficino and John Dee saw their work as a contribution to reuniting Christendom. Their universal religion, however, turned out to be based less on secret wisdom than on false history. Humanist scholarship revealed that the *Corpus Hermeticum*, like the *Chaldean Oracles* (thought to be the work of Zoroaster, the most ancient of the prophets) and the Orphic hymns, was in fact written by various unknown authors between AD 100 and 300. With their congeries of ancient Egyptian, Greek, Jewish, and Persian wisdom, these Gnostic authors were themselves looking back to a magical Golden Age as an alternative to mainstream Christianity. The Renaissance Hermetists, therefore, were far more involved in a tradition of *renovatio* than they realised. Ironically, their desire for what Mircea Eliade calls 'a mystical restoration of man's original dignity and powers' furthered the cause of the new science by making a theological virtue of human *will*: 'Hermeticism raised man from the pious and awestruck observer of God's wonders and encouraged him to operate within his universe by using the powers of the cosmos to his own advantage.'[1] The Hermetists themselves, though, interpreted new developments in mathematics and physics not as rational evidence but as astrological symbolism; Dee and Bruno, for example, were supporters of the Copernican theory of heliocentricity, but only because it appeared to them to presage the return of magical religion. Bruno, a figure often praised for his 'forward-looking' idea that the Universe is infinite, was, as Frances Yates shows, 'an out-and-out magician . . . for whom the Copernican diagram was a hieroglyph of the divine, who defended earth-movement with Hermetic arguments concerning the magical life in all nature, whose aim was to achieve Hermetic gnosis, to reflect the world in the *mens* by magical means, including the stamping of magic images of the stars on memory, and so to become a great Magus and miracle-working religious leader.'[2]

The Humanists' deconstruction of the Hermetic texts and the rise of empirical science forced esoteric religions underground, leading to a proliferation of counter-Enlightenment secret societies and sects in eighteenth-century Europe. Romantic religious thought was dominated by Neoplatonic dissent from orthodox Christianity, but in the late nineteenth century 'occultism' (a term first used in English in 1881) takes on a renewed identity resolutely opposed to organised religion and to Christianity in particular. The chief reason for this is the countercultural development of the notion of 'secret history' derived from the Abbé Barruel's anti-Jacobin tirades at the close of the eighteenth century. Exploiting the method on which occult scholarship bases its own interminable narratives – essentially a principle of affinity drawn from sympathetic magic, which reads coincidence as fact – Barruel forged an elaborate account of the French Revolution's pagan origins. He claimed that the atheist *philosophes* were in league with the 'Occult Lodges of the Freemasons', the conspiratorial force behind all political movements that sought to destroy the social order of states founded on Christianity and monarchy.[3] By portraying Christianity as the spiritual voice of the Ancien Régime, directly opposed to Enlightenment and esoteric movements, Barruel secured its image as conservative and authoritarian. The occult, by contrast, came to be imbued with a radical, anti-authoritarian quality it has not lost even after becoming associated with Nazism. Masonry, however, was far from being a subversive movement, and was too locally differentiated to make up an international conspiracy; its carefully guarded secrecy was a gift to reactionary critics such as Barruel and Edmund Burke, who put a conspiratorial slant on what was already an invented tradition. In turn,

> [t]he eccentric and occult history that descends from Barruel adopts his hermeneutic, his reliance on private and unofficial information, his practice of tracing a tradition, and his identification of that tradition with Jacobinism and sedition. But occult history reverses his animus, regarding as oppressed heroes and martyrs those whom Barruel attacked as seditious heretics and revolutionaries. The secret history of Europe becomes the history of the struggle of an oppressed minority culture – typically regarded as morally, spiritually, and aesthetically superior to mainstream culture – against arbitrary authority.[4]

The proliferation of personal religions and cults in the last quarter of the nineteenth century springs, then, from the romantic invention of counterculture. But while the alternative spirituality of the period retained a seditious element – notably in the radical aesthetic of Rimbaud's 'alchemy of the word', a central influence on the modernist avant-garde[5] – its countercultural impetus was, unsurprisingly, at the farthest remove from the revolutionary politics exemplified by Marxism. The 'personalisation' of religious practices underwritten by occult tradition was brought about by an uneasy fusion of the progressive and reactionary components of modernity. These include: the humanisation and paganisation of the historical Christ by Strauss, Renan, and the Tübingen school scholars, who recast Jesus as a type of mythic man; Frazerian anthropology, which performed a similar role by simultaneously relativising world religions and reducing them to a set of primordial ritual impulses; the rise of *Lebensphilosophie* and the huge impact of Nietzsche's assault on Christian ideology; Stirner's Egoism; the positive reception of Social Darwinism in the form of Haeckel's monism (which was intended to be a religion based on the natural sciences but which quickly slid into advocacy of eugenics, nature worship and German nationalism); the negative reception of Social Darwinism resulting from the *fin-de-siècle* obsession with degeneration; and the use of scientific method to support parapsychology and speculative theories of the 'unconscious', as in the work of the Society for Psychical Research and Eduard von Hartmann (whose *Die Philosophie des Unbewussten* mixed Schopenhauer with evolutionary biology and went through ten editions between 1869 and 1890).

These factors were not homogeneous but fed a general desire for cultural renewal through redemptive individualism. This found its focus in a variety of heretical movements of which the Theosophical Society and the Hermetic Order of the Golden Dawn are only the tip of the iceberg as far as the cultic influence on modernism is concerned. Only recently, for example, has the impact of Spiritualism on British and US culture been taken seriously by literary scholars, and there is scant recognition of the part played by neopagan groups in central Europe between 1900 and 1920.[6] During this period the Swiss village of Ascona became a centre for alternative therapies and bourgeois-bohemian experimentation, the San Francisco or Brighton of its day, frequented by D. H. Lawrence, Hermann Hesse and Franz Kafka, among others.[7] Theosophy and its rival school Anthroposophy put down roots in California, and between the wars the state became a magnet for Westerners attracted by the messianic teachings of gurus such as Krishnamurti and Swami Prabhavananda, who were drawn there by wealthy patrons. Ironically, emigré intellectuals such as Aldous Huxley, whose anthology *The Perennial Philosophy* (1945) lays claim to a continuous gnostic tradition, made their 'journey to the East' by going West: another emblem there. In the 1930s Jung made Ascona the site of his Eranos conferences, which drew together a new generation of anthropologists and occult scholars (including Henri Corbin, Erich Neumann, Carl Kerényi and Joseph Campbell) persuaded by Jung's archetypal theories. Eliade, himself a leading member of this generation, argues that a new, scientifically informed, comparative study of ritual practices had, by the 1940s and 1950s, rid occultism of its associations with 'obscurantist fakirs and psychopathic black magicians'; Corbin's work on esoteric Persian tracts, Gershom Scholem's monographs on the Kabbalah and Jewish Gnosticism, Joseph Needham's history of Chinese alchemy, and Eliade's own investigations of shamanism and yoga all disclose 'a very coherent and profound world of meaning in texts that had generally been dismissed as magic and superstition'.[8] This revaluation of 'primitive' religious practices and holistic cosmogonies furthered the lines of enquiry begun by positivist anthropology, becoming as important to Olson and Prynne as Frazer, Lévy-Bruhl and Jane Harrison were to Pound and Eliot. But while Eliade warned that what he calls the 'occult explosion' conflates disparate elements of Eastern wisdom into a false unity, this did not prevent his research from helping to legitimise all manner of cultic fantasies in the Western world of the 1960s. For every poet and scholar seeking an alternative to the ills of modernity in what Robert Duncan calls a 'primordial reality that challenges the boundaries of convention', there is an L. Ron Hubbard, an Anton LaVey, a Charles Manson.[9] For every research centre, school or commune dedicated to organic living, there is a Thule Society, a Process Church of the Final Judgement, an Order of the Solar Temple. Late modernism's positive spin on 'secret history' may have been inspired by the need to counter the role played by orthodox Christianity in supporting Western expansionism – of which the Bush/Blair axis at the beginning of the twenty-first century is a prime example – but it ignores the fact that the occult, like all forms of religious mystification, yields more readily to regressive than to progressive elements. The New Age movements of the last half of the twentieth-century show a benign aspect in their concern for 'personal growth' and ecological awareness, but they are prone to charlatanry in the Blavatsky tradition, are prey to fantasies of male resurgence (e.g. the popularity of *Iron John* (1987) by the lyric poet Robert Bly), and are the favoured medium of neofascist intellectuals such as Julius Evola, Savitri Devi and Miguel Serrano (author of *C. G. Jung and Hermann Hesse* (1966) and *The Golden Band: Esoteric Hitlerism* (1978)).[10] Duncan was too sensitive a critic of US politics in the 1960s to be unaware of this problem:

> Today we play out in East Asia all the grievous patterns once enacted in Catholic crusades against gnostics and Jews or Protestant persecutions of Catholics and witches. The very inspiration that carries the artist through in a state that combines fear for form and faith in form to realize the imperatives of his poem, moves makers of history who write their works in the lives of men. Hitler moves as the wrath of God to show a terrible truth about Germany, about Europe, about our Western civilization itself; as Johnson today betrays the character of Babbit swollen with his opportunity in history.

> Where history becomes myth, men are moved not towards the ends they
> desire but towards their fates, the ends they deserve.

Yet he soon reverts to the affirmation of poetry as personal gnosis: 'The
poem that moves me when I write is an active presence in which I work.
I am not concerned with whether it is a good or a bad likeness to some convention men hold; for the Word is for me living Flesh, and the body of my
own thought and feeling, my own presence, becomes the vehicle for the
process of genetic information.'[11]

In the following discussion, I describe Pound as an 'occult' poet. By this
I do not mean that his interest in the cultic practices indulged by Yeats and
Blavatsky et al. was anything but marginal to his *Lebenskraft*. His interest
in darker magi associated with the Golden Dawn, such as Aleister Crowley,
is non-existent. Although Pound put great faith in the regenerative value of
the fertility rituals known as the Eleusinian Mysteries, he was primarily
attracted to them *because* they are mysterious – it is hard to imagine him
getting involved in the nudist ceremonies of the Feraferia, a Californian
sect dedicated to the Eleusinian goddess Kore. Pound reserved his expression of faith for a more complete artifex, Mussolini. As I will argue in this
chapter, the study of comparative mythology and the use of Hermetic
tradition to sponsor a Nietzschean project of 'self-renovation' have more in
common than historians of modernism suppose. Specifically, Pound's Neoplatonic writings show that modernism destroyed the conceptual opposition between positivist theories of the human sciences and aesthetic
mysticism. The legacy remains today in a residual attachment to the belief
in the poet as 'seer' and the redemptive function of art in general. Tim Redman, for example, prefaces his empirical study of Pound and Italian Fascism
by lamenting the demise of the poet as 'cultural preceptor'. For Redman,
Pound's combination of 'undoubted poetic mastery and questionable political beliefs has contributed to the widespread retreat of American poets
from political engagement . . . what is germane, even vital, is the fact that
since Pound our culture has been without strong poetic guidance.'[12] In Redman's view, therefore, by tainting the 'hermetic lyric' with a discreditable
politics, Pound has reduced the tradition of *religio poetae* to propaganda. If
my study achieves anything, it is to show that this separation of aesthetic
mysticism from reactionary politics is utterly false; the ideological significance of Pound's poetics is not that it allows wise-after-the-event critics to
pontificate about the evils of fascism but that it exposes the intimate connection between modernist myth and cultic power. That that power does
not automatically result in the fascist *Geschlecht* – ultra-nationalism,
racism, and the reification of gender-identity – should be clear from its
involvement in countercultural politics throughout the twentieth century.
But its dependence on bogus scholarship, conspiracy-theories, charismatic

leaders, elitist tribalism and self-mystification makes it part of the problem of the ethics of difference rather than the solution. Far from being the alternative to capitalism's abuse of power, mythic consciousness is implicated in the rise of a new and subtle authoritarianism; as Eric Hobsbawm points out, 'After the 1870s . . . and almost certainly in connection with the emergence of mass politics, rulers and middle-class observers rediscovered the importance of "irrational" elements in the maintenance of the social fabric and the social order.'[13] In order to grasp the poetic implications of this cultural shift, we need to confront Pound's obsession with Eleusis and the central figure of Kore.

Cora, Persephone, Proserpine, Flora: names for the daughter of Zeus and Demeter (or Ceres) abducted to the underworld by Zeus's brother Plouton (or Aidoneus, Hades, Dis) and guided back to the sunlit world by Hermes. When associated with her mother, the goddess of fertility, she is the personification of spring, a symbol of the cyclical renewal of nature and of the rebirth of the soul; when associated with Plouton, as in Orphic myth, she becomes the queen of the dead, a dark and erratic goddess. This double, transformative identity makes Kore a powerful figure in art and literature, but her power is compromised by the fact that she is always subject to another, more forceful deity. Whether as innocent maiden or demonic bride, her character is essentially passive and subordinate, a status that makes her particularly vulnerable to male fantasy. Kore's importance for Hellenistic and Roman writers carries over into medieval and Renaissance literature: she is a model Primavera for Dante and Cavalcanti, and both a radiant and shadowy figure for Chaucer, Spenser, Shakespeare and Milton. Retreating into obscurity for the eighteenth century, she reemerges into the literary field in Keats's 'Ode on Melancholy' and in Shelley's translation of the *Homeric Hymn to Demeter* and 'Song of Proserpine'. By the late nineteenth century, she has joined a pantheon of ethereal beauties poised between Tuscany and the drawing-room, heralded as Flora and demonised as Circe. She is the heroine of Pater's religion of pure ideas and the presiding spirit of Ruskin's botanical monograph *Proserpina*; and she is the central figure in the argument between Swinburne and Tennyson over pagan and Christian eschatology.

For the Modernists, Swinburne's darker vision carries the day, though only as a negative image of Proserpine waiting to be reborn. In twentieth-century poetry, therefore, Kore becomes an alluring, problematic figure, clouding the opposition between darkness and light, obscurity and revelation, even as she preserves the ideal of enlightenment. She appears in various guises throughout Pound's work, is invoked as a curative for Pound's 'blight of the imagination' in William Carlos Williams's *Kora in*

Hell, and becomes a guiding star for late modernist poets such as Robert Creeley and Robert Duncan, 'the girl the man knows nothing of'.[14] While for these male poets she is a liminal, eroticised figure, for women poets such as Edna St Vincent Millay, Eleanor Wilner, Sylvia Plath and Veronica Forrest-Thomson, she is more a symbol of maternal loss, an oppressed figure with whom to be identified. H. D. prefers the stronger figure of Demeter, the still centre of a feminine archetype based on virgin, mother and daughter. This feminine axis is conspicuously absent from Guy Davenport's essay 'Persephone's Ezra', which presents itself as a compendious survey of allusions to Kore and her metonyms, but while it locates the origin of Pound's interest in metempsychosis ('*The Flowered Tree as Koré*') in the unpublished *Hilda's Book* (c. 1906), no consideration is given to H. D.'s own investment in myths of female transformation. Nor, for that matter, are there any references to female poetry; the focus is entirely on male representations of the feminine reduced to a cosmic opposition between darkness and light. Davenport is intent on releasing Pound from 'the neurasthenic dark of the nineteenth century Circe-world and its Hell-like *cul de sac*', hiding the issue of gender in luminous detail: 'everywhere we turn in his poetry there is the clear emergence of Persephone as a persistent image and symbol'.[15] From this perspective, the aim of the *Cantos* is to make 'Persephone's transformation back to virginity' emblematic of a moral order of 'lost form, lost spirit' which depends on the chasteness of an ideal femininity.[16] That Pound's identification of feminine virtue with natural law (*virtù*) has its complement in a mystical biology which equates intellection with male fertility is not part of the reckoning – the virginal Kore is simply a metaphor of light and universal redemption.

Since I am specifically concerned with the relationship between a Gnostically inspired poetics of obscurity and male fantasy, in the following discussion I do not propose to rectify Davenport's omissions by speaking for the alternative configurations of women's poetry. I explore the 'persistent image' of Kore as it translates from antiquity into Pound's occulted history of Provençal and Tuscan poetry, and from there into a late modernist symbol. While Pound's 'theory of love' has been the subject of extensive discussion elsewhere, with prominence given to the Eleusinian Mysteries, the *Trobar clus*, and Cavalcanti's *Canzone d'Amore*, little has been made of its influence on later poetry in the Pound tradition.[17]

Tennyson's 'Demeter and Persephone' projects the earth-goddess's thoughts on the return of her daughter; redeemed by the 'deathless heart of motherhood', Persephone is 'Queen of the dead no more'.[18] Demeter looks forward to the full release from cyclical time, when Persephone will no longer be required to spend part of each year in Hades. Then, she announces, even Plouton shall

> accept and love the Sun,
> And all the Shadow die into the Light,
> When thou shalt dwell the whole bright year with me

Likewise, freed from the grip of deified nature, men will have no need of the conceit by which they 'made themselves as Gods against the fear/Of Death and Hell': the Christian God illumines Gnostic glimmerings. The poem forms a riposte to Swinburne's gloomy musings in 'The Garden of Proserpine' and 'Hymn to Proserpine', texts that maintain Persephone as a chthonic figure. 'The Garden' takes place in a narcotic, blighted version of the coastal reaches of that part of north-east Norfolk known to Victorian tourists as Poppyland. Here, Swinburne's blown poppies, 'green grapes of Proserpine', presage death as a sleep that will end the weariness of the diurnal round. Proserpine 'forgets the earth her mother/The life of fruits and corn', crushing deadly wine for dead men who are 'safe' in the fact that they will not 'wake with wings in heaven,/Nor weep for pain in hell.'[19] Meanwhile the 'Hymn' turns the tables on the Emperor Constantine's 'proclamation in Rome of the Christian faith' by suggesting that Jesus has only temporarily displaced Venus, the Vergilian goddess associated with the allegorical Roma and linked with Fortuna (herself a Demeter-figure) and Tyche, goddess of the random workings of fate. For Swinburne, Christianity tries to suppress the irrational forces to which Venus and Persephone attest but, he says, such religions will come and go, leaving only one certainty:

> Thou art more than the Gods who number the days of our temporal breath;
> For these give labour and slumber; but thou, Proserpina, death . . .
>
> For there is no God found stronger than death; and death is a sleep.[20]

This paganism, however, seems far removed from the world of antiquity, which unlike Christendom was not tormented by infernal visions of the lower depths. Haunted by the loss of the faith he seeks to reject, Swinburne labours to find something in the Eleusinian myth that might compensate mercantile society for the loss of the old gods, but his Persephone is an enervating rather than a revitalising figure. For his part, Ezra Pound never lost faith with Swinburne's desire to reinstate the pagan gods, but in his own poetry he soon tired of evoking a netherworld of languid dreams and looked to Eleusis for a new redemptive order.

Heretical poetry and thought in the twentieth century aims to exorcise Victorian fatalism by recourse to either a *coincidentia oppositorum* for which high and low, darkness and light, are figured as Blakean contraries, or as a Neoplatonic metaphysics of light. The two positions are not mutually exclusive and indeed converge under the sign of spiritual alchemy, which entails a belief in palingenesis, the transformation of the self through a mystical or symbolic death into rebirth as a higher being. For G. R. S. Mead, theosophist, author of countless scholarly guides to secret wisdom, and editor of the journal *Quest*, which published Pound's most theosophical essay 'Psychology and Troubadours' (1912), this metamorphosis is the very essence of Gnosis.[21] Occultists tend to view history as evolutionary and/or apocalyptic: always, humanity is nearing the end of its current stage of existence and is ready to be superseded by an advanced form of consciousness; only those individuals to whom the truth has been revealed may ascend to the next level of being. Madame Blavatsky, for example, promised the advent of a 'new race' of 'peculiar children who will grow into peculiar men and women – will be regarded as abnormal, oddities, physically and mentally. Then, as they increase, and their numbers become with every age greater, one day they shall awake to find themselves in a majority. Then present men will begin to be regarded as exceptional mongrels, until they die out in their turn in civilized lands.'[22] The concept of the New Age is everywhere at the turn of the nineteenth twentieth century; it is constantly reprised in Mead's writings and is the inspiration for A. R. Orage's journal of the same name. A mysticised revision of Darwinism, it offers a way of overcoming the *fin-de-siècle* obsession with degeneration, still current in Pound's 'The Garden' (1913), which condemns the *hauteur* of its Kensington damozel as the 'end of breeding', while

> round about there is a rabble
> Of the filthy, sturdy, unkillable infants of the very poor.
> They shall inherit the earth.[23]

The poem is one of a number of satirical pieces included in *Lustra* (1916). Its splenetic view of a society in which the anaemically genteel are losing the battle against lumpen proletarian vermin makes no overtures to theosophical accounts of a coming race that will supplant the 'mongrel' classes. Yet its reverie of the poet as a eugenically discriminating *flâneur* nods to the attendant belief in an advance guard of intellectually, spiritually and even racially superior individuals. Where Blavatsky speaks of a benign, supernatural transition from inferior to superior forms of consciousness, Pound is drawn to a fantasy of ethnic cleansing. The poem's devolutionary pessimism isolates the speaking subject from both excessive feminine *ennui* and a virulent underclass, and provides an early example of Pound's equation of cultural decline with the lack of sexual restraint, introducing an erotics of sanitation that comes to govern his aesthetics (the preference for the 'clean' over the 'thickened' line), his economic theory (the flow of state-sponsored credit over the anal clog of private usury), and his politics (the decisive ruler over the soft masses).

> The atrophied lady
>   would like someone to speak to her
> And is almost afraid that I
>   will commit that indiscretion.

The indented final line lengthens the pause which leaves the 'I' teetering on the edge of compliance, but the speaker is merely toying with the idea, knowing that discretion maintains his phallic self-control. This holding-back of desire might seem at odds with the correlation between coition and cerebral development Pound derived from Remy de Gourmont's *Physique de l'Amour* (which he translated in 1922) and which he associates with artistic energy: 'even oneself has felt it, driving any new idea into the great passive vulva of London, a sensation analogous to the male in copulation.'[24] However, for Pound the whole point of healthy sexuality and its extension into civic *virtù* is its control over the passions, its avoidance of immediate satisfaction in favour of unswerving commitment to the object of desire. I will show later how this libidinal economy achieves its ideal form in Pound's translations of Guido Cavalcanti's *Canzone d'Amore*, a notoriously obscure poem which was rarely far from his attention. For now, it is enough to note that Pound saw Guido as the prime inheritor of the Provençal verse tradition that, Pound believed, had an esoteric significance that reached far beyond the artificial medievalism imposed on it by the late Romantics. According to Peter Makin,

> Pound has the troubadour developing his knowledge of the 'universe of fluid force' by attacking the great barrier between himself and that elemental other, the female, and hence generating a tension that increases his psychic sensitivity. From this come all the electrical metaphors for creativity – sparks across polar gaps – in the early 'Psychology and Troubadours'. Provence, Pound felt, had favoured this sexual tension because 'the living conditions . . . gave the necessary restraint'; by 1928 he thought that the cause was not such a sociology but 'the dogma that there is some proportion between the fine thing held in the mind, and the inferior thing ready for instant consumption', but that this was still in opposition to the Hellenic 'Plastic plus immediate satisfaction'. Ritual reflected this resistance and this breakthrough, so that the troubadour was in some sense a priest; his poem was like a rite; and Pound in fact believed that a sexual rite was behind the troubadours.[25]

The sexual rite is, at core, a mystery, but one that is fundamentally mascu-line, heterosexual and genital. Its mysticism privileges intuitive wisdom over scholarly analysis, interpretive cults over revealed religion, and is alchemically inspired: 'Prose corresponds to disgust, rejection, anality, refuse, excrement, and the task of poetry is to transmute these inferior elements into a phallic drive toward heaven, aesthetic imagination and paradise. Analysis and anality go along together, and the "arsethetic" . . . is always related to Hell.'[26] This Dantesque vision of paradise mingling with abject eroticism fuses Christian and occult imagery, reminding us that Pound's arcane bent, at least in intention, is towards white magic, the light of Neoplatonism, rather than to the resolutely chthonic mysticism of that other modernist priest of the phallus, D. H. Lawrence, whose 'Purple Anemones' ridicules Persephone as an archaic suffragette trying to escape the 'Hell-glamorous, purple husband-tyranny' of her 'master':

> Who gave us flowers?
> Heaven? The white God?
>
> Nonsense!
> Up out of hell,
> From Hades;
> Infernal Dis![27]

Where Pound is syncretic, retaining the Christian values of Heaven and Hell in an expansively pagan *Lichtmetaphysik*, Lawrence inverts the hierarchy, giving Dis the power of regeneration traditionally associated with the Primavera. As elsewhere in Lawrence's work, this Dionysian polemic is based on a crude reduction of psychoanalysis to 'primal forces', in turn derived from occultist hostility towards asceticism. Lawrence mocks Persephone's feminism as the denial of her true, earthly, feminine status as 'husband-tilth'. Her return to the light may look like emancipation, but this is all part of Dis's 'strategy': she is allowed her moments of freedom so that he has the sport of tracking her down and reclaiming her. Crass though this reading of the myth may be, it works as an allegory of individuation, which in cultic terms means that access to self-knowledge and spiritual transformation depends on the adept's willingness to face the darkest aspects of the psyche – everything repressed as evil by dualist theology. The occult heresy, therefore, is to regard good and evil not as external realities but as constructs imposed on the subject which, unless reconciled and sublated through personal revelation, block the will to power. While this Nietzschean transvaluation has contributed to various emancipatory movements, its extreme subjectivism has ultimately no way of distinguishing between self-interest and self-harm; nor can it ground any judgements about conflicting desires between individuals other than by appealing to some kind of super-egoic force which by directing the play of individual desires reclaims them as subject to a higher ('higher' or 'lower'?) will. When supported by a rhetoric of evolution, destiny or *phusis*, individuation falls prey to any charismatic figure, whether guru or dictator, whose claim to be the messenger of secret wisdom asserts itself over those struggling to 'find themselves'.

Hermann Hesse's novel *Demian* (1919), which was to become required reading for the psychedelic generation, is a classic example of this mirage of self-identity. The book begins as a romantic *bildungsroman* in the style of Hesse's earlier work but turns into a Gnostic tract dedicated to the idea of spiritual rebirth through the cataclysm of war. Its protagonists – Emil Sinclair, a soul-searching youth, Max Demian, a student Tiresias, Pistorius, a gifted musician, alchemist, and general smart-aleck, and Demian's mother, Eva, a clairvoyant earth-mother – are drawn together by their shared perception of an invisible 'mark of Cain' which sets them apart from the complacent burghers and vicious urchins with whom they are forced into day-to-day contact. As the story progresses, the adepts become increasingly less like individual 'characters' (though they are pretty thin to begin with) and begin to resemble aspects of a single, directed consciousness. The narrator, Sinclair, is guided through the terrors of adolescence by his otherworldly friends, who exist in a state of constant anamnesis and telepathic knowingness, posing tricky existential questions to which they always already have the answer. No matter who speaks, he or she reveals the same monologic truth awaiting Sinclair's epiphany:

> What Demian had said about God and the Devil, about the godly-official and the suppressed Devil's world fitted in with my own ideas on the subject, my own myth, the conception I had of two worlds or two different halves of the world – the light and the dark. The realization that my problem was a problem of all humanity, a problem of all life and philosophy suddenly swept over me like a holy shadow and I was overcome with fear and awe when I realized how deeply my own personal life was caught up in the eternal stream of great ideas.[28]

The eternal 'problem' is how to reconcile the two worlds. The answer, proposed by Demian, explicated by Pistorius and confirmed by Eva, is represented by the Gnostic god Abraxas, who collapses the distinction between light and dark, good and evil, and binary oppositions in general. Thus, the only way forward is to live without the either/or certainties imposed by official morality, and to hurl oneself into pure experience:

> There was only one true vocation for everybody – to find the way to himself. He might end as poet, lunatic, prophet or criminal – that was not his affair; ultimately it was of no account. His affair was to discover his own destiny, not something of his own choosing, and live it out wholly and resolutely within himself. Anything else was merely a half-life, an attempt at evasion, an escape into the ideals of the masses, complacency and fear of his inner soul.[29]

One chooses to find oneself, but finding oneself is not a matter of choice. At this point 'destiny' means nothing more than the realisation of what is latent in a given personality – on condition, that is, that the human essence revealed be extreme in nature. One might find one's destiny as an Allen Ginsberg or a Charles Manson, but not as a chartered accountant with a passion for finely tooled bindings. Light and dark remain necessary if illusory symbols of human transcendence; desires that fall between these poles and their synthesis merely preserve the status quo:

> We who bore the 'sign' might rightly be considered odd by the world, even mad and dangerous. We were 'awake' or 'wakening' and our striving was directed at an ever-increasing wakefulness, whereas the striving and quest for happiness of the rest was aimed at identifying their thoughts, ideals, duties, their lives and fortunes more and more closely with that of the herd. That too was striving, that too was power and greatness. But whereas we, in our conception, represented the will of nature to renew itself, to individual-ize and march forward, the others lived in the desire for the perpetuation of things as they are . . . For us humanity was a distant goal towards which we were marching, whose image no one yet knew, whose laws were nowhere written down.[30]

Now the urge to individualise becomes inseparable from a group con-sciousness which, although distinguished from the 'herd', takes on its own species-being, called to its collective destiny by 'the will of nature'. The call is occult: ineffable, without image or inscription, yet somehow, like the mark of Cain, always present to those it has selected.

The obscurity of secret wisdom gives it endless speculative power and hermeneutic licence. Its division of knowledge into the limited, chaotic experience of ordinary men and the expanded consciousness of the new race is close to Eliot's opposition between dissociated sensibility and the poet's mind 'constantly amalgamating disparate experience . . . always forming new wholes.'[31] The drive to wholeness plays down difference and elevates continuity to the point where random and coincidental phenom-ena are pressed into the service of a supra-personal *Gestalt*. For the adept, the world of antiquity is only superficially governed by chance, its accep-tance of the irrational confirming the belief that human actions are guided by cosmic forces. As Plotinus has it, 'Everything is everywhere and every-thing is everything and every single thing is everything.'[32] In occult cos-mogony all meaning is in the position of a non-arbitrary sign, uncannily motivated by the gods and encoded in the text of nature. Jungian 'analytic psychology', for example, rejects Freud's materialist account of the dream-work as confining its veiled messages to provisional, context-bound unities. Instead, dreams speak in fragments of an imaginative totality denied by the rational mind, and/or they are auguries of collective destiny divined less by analysis than by a flash of intuition. Jung's own dream-interpretations are typological, reading back variable images into a perennial tradition of fixed identities. In 'The Psychological Aspects of the Kore', a woman recounts a dream in which she is raped by a man in a golden carriage. Jung seizes on the dream's vague similarity to Persephone's ritual. The woman, therefore, is 'identical' to the young girl, who 'often appears a a *youth*'; the youth embodies the 'masculine element in a woman', and so this ambiguous image forms 'a syzygy or *coniunctio* which symbolizes the essence of wholeness (as also does the Platonic hermaphrodite, who later became the symbol of a perfected wholeness in alchemical philosophy)'.[33] The specific details of the dream are quickly discarded in favour of the self-evidence of the *coincidentia oppositorum*. The interminable task of Gnostic scholarship is to draw out such conjunctions hidden in the most apparently disjunct material. Similarly, history is thought to follow patterns concealed beneath the surface-world of random 'facts'. What to the untrained eye looks like an immense panorama of futility and anarchy, to the occult historian yields a single esoteric significance, albeit one that can be represented only symbolically, since its true meaning is not open to view but epiphanic. This is why there is an endless proliferation of occult 'theories' and cults, all laying claim to be the chosen vehicles of a secret wisdom to which only they have access. To complicate matters, the 'mythic method' of occult speculation cannot always be distinguished from euhemerism, a sceptical approach which treats myths as primitive explanations for irrational phenomena and allegories of historical events. The classical world had its euhemerists, such as Herodotus and Strabo, and modern exponents are represented by the wave of positivist scholarship that ran in tandem with the occult revival of the nineteenth century, its most influential figure being Sir James Frazer, whose *The Golden Bough* (1890–1915) appears *ad nauseam* in modernist criticism. Theosophists and euhemerists seem unlikely bedfellows, yet, according to Surette, there were many points of contact between the two traditions, not least being the fact that the relativism of anthropologists such as Frazer, Jane Harrison and Lucien Lévy-Bruhl questioned the authority of orthodox religion and so put the 'conquered' faiths on an equal footing: 'Frazer's findings reduced the putatively unique event of Christ's passion, death, and resurrection to just one of hundreds, perhaps thousands, of such deaths and resurrections that have been enacted around the world from the earliest times.'[34] Consequently, this unitary concept of myth gave greater credence to notions of a 'secret tradition' stemming from antiquity and running as an undercurrent throughout official history: 'the Frazerians, the aesthetes, Pound, and the occult clung to the belief that some of the lost virtue or wisdom of the past could be recovered through scholarship or meditation, thereby saving civilization.'[35]

The contentious yet complicit relationship between anthropology and the occult helps to account for academic confusion over the nature of modernist myth. Modernist scholarship has tended to emphasise the provisional aspects of the mythic method in the work of Yeats, Eliot, Pound and their contemporaries, sidelining their occult investigations as if these were at best handy tools for freeing-up ingrained habits of thought and at worst mere cranky affectations. Yet at the same time modernism is seen as a reaction to the sceptical project of modernity, striving to reassemble the fragments of a forgotten faith. This inconsistency may be no more than unwillingness to see a radical artistic movement tainted by religious fanaticism of a particularly naff kind, an impulse shared by the historians of science who wish to explain away Newton's lifelong respect for alchemy. Yet the complexity of modernist poetics results to a large extent from its conflation of scientific paradigms with the older concept of natural philosophy and its esoteric offshoots. Of course, this does not mean that all modernist texts are equally problematic in their attempt to assimilate the conflicting factors of modernity to aesthetic forms. What makes Hesse such a straw man for criticism is the non-reflexive, univocal way in which his novels appropriate their subject matter. Hesse's disciples and admirers call this dearth of literary qualities 'lucidity'. Arguably, Pound's poetry is at base just as monologic, in that it requires the reader to follow a single, if fragmented, vision. But there the comparison ends. The *Cantos* display massive erudition in combination with a disjunct yet highly tendentious form to give the effect of sublime authority. The elisions of the text demand completion at every turn, cowing readers into accepting the poverty of their intellectual and imaginative grasp of the poem as a 'whole'. The lack of coherence at the exoteric level leads to the expectation that the text must cohere in another, esoteric, way.

That finally Pound himself could not claim with any confidence that his major work coheres shows this effect of authority to be a mirage. Pound continually invokes scientific criteria as the means to 'clarity', and his interest in ancient religion is described in positivist terms: 'Paganism never feared knowledge. It feared ignorance and under a flood of igno-rance it was driven out of its temples.'[36] Yet he also argues (having quoted Cavalcanti's line *'Che l'intenzione per ragione vale'* – 'the image prevails over reason') that 'Faith is totalitarian. The mystery is totalitarian. The sacred symbols are totalitarian . . . That fatal inclination to want to under-stand logically and syllogistically what is incomprehensible is Hebrew and Protestant.'[37] These views seem utterly incompatible, and, in an absolute sense, they are. In positivist methodologies such as euhemerism myths yield to facts, which are thought to exist independently from subjective interpretation. In esoteric speculation, however, facts are the fallen signs of a noumenal reality which acquire meaning through interpretation. Both approaches require a subject to sift through and order the evidence, therefore both believe that 'truth' is channelled though a subject. But the former insists that 'subjectivity' is merely a corollary to the facts, whereas the latter makes the (divinely chosen) subject the guarantor of revelation. In Pound's *coniunctio*, positivism is endorsed only to the extent to which it can be used to legitimate divinely inspired knowledge. When he argues that the pagans were open to knowledge and despised ignorance, Pound means that unlike Christianity, which assumes a kind of spiritual democracy, archaic religion was not afraid to separate the enlightened from the unenlightened: 'The glory of the polytheistic anschauung is that it never asserted a single obligatory path for everyone. It never caused the assertion that everyone was fit for initiation and it never caused an attempt to force people into a path alien to their sensibilities.'[38]

The double standards in this passage are a constant feature of Pound's writings and form the central contradiction of the politics of mystic counterculture. On one hand, paganism champions personal gnosis against orthodoxy, on the other, it holds that only those who are 'fit' may join the elect. Freedom of choice exists only insofar as one's *virtù* – not a moral quality but biological/spiritual destiny – fits one to the task of initiation.[39] Thus, while Pound's thought is closer to Hesse's New Age sensibility than at first appears, its rhetorical strategy is far more sophisticated, negating romantic subjectivism in favour of a new poetic designed to 'give the illusion of impersonal objectivity'.[40] The *Cantos*' extensive use of historical documents and quotations is presented as a 'deductive' method based on 'violently contrasted facts'.[41] In practice, however, the decontextualised mass of data not only resists analysis but is virtually indecipherable. As Lawrence Rainey has shown, the raw, contradictory transcriptions of the Malatesta Cantos succeed one another 'without logic or principle, each bristling with cryptic names and dates', defying any 'rationalist criteria of evidence and proof, logic and argument, and instead can appeal only to a hermeneutics of experience, to what must be only felt and not analysed, shown and not clarified.'[42] If, as James Longenbach argues, 'Pound's removal of the signs of authorial presence from *The Cantos* is finally a political strategy designed to make his idiosyncratic interpretations of history and economics seem as inevitable as nature itself', it is also a way of destroying historical analysis, so that a vitalist mythos based on will, faith and memory may gather the ruins of the empirical.[43]

So, while Pound has no interest in the supernatural visions of Blavatsky, Jung and Hesse, and distances himself from the 'disagreeable sensations' of Lawrence, preferring to align his work with the classical virtues of science, nature, clarity, intellect and proportion, he is nevertheless committed to ideas that are occult in two crucial respects.[44]

Firstly, Pound's hermeneutic principle is fundamentally, not incidentally, hermetic. He believes that there can be illumination only where there is obscurity. Truth is an essential mystery which cannot be revealed to everyone but is transmitted symbolically through a secret tradition or 'conspiracy of intelligence'.[45] Conspiracy here means a transhistorical line of Gnosis handed down from high antiquity to generations of artists and thinkers who preserve it from being assimilated into official culture. One such theory, supported by a mass of outdated scholarship and dodgy speculative literature (as well as much Pound scholarship), holds that the Eleusinian cult of fertility originated in Ancient Egypt, and was passed on through Hellenic civilisation to medieval Provence, where by way of the troubadours' Cathar links it entered the European minstrel tradition and became the spiritual force behind the poetry of the *dolce stil nuovo*.[46] (*Trobar clus* means 'enclosed'.) Pound was attracted to this heretical tradition primarily because it allowed him to set an elite, life-affirming and eroticised spirituality against what he saw as the ascetic, pain-loving religious doctrines of Mithraism, Buddhism and Christianity. He endorses Church ritual only when it can be traced to older, pagan symbols, and approves of scholasticism in so far as it supports 'natural demonstration' and the Neoplatonic concept of the divine *mens*.[47] The belief in a benign conspiracy has its counterpart in the fear of malign influences, and Pound, in common with many occult scholars, is notoriously prone to fantasies of this kind. His economic theories, not in themselves an unreasonable response to social conditions between the wars, are completely undermined by the attendant notion, promulgated by the forged *Protocols of the Learned Elders of Zion*, that a conspiracy of Jews maintained the instability of global markets in their own self-interest. Pound's somewhat sceptical approach to this document did not prevent him from recommending it as a 'clear description of process'.[48]

Secondly, Pound follows the holistic, continuous approach to 'evidence' favoured by occult scholarship. The conflation of science and mysticism is typical esoteric practice and informs the vitalist philosophy espoused by modernist gurus such as Nietzsche, von Hartmann, Haeckel, Bergson, Klages and Jung. Pound supports his Eleusinian tradition of Amor with anti-Darwinian biological theories drawn from de Gourmont, J. H. Fabre and Louis Agassiz, all of which have something in common with Bergson's *élan vital*. 'Fabre and Frazer', Pound writes, 'have been the essentials in the mental furnishings of any contemporary mind qualified to write of ethics or philosophy or that mixed molasses religion' and the '*Physique de L'Amour* should be used as a text-book of biology'.[49] Bergson, at one time President of the Society for Psychical Research, posited a biological theory of the unconscious whereby human beings have intuitive access to their evolutionary past. As we have seen, Pound's *Paideuma* is similarly concerned with racial memory and cultural 'instinct', and his bizarre reading of de Gourmont's erotic thesis is rooted in phylogenesis. Surette argues that the phallocentrism of Pound's sexual theory is 'thoroughly out of step with mainstream occult attitudes', observing that the theosophists were 'gynocentric' and that Mead, Edouard Schuré, Friedrich Creuzer and Jung were all attracted by the *'theacentric'* nature of the Eleusinian mysteries.[50] While it is true that, as an institution, theosophy was free from patriarchy – Madame Blavatsky could hardly have become such an important figure otherwise – and that Jung's privileging of goddess archetypes led to what Julia Kristeva calls a second wave of feminist consciousness, Surette underestimates the extent to which the occult's essentialist concepts of the feminine relegate women to the status of subordinate, nurturing figures of male fantasy. Likewise, the *Cantos* can be said to be gynocentric in that they teem with powerful goddesses, but in Pound's mythos they remain the objects of the male gaze. The lack of doctrinal consistency is, in any case, not an exception to Pound's esoteric leanings but precisely what defines them; what he calls the 'exciting and exhilirating hotch-potch' of 'a "Platonic" academy messing up Christian and Pagan mysticism, allegory, occultism, demonology, Trismegistus, Psellus, Porphyry' allows him to pull in any material he deems sympathetic to the vitalist principle, irrespective of 'mainstream attitudes'.[51] In 'Terra Italica', for example, Pound condemns the cult of the Iranian sun-god Mithras because, unlike the cult of Eleusis, it was a survival of the dualist Zoroastrian religion and contained 'sadistic and masochistic tendencies', which allowed it to be absorbed by the early Christian church.[52] But for Mead, Franz Cumont and Jung, Mithraism is directly antagonistic to the Judaeo-Christian tradition, a phallic, Aryan form of nature worship which represents the true *Urreligion* perverted by two thousand years of Christianity. The whole issue is complicated by the fact that, since the publication of Cumont's *Mysteries of Mithra* at the end of the nineteenth century, archaeologists have been unable to discover a single recorded account of the myth, and the iconographical evidence offers only tableux devoid of explanation. 'Any attempted interpretation of the myth of Mithras, then, is an imagining, a reconstruction, a fantasy.'[53] There are similar problems with Eleusis. Since Herodotus, the secret rites dedicated to Demeter and Persephone were thought to have been introduced to the Hellenic world by the ancient Egyptians, the story of Isis and Osiris having an affinity with the (c. 600 BC) *Homeric Hymn to Demeter* (hence Pound's 'I Gather the Limbs of Osiris'). However, as George E. Mylonas notes, 'not a single object of Egyptian origin, or indicating Egyptian influence, dating from the second millennium was found in the Sanctuary of Eleusis' near Athens.[54] Moreover, we know nothing of the substance of the Mysteries, of the meaning derived even from the Sacred drama which was performed. Explanations suggested by scholars thus far, and philosophic conceptions and parallels, are based upon assumptions and the wish to establish the basis on which the Mysteries rested. These accounts do not seem to correspond to the facts. The secret of the Mysteries was kept a secret successfully and we shall perhaps never be able to fathom it or unravel it.[55]

Scholarly conclusions of this kind will never do for occultists, who are drawn to the history of arcana and irrational phenomena by a strong desire to *explain* the mysterious, if only by translating it into further myths and mysteries. Their interminable researches into mythic origins, biological and racial theories, psychological types, chemical experimentation and the like, are designed to legitimate an ineffable spiritual tradition. The condition of modern hermeticism is to attest to the essential mystery of secret wisdom while determining it as both *myth* and *fact*, discounting any evidence (or lack of evidence) that breaks continuity. Pound's poetry and thought derive from this *via negativa* and not, therefore, from a tradition of philosophical scepticism.[56] There is no reason to suppose that his 'tradition' is anything other than what he repeatedly says it is, a psychic universe composed of 'real' symbols reaching towards a non-artificial paradise. The oft-quoted 1927 letter to Homer Pound defines the *Cantos* as a journey to the underworld, translating the myth of Persephone into a masculine Odyssey:

A.A.   Live man goes down into world of Dead
C.B.   The 'repeat in history'
B.C.   The 'magic moment' or moment of metamorphosis, bust thru from
        quotidien into 'divine or permanent world.' Gods, etc.[57]

The metamorphic moments of water, light, and stone punctuate the epic as oases in a desert of broken historical documents:

Thus the light rains, thus pours, *e lo soleils plovil*
The liquid and rushing crystal
                beneath the knees of the gods.
Ply over ply, thin glitter of water;
Brook film bearing white petals.[58]

Arnaut Daniel's lyric '*Lancan son passat li giure*', the source for this passage, is transformed into the fructive image of crystal, which Carroll F. Terrell glosses as 'the transmutation of the fluid transparency of subjective experience into the objective solidity of stone through poetry, or, in another relevant terminology, the alchemist's fabrication of the philosopher's stone by palingenesis'.[59] And, for Richard Sieburth, 'these terms, clarity (*claritas*), process (*tao*), and liquid light ... in conjunction – chthonic, sexual forces joined with love, lustre, fidelity – form an epiphanic ideogram absolutely central to the *Cantos*.'[60] All the further metamorphoses of the *Cantos* fan out ('ply over ply') from this principle, linked in *The Pisan Cantos* to Aphrodite's emergence from the sea ('Cythera potens') and Kore's journey from the dark world (where, in 'The Alchemist' (1912), she is 'Queen of Cypress'[61]) to a beatific state in which she is both virgin and goddess:

> Cythera potens, Κνθερα δεινα
> no cloud, but the crystal body
>> the tangent formed in the hand's cup
>> as live wind in the beech grove
>>> as strong air amid cypress
>
> Κορη, Δελια δεινα/et libidinis expers
> the sphere moving crystal, fluid,
>> none therein carrying rancour
> Death, insanity/suicide degeneration
> that is, just getting stupider as they get older
> τολλα ταθειν,
>
>> nothing matters but the quality
> of the affection –
> in the end – that has carved the trace in the mind
> dove sta memoria[62]

Kore is associated with 'powerful Delia' or Artemis, the eternal virgin, 'to whom passion is unknown'. Identified with crystal, she is an image of sanity removed from the Odyssean sufferings of men, and she also shadows the love-object which justifies the metaphysics of Duocento poetry: *Ingenium nobis ipsa puella fecit*. Pound's splicing of Propertius and the courtly tradition goes back to *Canzoni* (1911), verse dedicated to the Kore of *Elegies* II.8 (*quos ego Persephonae maxima dona feram*), with its 'Prayer for His Lady's Life':

> Here let thy clemency, Persephone, hold firm,
> Do thou, Pluto, bring here no greater harshness.
> So many thousand beauties are gone down to Avernus
> Yet might let one remain above with us.[63]

In the essay 'Cavalcanti' (1928–1934), Propertius plays second fiddle to the troubadours, who renounce the 'classic aesthetic' centred on 'immediate satisfaction' preferring a nobler eroticism based on the idea of 'the fine thing held in the mind'.[64] This reservation notwithstanding, Pound retains the Propertian sentiment that men's genius is invested in the maiden. This 'genius' is preserved in memory; the line from Cavalcanti's *Canzone d'Amore* 'dove sta memor[i]a', translated in Canto XXXVI as 'Where memory liveth', has a key significance for Pound, along with the same poem's 'formato locho' or 'forméd trace' in the mind. This has long been recognised by Pound's commentators, yet they remain either uncertain or too certain as to what it means, mirroring Pound's own assertive yet equivocal responses to Cavalcanti's obscure text.

In a chapter of *Ezra Pound: Poet as Sculptor* (1964) written with the assistance of J. H. Prynne, Donald Davie observes that 'From the first translation of 1912 through to his edition of *Tre Canzoni* in 1949, Pound has worried away at the poems of Cavalcanti more doggedly than at any other body of literature, even the Confucian scriptures.'[65] In fact, Pound had declared himself a disciple of 'Ser Guido of Florence, master of us all' as early as 1909, and shortly afterwards published a loose translation of the sonnet 'Chi E Questa?'.[66] Thereafter, except for the canzone 'Io non pensava' and the ballata 'Fresca rosa novella', he made translations of all of Cavalcanti's poems. These were published in various versions in numerous places, but between the *Sonnets and Ballate* of 1912 and the scholarly edition of the *Rime* prepared in 1932, a formal shift occurs from overdependence on the English pentameter to more flexible rhythmic units. This prosodic 'heave' is what makes Pound such a great translator and a radical theorist of the art, enabling him to mime the sound-world of the original while drawing attention to differences between what he calls his 'traductions' and the poems themselves. Less successful is his penchant for archaic diction, which actually increases in the later versions. Like Rossetti before him, Pound seems unable to grasp the fact that the *stilnovisti* poets were creating a new vernacular language, and in spite of his claims to have discovered a new '*robustezza*, a masculinity' forcing its way through 'the crust of dead English', the translations never lose the taint of 'Merrie England'.[67] In addition to the translations, Pound constantly refined his thoughts on Cavalcanti and the Hellenic and medieval influence on Tuscan poetry (the assembled parts of the 'Cavalcanti' essay date from 1910–1931) and composed an opera based on poems by Cavalcanti and Sordello (1932).

The long concentration on musical properties in the work of a single poet enabled Pound to modulate the aural qualities of his own poetry. But his special interest in the canzone *Donna me prega* extends beyond these formal considerations to the metaphysical and erotic basis of his poetics. The canzone represents Cavalcanti's attempt to give a psychological account of the Provençal Amor tradition. Its use of Neoplatonic and Scholastic terminology is more rigorous than the 'philosophical' component in the work of his contemporaries, yet its deployment of highly technical language in the context of a lyric poem designed to be understood only by the 'conoscente' makes it strangely opaque. This double presentation of scientific and obscurantist elements was bound to appeal to Pound, and he describes the canzone as combining 'the suavity of song ... the neatness of a scalpel-cut' with an eclectic approach to its material that suffers no 'dogma unsupported by nature'.[68] By 'dogma' he means rational exposition motivated by the need to conform to religious orthodoxy, which is therefore opposed to Cavalcanti's 'natural dimostramento', a method that is 'Non razionale/mà che si sente dicho' ('not by the reason, but 'tis felt, I say').[69] Cavalcanti's mindset, therefore, is quite different from 'Dante's willingness to take on any sort of holy and orthodox furniture'.[70] The canzone appears to be offering a secular account of the nature of love, which moves from luminous affirmation to deep pessimism: formed by a pellucid intellectual light ('sì formato come/diafan, da lome') but also by a dark, irascible ('ira') passion said to be influenced by the planet Mars, the bringer of war ('D'una scuritate/la qual da Marte'), love seems to illuminate itself perpetually ('resplende in sé, perpetuale effetto'), yet its intending towards its desired object voids reason ('ché la 'ntenzione per ragione vale'). Submerged in a dark medium, it finally erases light, or shines faintly through the darkness ('asciso 'mezzo scuro, luce rade'), finding its reward ('mercede') only in the painful recognition of its own transience.

What Cavalcanti appears to be saying, then – and I stress again the provisional nature of interpretation, since the canzone is not only subject to numerous textual variants but highly paratactic in form – is that the courtly tradition of sincere love, or *fin'amors*, continued in the *stilnovisti* doctrine of the *cor gentil*, is an idealisation of the true condition of love, which is an amalgam of fantasy and aggressive desire. While they differ as to the precise details of the poem's meaning, most modern commentators agree that it attests to the absence of a *rapport sexuelle*; that is to say, in Lacanian terms, there might be a *sexual* relationship, but there is no sexual *relationship*. Love is actualised only when fantasy is moved by passion to draw the admiring glance ('sguardo') of one whose 'complessione' appears to match the lover's own. Even so, it does not last long ('poco soggiorna') since the same *ira* that inspires action also impairs judgement. Therefore, as J. L. Shaw puts it, 'the promise of the "sguardo" is delusive, it can never be maintained. The complete satisfaction of sense and intellect can be imagined but never realized.'[71] The lover is faced with the symbolic death ('morte') of those who have turned away from the life of reason ('buon perfetto'). The final, redemptive word of the poem before the *envoi* becomes ambiguous. 'Mercede' (less 'mercy' than 'reward') is a conventional term in courtly lyrics referring to the correspondence between the lover and his *damozel*; the lady repays the lover's attention 'in some special way or in no special way.'[72] The summational use of the term in the canzone suggests both that *mercede* results from the destruction of love (therefore, paradoxically, there *is* love, in kind) and that it is merely an irony of the (non-) relation of love. This provisional understanding reaffirms the canzone's opening proposition, that love is an *accident*:

Donna me prega, per ch'io voglio dire
d'un accidente che sovente è fero,
ed è sì altero, ch'è chiamato amore . . .

'Accident' is an Aristotelian term meaning an attribute of a substance. It is something which may happen to a subject, but which cannot define its essence. Love, therefore, is not itself substantial but fortuitous. Hence Cavalcanti writes of psychology, not essences, divine or otherwise.

If *Donna me prega* is far removed from Dante's 'holy furniture', it is just as far from the occult mysticism I have ascribed to Pound's conspiracy of intelligence and secured by the Eleusinian tradition. ('Terra Italica' states clearly that 'the cult of Eleusis will explain not only general phenomena but particular beauties in Arnaut Daniel or in Guido Cavalcanti'.[73]) So why does Pound see Cavalcanti as the inheritor of Eleusis and Provence? The obvious answer would be that he simply doesn't recognise the reading of the canzone proposed above, nor any reading along similar lines. After all, to say that the whole poem 'is a sort of metaphor on the generation of light' consonant with the Neoplatonic writings of Robert Grosseteste is to ignore the critical aspects of its treatment of Amor. As Line Henriksen argues, 'Pound reads light where Cavalcanti wrote darkness'.[74] The assumption governs pretty much all commentary on Pound's Cavalcanti, Makin and Surette included. Michael Bernstein writes that the stress on 'Risplende/in sé perpetuale effecto' 'suggests a cry of joy, as if both the light and the illuminated world are together shouting out their d*elight* at the beauty of the divine process'[75] and Peter Nicholls defines Pound's metaphysics of light as

a two-fold knowledge, at once visionary and 'scientific'. In Grosseteste's thought, light is a mediating form between soul and body, and it permits a frame of intelligibility which contains the potential of all forms active between the two modes of enquiry . . . there is a movement between empirical knowledge (of the physical properties of light and the manner of its propagation) and cosmogonic speculation. Grosseteste describes light as 'a spiritual body, or if you prefer, a bodily spirit', and the chiastic structure of this phrase neatly defines the main focus of Pound's interest, since for him the melodic precision and balance of the Canzone express an achieved 'proportion' between the real and the ideal, between 'natural demonstration' and visionary insight.[76]

Grosseteste's theory, which combines Aristotelian physics with the alchemical principles of sublimation and humiliation, describes the quest for knowledge as a movement from the mutable to the incorruptible in the achievement of *intelligentia*. Etienne Gilson, Pound's source for Grosseteste's *De Luce*, explains that

> the soul, having become torpid, so to speak, in the body, awakens little by little to the intelligible, under the repeated shock of sensations, analyses the complexity of objects, divides colour from size, shape and mass, then the shape and size from the mass, and so on, until it thus gets to know the corporeal substance which bears these various accidents. If we have thus to put up with sensations, it is because our soul, blinded by the love it has for its own body, can see only what it loves. In casting off the love of the body, the soul is, on the contrary, purified, open to the influence of divine Ideas and it discerns by their light the truth of things, which are so to speak their reflections.[77]

Grosseteste is not exactly an ascetic, since he does not identify the body with evil, yet his association of the corporeal with blindness is difficult to square with Pound's assertion that the Tuscan conception of 'the body as perfected instrument of increasing intelligence . . . invalidates the whole of monastic thought'.[78] But Pound also claims that such 'heresy' is in line with 'Averroes's specifications for the degrees of comprehension; and we may perhaps consider Guido as one of that "tenuous line who from Albertus magnus to the renaissance" meant the freedom of thought, the contempt, or at least a moderated respect, for stupid authority.'[79] This notion derives from the religious historian Ernest Renan, who falsely attributed Averroism to Grosseteste and the Oxford Franciscans. Averroes believed that human beings are distinguished from other life-forms by their ability to cultivate the intellect according to reason; yet he did not include love in the intellectual sphere, and his philosophy is therefore quite different from Pound's Neoplatonic equation of love with intellectual light.[80] In his review of the 1932 *Rime*, Gilson says 'there is not the slightest evidence' that Guido was an Averroist, and he objects to the idea that Cavalcanti was a 'natural philosopher' in the first place: 'I feel very strongly inclined to think that he was a poet, using a commonly received terminology and trying to turn it into beautiful verses.'[81] The canzone's obscurities, therefore, are due to its poetic nature, and we will never know the exact significance of its philosophical terminology. To further complicate matters, Gilson offers corrections of the translations based on a fourteenth-century commentary by Dino del Garbo, an authority Pound considers to be Averroist. According to Gilson, the lines

E l antenzione

per ragione

vale

Discerne male

in chui é vizio amico

do not mean, as Pound has it

> Maintains intention reason's peer and mate;
> poor in discernment, being thus weakness' friend

but

> For intention's value rests on reason
> And it sees but little in whom has vice for friend.

Bafflingly, the revision is glossed as meaning, via Dino, that love corrupts judgement. While Pound incorporates many of Gilson's corrections in his 1934 translation, he retains this version with only slight modification, most likely because on this point he could not make sense of Gilson. In any case, he continues to mark his puzzlement over the word *intenzion* by holding on to its ambiguity:

> Deeming intention reason's peer and mate,
> Poor in discernment, being thus weakness' friend

'[D]oes *intenzion* mean intention (a matter of will?) does it mean intuition, intuitive perception, or does the line hold the same meaning as that in Yeats's Countess Cathleen, *intenzion* being intention, and *ragione* meaning not reason, but "being right"?'[82] The note only makes it more unclear as to why Pound should prefer to see love both as a kind of weakness and reason's peer and mate. For Surette, 'Gilson's translation is obviously correct', and it is a mystery that Pound 'wanted Amor to be weakness' friend even though Cavalcanti's meaning is that Amor will have nothing to do with the vicious.'[83] The variations on this passage in other translations show that Gilson is not 'obviously' correct: 'Its judgement is without regard for well-being, for absorbed attention takes the place of reason' (Shaw); 'because it's intention/by natural law/prevails:/recognizing evil/vice's friend' (Cirigliano); '[Love] keeps its judgement independent of well-being, since intention is operative in place of reason, discerns poorly who is a friend to vice' (Ardizzone). Like Dino, Gilson limits the canzone's definition of love to a 'poetic' passion of the senses, while more recent evidence, i.e. post-1400, suggests that Guido attached great importance to its intellectual aspect. The precise distinction between the sensual fantasy of an ideally beautiful woman and the intellectual concept of ideal femininity is easy to lose. Shaw explains it as follows:

> The Possible Intellect in itself, as the receptacle of abstract concepts ('locus specierum') is not a communication with the body, but when it is in action, as Speculative, it communicates with the body by means of the Fantasy. In order, then, to consider the concept Feminine Beauty, Intellect and Fantasy construct a *phantasma* which is an image of ideal feminine beauty,

corresponding to the idea as faithfully as a particular image can correspond to an abstract idea. They construct it out of the materials that are available to the inner senses, images and notions ('intentiones') in the 'Imaginatio' and 'Memoria', and combinations of images and notions, the previously constructed *phantasmata* out of which the pure concept itself has already been abstracted by the *Intellectus Agens*. These previously constructed *phantasmata* were beautiful and attractive, but this new *phantasma*, the best representation of ideal feminine beauty the mind can contrive, is satisfactory to it, for it sees in it its own ideal of feminine charm.[84]

Hence the 'dove sta memora', that part of the brain supposed to be the place where the faculties of sense are at their most intellectual. Memory stores the ideal concept of the feminine prior to the appearance of an actual physical object of desire, a woman who, seeming to match the feminine ideal, disrupts contemplation by arousing the *ira*. The Sensitive Intellect ('in quella parte dove sta memora') is informed by diaphanous light, but it becomes darkened by the martial desire to realise love in its physical incarnation. This darker aspect of love allows the lover to act, as it were, on impulse in order to achieve satisfaction. But because it obscures the seen form ('veduta forma') in the Sensitive Intellect, *irascibilis* deprives him of reason so that he misrecognises passion for permanent love.

For Pound, 'dove sta memoria', with its Neoplatonic emphasis on light, is the guiding force of the canzone. It becomes talismanic in the Pisan Cantos, protecting radiant images:

> And the sun high over horizon hidden in cloud bank
> lit saffron the cloud ridge
> > dove sta memora[85]

In the translations, Pound transforms the canzone's darker passages into reaffirmations of celestial light. Where Cavalcanti writes that the accidental 'whiteness' which is the origin of colour becomes obscured by a dark medium (love under the influence of Mars), Pound makes it continuous with the 'risplende in sé':

> taken in the white light that is allness   (1934)

> There, beyond colour, essence set apart,
> In midst of darkness light light giveth forth
> Beyond all falsity   (1932)

> Being divided, set out from colour,
> Disjunct in mid darkness
> Grazeth the light, one moving by other,
> being divided, divided from all falsity   (1934)

Both translations use subtle repetition to displace negative connotations in the original. The earlier version has light giving forth light in the midst of darkness, and the whole passage is given greater rhetorical intensity (if less immediacy) in the later version, with its echoing 'essero diviso' ('being divided'). In case the disjunction and division appear to rupture the grazed light, a third 'divided' insists on their distance from falsity. The second version's tortured dialectic is less successful in conveying the sense ('Grazeth' presumably means to touch lightly in passing, but it also conjures the comical image of bovine light feeding on grass), yet it shows the poet grappling with a question that pervades the entire project of *The Cantos*: how may an obscure, disjunct poetics establish truth by natural demonstration? Pound's reading of this passage is justified by the text, which links 'without colour, being divided' to 'without all falsity' in the repetition of 'Fuor' ('Fuor di cholore essero diviso . . . Fuor d'ogni fraude'), though 'fraude' may be connected with the following 'dice dengno in fede', so that the sense is less that light's essence is without falsity than that 'light, being divided, is obscured by a dark medium, says one who is without deceit and can be trusted'. Cirigliano's translation maintains this paratactic openness by the use of elision:

> Colorless, a being divided,
>   sealed
>
>   in the middle of darkness, erasing
>   light . . . Beyond deceit
>   I say in good faith
>   mercy comes only from Love . . .

Pound's version allows him to place greater emphasis on 'the fine thing held in the mind' ('dove sta memoria') as the guardian of erotic restraint. If light is corrupted by the *ira* rather than sustained by it, it is akin to the falsity of 'the inferior thing ready for instant consumption.'[86] Pound therefore takes the *ira* to be a positive phallic impulse or anger, the mark of a man's strength of character, and not a dark force dividing love from reason. In Canto LXIII, '*in quella parte/dove sta memora*' graces the actions of Colonel Chandler, ally of one of the poem's great legislators, John Quincy Adams, who noted in his diary of 26 May 1760 that 'the mind must be agitated with some passion, either love, fear, hope, &c., before she will do her best'.[87] Pound brilliantly converts this into the language of the canzone:

> must be (IRA must be) aroused ere the mind be at its best
> *la qual manda fuoco*[88]

Cavalcanti acts here as the mediator between eighteenth-century America and modern Italy. Adams's sense of judgement is seen as the model for a 'vigorous realignment' of political life in the United States which could be achieved if American citizens take their cue from Mussolini. This does not mean that revolutionary mechanisms adapted to Italian society can be simply imported, but 'Mussolini will have acted as a stimulus, will have entered in American history, as Lenin has entered world history'.[89]

More problematic from a textual point of view is 'un formato locho', which Pound first renders as 'unformèd space' and then as 'forméd trace'. He was aware that some manuscripts give not 'un formato' but its opposite, 'non formato', but believes that the latter 'does not cohere in the general exposition.'[90] In fact, his text, the Laurentian XL, 46, 'is one of the less authoritative manuscripts for our poem, and the Italian text is consequently unreliable.'[91] All modern editions have 'non formato'. The difference is crucial to any reading of the canzone, since 'non formato' makes passion a force which unhinges reason, inducing a man to 'stare into empty space', hardly a defence of Amor as the conjoining of intelligence and imagination in a mental image. Pound's first go at the phrase cleverly fuses both variants, so that 'unformèd' may mean either that space is without form or that it has yet to be formed, but Canto XXXVI demands the less equivocal sense offered by 'forméd trace'. Now, love's 'uneasiness' ('Destandos'ira') creates the necessary resistance or difficulty that Adams understood as rousing the flame ('la qual manda focho') of action. Passion and intellect are joined in reason, which Pound comes increasingly to identify with intuition and Gestalt ('un formato locho') and against 'the tyranny of the syllogism, blinding and obscurantist'.[92] Such 'inspired overinterpretation' (as Makin calls it) allows Pound to 'build unassailable myth' on the canzone's 'insoluble cruces'.[93] Although the interpretation of *Donna me prega* is based on the notion that Cavalcanti disturbs the peace of the medieval mind by introducing 'proof by reason' and 'proof by experiment' into the Amor tradition, this new scientific paradigm comes to stand for the occult biologism of Pound's phallic theory of sexual and civic health, and eventually to the affirmation of totalitarian faith, pitted against the rationalist 'Hebrew and Protestant' desire to explain mysteries that should remain incomprehensible to all but the 'present knowers' ('a'l presente/chonoscente/chero'): 'It is a truth for elect recipients, not a truth universally spreadable or acceptable.'[94]

Here, then, is why Pound chooses Cavalcanti and not Dante to represent the culmination of the Amor tradition inherited from Provence. Considering that the *Commedia* remained almost as important a model for the *Cantos* as the *Odyssey*, Dante should be the prime focus of the tradition. But Pound's interest in Dante's poetry lies chiefly in its epic qualities, its consonance with the Eleusinian/Homeric theme of the journey through darkness to light, and not in its more local aspects: 'despite Dante's Provençal studies and the melody of his own lyrics, and despite the tremendous music of the *Commedia*, Dante, in taking up narrative, chucked out a number of MINOR criteria, as any writer of a long poem must in favour of a main virtue'.[95] When it comes to the matter of love, Dante parts company with the troubadours. By idealising objects of sexual desire, usually in the context of adulterous longing, the Provençal poets ran the risk of blaspheming against the medieval church. Arguably, their capricious use of expressions borrowed from the Scholastics and equation of the beloved with the Virgin Mary were ways of making carnal love more acceptable to the authorities: 'it is significant that at Toulouse, after the crusade against the Albigenses, when profane love was forbidden, the poets wrote sacred hymns to the Virgin instead, using the same language as before.'[96] Dante, however, reconciles the courtly tradition with Christian orthodoxy by stripping away the sensual aspects of his *donna angelicata* so that she becomes the embodiment of moral goodness. As we have seen, Pound objects to this holy 'dogma' because he relates it to the fear of the 'body as perfected instrument of the increasing intelligence'. Thus, he argues that the troubadours and Cavalcanti belong to a 'conspiracy of intelligence' derived from the celebratory sexual rites at Eleusis and not to Manichaeanism, an ascetic religion associated with the Cathars. The idea that thirteenth-century Provence was full of heretics who believed the world to be so evil that it could not have been created by God, and that this lugubrious theology informs the Amor tradition is, Pound argues, 'pure bunkumb'.[97] As Makin shows, Pound was right to see the Crusade against these so-called heretics as based on fear and slander, since all evidence suggests that 'Catharism' was largely an invention of the Catholic Church, determined to suppress the independent region of the Languedoc.[98] The secret history of the Cathars, and the minstrel tradition presumed to derive from it, is a conspiracy theory on the same lines as Barruel's fantasy of occult sedition.

Pound's association of Manes with Mussolini in the Pisan Cantos indicates that he is more interested in forging trans-historical and trans-mythic identities than in any consistent analysis of the issues. Manes may have founded a cult which, unlike Eleusis, 'produced nothing to match the grace of the well-curb at Terracina', but the similarity between his execution and Mussolini's (both, according to Pound, 'tanned and stuffed' by the faithless mob) is enough to earn him a place in the pantheon of those martyred in the name of elect wisdom.[99] Barruel argued that the Templars, Masons, Cathars, and Jacobins were all part of a conspiracy against Christianity and monarchy which began with the evil doctrines of the Manichaeans. In principle, Pound buys into this idea of a secret tradition opposed to Judaeo-Christian authority and what he believes to be its usurious economics, but he regards both Manichaeanism and

Christianity as part of a universal conspiracy against the sane and the sanitary which includes 'the Hebrew disease, the Hindoo disease, fanaticisms and excess that produce Savonarola, asceticisms that produce fakirs, St Clement of Alexandria, with his prohibition of bathing by women.'[100] All these manifestations of anality are without the *intelletto* he sees at work in Cavalcanti's theory of love and the 'exact and diversified terminology' of the troubadours, men who display 'considerable penetration' in their psychology.[101]

By linking the Amor tradition to the cult of Persephone instead of to Manichaeanism, Pound saves it from the taint of the unclean line, the hatred of the body, fertility and intelligence, and the usurers who, *contra natura*, have 'brought whores for Eleusis'.[102] He therefore replaces the secret history of Catharism promulgated by Gabriele Rossetti, Eugene Aroux, Josephin Peladan, Luigi Valli and others, who make esoteric virtue from Barruel's reactionary theories, with a metaphysics of light, no less occult in its fusion of intellect and irrationalism. This spirit of illumination, claiming freedom from centuries of ascetic repression while seeking organic wholeness in forms of mysticised authoritarianism, is central to the politics and poetics of late modernism. As we shall see in the next chapter, Olson's masculine poetics of self-transcendence is underwritten by occult psychology.

Notes

1 Mircea Eliade, *Occultism, Witchcraft, and Cultural Fashions* (Chicago: University of Chicago Press, 1976), 52; Peter French, *John Dee: The World of an Elizabethan Magus* (London: Ark, 1984), 85.

2 Frances A. Yates, *Giordano Bruno and the Hermetic Tradition* (London: Routledge and Kegan Paul, 1964), 451.

3 See David Simpson, *Romanticism, Nationalism, and the Revolt Against Theory* (Chicago: University of Chicago Press, 1993), 87–9.

4 Surette, *The Birth of Modernism*, 98.

5 'Like Blake, Swinburne, and Nietzsche, Rimbaud sees Christ as "the eternal thief of vigour", and his thought is permeated with anti-clericalism, communism . . . illuminism, and, above all, with a belief that imaginative energy is the motor of revolution . . . ' (Peter Nicholls, *Modernisms*, 31).

6 See Helen Sword, *Ghostwriting Modernism* (Ithaca: Cornell University Press, 2002); Richard Noll, *The Jung Cult: Origins of a Charismatic Movement* (London: Fontana, 1996), 75ff.

7 Noll, *The Jung Cult*, 107–8. Ascona was to a considerable extent the offspring of the Tübingen scholars: 'The search for the historical Jesus proved to be the turning point for nineteenth-century critical theology and European culture as a whole, for by the end of the century, widespread skepticism about the divinity of Jesus and the truth of the stories in the Gospels of the New Testament opened the way for social experimentation with alternative religious, neopagan, occultist, or atheistic lifestyles' (33–4).

8 Eliade, *Occultism, Witchcraft, and Cultural Fashions*, 55–6.

9 Robert Duncan, *The Truth and Life of Myth: An Essay in Essential Autobiography* (Fremont, Michigan: The Sumac Press, 1968), 22.

10 Evola tends to be linked to neofascism, though it is perhaps true to say that his writings, like Nietzsche's, only lend themselves to fascist interpretation. In *Phoenix: Fascism in Our Time* (New Brunswick: Transaction Publishers, 1999), A. James Gregor argues that 'What Evola liked were "secret" supranationalisms; gnostic wisdom from "on high", transmitted in signs and wonders; society organized in hereditary castes, all subordinated to warrior-bands of men; and led by divine rulers who represent the transcendent "light" of the world . . . What he did not like was Fascism' (15). On Devi and Serrano, see Gary Lachman, *Turn Off Your Mind: The Mystic Sixties and the Dark Side of the Age of Aquarius* (London: Sidgwick and Jackson, 2001), 139–43.

11 Duncan, *The Truth and Life of Myth*, 23.

12 Tim Redman, *Ezra Pound and Italian Fascism* (Cambridge: Cambridge University Press, 1991), 13. 'Donald Davie commented years ago that awarding the Bollingen Prize to Pound meant recognizing the "absolute disparity between the life of the poet and the life of the man"' (12). The Bollingen Foundation at Princeton was set up by Paul and Mary Mellon and dedicated to the work of Jung (whose rural retreat, a tower in the Swiss village of Bollingen, gives it its name). There is little acknowledgement by the academic community today of the reach of Jung's influence. From the 1950s to the 1970s, many academics were weaned on existentialist readings of Heidegger and Jung's analytic psychology. Criticism drawn from the 'myth-kitty' was once as much stock in trade in the universities as the congeries of 'theory' is now. Jung was seen as a spiritual father guiding scholars through the dark wood of their projections and misconceptions. Now, away from the more remote campuses of the Western seaboard, he has become an intellectual *persona non grata*, his tomes (Routledge/Princeton University Press, 'Bollingen Series'. Ed. Sir Herbert Read) relegated to the 'inner bookshops' that mark the fringes of university towns, the hardback edition still commanding high prices among initiates.

13 Eric Hobsbawm, 'Mass-producing Traditions: Europe, 1870–1914', in Eric Hobsbawm and Terence Ranger, eds, *The Invention of Tradition* (Cambridge: Cambridge University Press, 1983), 268.

14 Robert Duncan, 'The Maiden', in *The Opening of the Field* (New York: Grove Press, 1960), 27–9: 'No goddess, She/must be revived,/Cora among the grasses./Hearts/revive with her.' See also Robert Creeley, 'Kore' (1959), in *The Collected Poems of Robert Creeley 1945–1975* (Berkeley: University of California Press, 1982), 206.

15 Guy Davenport, 'Persephone's Ezra', in Hesse, ed., *New Approaches to Ezra Pound*, 147.

16 Davenport, 'Persephone's Ezra', 155.

17 See Peter Makin, *Provence and Pound* (Berkeley: University of California Press, 1978); Leon Surette, *A Light from Eleusis: A Study of the Cantos of Ezra Pound* (Oxford: Clarendon Press, 1979); Alan Durant, *Ezra Pound, Identity in Crisis: A Fundamental Reassessment of the Poet and His Work* (Brighton: Harvester Press, 1981); Smith, *Pound Revised*; Rabaté, *Language, Sexuality, and Ideology*.

18 'Demeter and Persephone', in *The Poems of Tennyson*. Ed. Christopher Ricks (London: Longman's, 1969), 1373–8.

19 Algernon Charles Swinburne, *Poems and Ballads and Atalanta in Calydon*. Ed. Kenneth Haynes (London: Penguin, 2001), 136–9.

20 Swinburne, *Poems and Ballads*, 55–61.

21 On the relationship between Pound and Mead see Surette, *The Birth of Modernism*, esp. 17–18; 130–5, and Demetres P. Tryphonopoulos, *The Celestial Tradition: A Study of Ezra Pound's* Cantos (Waterloo: Wilfrid Laurier University Press), 1992.

22 Helena Petrovna Blavatsky, *The Secret Doctrine* (Pasadena: Theosophical Universe Press, 1970), 445.

23 Ezra Pound, *Selected Poems 1908–1959* (London: Faber & Faber, 1977), 41.

24 Pound, Postscript to Remy de Gourmont, *The Natural Philosophy of Love* (New York: Rarity Press, 1931), 170.

25 Peter Makin, *Provence and Pound*, 32. As Makin points out, Pound's early Provençal-based verse 'went along with the "artistic" costume that he wore: he was not at this time [c. 1909] a budding neo-Platonist, but a late Romantic' (18). Nevertheless, the spirit of troubadour romance was important enough to him for him to persist with it even after he had rejected the fusty aesthetic posturing admired by Bridges et al. Makin argues 'that Pound brought Provençal culture not only into the modern world but also into the heights of his personal late-achieved Paradise' (4).

26 Rabaté, *Language, Sexuality, and Ideology*, 218.

27 D. H. Lawrence, *Birds, Beasts and Flowers* (London: Martin Secker, 1931), 56–9.

28 Hermann Hesse, *Demian*. Trans. W. J. Strachan (London: Granada, 1979), 59.

29 Hesse, *Demian*, 120.

30 Hesse, *Demian*, 136.

31 T. S. Eliot, 'The Metaphysical Poets', in *Selected Prose of T. S. Eliot*. Ed. Frank Kermode (London: Faber & Faber, 1975), 64. Eliot finds in Hesse's *Blick ins Chaos* a diagnosis of cultural decline which squares with his criticism of 'the ordinary man's experience' as 'chaotic, irregular, fragmentary'. The passage included in the notes to *The Waste Land* – quoted in German, though Eliot must have first come across it in an English translation for the July 1922 issue of the *Dial* – concludes Hesse's analysis of 'that strange, occult, godlike faculty' which allows the modern shaman (prophet/maniac/poet) insight into the sickness of Europe. According to James Longenbach, Eliot felt that he too had been beset by a visionary illness that showed him nightmares of Western decay. But this signified more than mere pessimism; like Hesse he believed that the descent into chaos presaged a new era. See Longenbach, *Modernist Poetics of History: Pound, Eliot, and the Sense of the Past* (Princeton: Princeton University Press, 1987), 233–7.

32 Plotinus, *Enneads*, V.8.4, in Luck, *Arcana Mundi*, 365. See also Stephen MacKenna's translation: Plotinus, *The Enneads* (London: Faber & Faber, 1956), 425.

33 C. G. Jung, 'The Psychological Aspects of the Kore', in Jung and Kerényi, *Essays on a Science of Mythology*, 165–6.

34 Surette, *The Birth of Modernism*, 57. See also John B. Vickery, *The Literary Impact of* The Golden Bough (Princeton: Princeton University Press, 1973).

35 Surette, *The Birth of Modernism*, 57–8.

36 Pound, 'Terra Italica' (1931–32), in *Selected Prose 1909–1965*, 56.

37 Pound, 'Idee Fondamentali' (1942), translated by Peter Nicholls in 'Lost Object(s): Ezra Pound and the Idea of Italy', in Taylor and Melchior, eds, *Ezra Pound and Europe*, 171–2. (My translation of Cavalcanti.)

38 Pound, 'Terra Italica', 56.

39 See J. E. Shaw, *Cavalcanti's Theory of Love: The Canzone d'Amore and Other Related Problems* (Toronto: University of Toronto Press, 1949), 56: 'St Thomas says that the *virtue* of any particular thing is its *excellent faculty*, that which makes its operation good, so that the virtue of a horse is its ability to run fast. (Morality of the race-track.)'

40 Longenbach, *Modernist Poetics of History*, 142.

41 Pound, 'Pastiche. The Regional', 284.

42 Rainey, *Institutions*, 124–5.

43 Longenbach, *Modernist Poetics of History*, 142–3. It is easy to underestimate the extent to which Pound became an *Italian* poet. The *Cantos* can be seen to engage with deep-rooted and conflicting tendencies in modern Italian society: the cult of beauty, the belief in self-governing provinces, the yearning for a political figure who will cut through bureaucracy and misrule, the respect for tradition, the fear of history, the obsession with cover-ups and conspiracies, and the need to '[c]odify, recodify, encrypt. Quod non est in actis non est in mundo: anything not written down, documented, simply doesn't exist. The standard compliment for a history book here isn't that the argument seems convincing, it's simply that the book is *documentato*, that it's based on documentary evidence . . . Here, laws or facts are like playing cards: you simply have to shuffle them and fan them out to suit yourself.' (Tobias Jones, *The Dark Heart of Italy: Travels Through Time and Space Across Italy* (London: Faber, 2003), 57.)

44 Pound, 'D. H. Lawrence' (1913), in *Literary Essays of Ezra Pound*. Ed. T. S. Eliot (London: Faber and Faber, 1968), 387. In this review of *Love Poems and Others*, Lawrence's erotic verse is rubbished as 'pre-raphaelitish slush, disgusting or very nearly so.' However, in 1910 Pound had told Lawrence of his desire to write a history of Dionysian erotic cults but feared no English publisher would touch it. (Recounted in Surette, *The Birth of Modernism*, 131.) Eighteen years later, he distinguishes the Tuscan aesthetic from that of the 'northern race' in terms which are meant clearly to go beyond Lawrence's fetishism of the lower body; unlike his northern counterpart, who is forced to spend his time guarding his body against 'assaults of the weather, the 'man' of the south is spurred by the 'effect of a decent climate', to leave his 'nerve-set open', eventually declining 'to limit reception to his solar plexus.' ('Cavalcanti', in Anderson, ed., *Pound's Cavalcanti*, 206.)

Surette notes the close proximity between Jung's cosmological and theological account of personality and Pound's biological and psychological theory of creativity, based on 'the same Gnostic texts' (147) which were also those 'available to Mead – primarily patristic condemnations' (138): 'Such incidents suggest that the cognitive scene in which the modernist drama was staged was stranger than scholarship has so far imagined' (147). The drama is not so strange when one considers the huge impact of vitalist philosophies on modernist theories of psychology and aesthetics. Pound and Jung could and do share a number of influences without having any professed allegiance. Both, for example, were heavily indebted to Frobenius. In his later years Pound greeted any mention of Freud with a torrent of racist abuse, but when asked whether he preferred Jung he replied that he 'couldn't distinguish between contents of the sewer'. (See Torrey, *The Roots of Treason*, 250; Noll, *The Jung Cult*, 38–9.)

45 Ezra Pound, *Guide to Kulchur* (New York: New Directions, 1968), 263.

46 See George E. Mylonas, *Eleusis and the Eleusinian Mysteries* (Princeton: Princeton University Press, 1961), 15ff; Makin, *Provence and Pound*, 217–21: 'Pound explains that what I have called "natural esotericism" does not apply merely to some separate, mystical area: it applies to every branch of knowledge, including what is called "science" . . . "Eleusis" contains the summation or concentration of the wisdoms thus gained.' (218–19); Surette, *The Birth of Modernism*, 102–8; 122ff.

47 See Pound, 'Cavalcanti', 210–11; Boris de Rachewiltz, 'Pagan and Magic Elements in Ezra Pound's Works', in Hesse, ed., *New Approaches to Ezra Pound*, 193–4;

Makin, *Provence and Pound*, 173, and *Pound's Cantos* (London: George Allen and Unwin, 1985), 184–5.

48 This was in 1940. Pound was still extolling the virtues of the Protocols to his visitors at St Elizabeth's in the 1950s. Tim Redman, *Ezra Pound and Italian Fascism*, 69–70, 202; Torrey, *The Roots of Treason*, 226. It is worth pointing out that, of Pound's two early economic mentors it is C. H. Douglas who entertains the theory of a Zionist conspiracy, not the occultist A. R. Orage, even though he published Arthur Kitson's anti-Semitic tirades in *The New Age* (see Redman, *Ezra Pound and Italian Fascism*, 39–40, 69–70).

49 Pound, 'Remy de Gourmont' (1920), in *Literary Essays*, 343.

50 Surette, *The Birth of Modernism*, 148–9.

51 Pound, *Gaudier-Brzeska*, quoted in Walter Baumann, 'Secretary of Nature, J. Heydon', in Hesse, ed., *New Approaches to Ezra Pound*, 310. While Pound grew increasingly disenchanted with Yeats's world of spooks and fairies, Baumann shows that he did not throw out, as James Longenbach supposes, the Neoplatonic baby with the Spiritualist bathwater. See Longenbach, *Stone Cottage*, 238ff; Baumann, 'Secretary of Nature', 311ff.

52 Pound, 'Terra Italica', 58.

53 Noll, *The Jung Cult*, 125. See also Luther Martin, *Hellenistic Religions: An Introduction* (Oxford: Oxford University Press, 1987), 114–15.

54 Mylonas, *Eleusis and the Eleusinian Mysteries*, 15.

55 Mylonas, *Eleusis and the Eleusinian Mysteries*, 281. Fragmentary evidence takes on a speculative life of its own. Of the few details known of the Eleusinian ritual, one is that at a key point in the ceremony initiates drank a potion, or *kykeon*, generally thought to be symbolic of the harvest. But Robert Gordon Wasson, the first Westerner in recorded history to eat magic mushrooms and co-author of *The Road to Eleusis* (1978), argues that the initiates made use of hallucinogenic fungi as a way of communing with the world of the spirits. Since the ritual ingestion of fly agaric and *Psilocybe mexicana* is a known shamanic technique, this thesis is not implausible. It is, however, unprovable and probably has more to do with Western fantasies of primitive consciousness than with ritual practice in Ancient Greece. See Gary Lachman, *Turn Off Your Mind*, 144–61.

56 See for instance Surette, *The Birth of Modernism*, 4–5: 'Postmodernism – whatever this volatile force might eventually turn out to be – clearly has as a common element the rejection of the modernist fantasy of decontextualized or positive knowledge and the adoption of a relativism or perspectivism that is most commonly traced to Friedrich Nietzsche . . . The modernists have become "adopted" as the self-assured, oppressive fathers of the postmodernists, just as the Victorians were for the modernists themselves'; hence, 'Eliot scholars may well not be "interested" in an argument claiming that *The Waste Land* should be placed within the occult enterprise of assembling the fragments of a lost faith rather than within the Nietzschean enterprise of "calling into question" all religious faith.' A complicating factor here is that Nietzsche's early theory of tragedy was a primary source for the ecstatic, Dionysian strain in twentieth-century occultism. Surette's chapter on 'Nietzsche, Wagner, and Myth' charts the influence of Nietzsche's 'resacralization of pagan mythology' (193) on Yeats, Mead, Orage, Jessie L. Weston, Jane Harrison, C. G. Jung and Pound. Richard Noll shows that Nietzsche's importance for European occultism was hardly restricted to this early work: 'The Nietzsche of *The Birth of Tragedy* (1872) was not the Nietzsche of *Also Sprach Zarathustra* (1892). Gone was the Apollonian cultural idealist, the lover of the Dionysian in the musical tragedy of Wagner. Nietzsche *was*

Dionysus, the pagan god of irrationality, the "loosener", the "breaker of bonds", the catalyst of reversals, the seducer through sudden cacophonies and equally sudden silences, the iconoclast who could proclaim the death of the Judaeo-Christian god and dare to overthrow even his own beloved "Divine Hero", Richard Wagner: this was the image of Nietzsche as Dionysian Hero adopted by individuals and groups seeking *Lebensreform* ("life-reform"), whether spiritual or political.' (*The Jung Cult*, 4.) I should also mention in this context the black magician Aleister Crowley, arguably the greatest single influence on countercultural subjectivism, whose mantra 'Do what thou wilt shall be the whole of the Law' owes much to Nietzsche's concept of the will to power, and is anything but sceptical. In October/November 1909 a Swinburnean extravaganza written and produced by Crowley, 'The Secret Rites of Eleusis' was performed at the Caxton Hall, London. Evidently, the rites were not so secret that they could not be divined by Crowley and his assistants.

57 Pound, Letter to Homer L. Pound, Rapallo, 11 April 1927, *The Selected Letters of Ezra Pound 1907–1941*, 210. 'Afraid the whole damn poem is rather obscure, especially in fragments.'

58 *The Cantos of Ezra Pound*, 19.

59 Carroll F. Terrell, *A Companion to* The Cantos *of Ezra Pound* (Berkeley: University of California Press, 1993), 13.

60 Richard Sieburth, *Instigations: Ezra Pound and Remy de Gourmont* (Cambridge, MA: Harvard University Press, 1978), 135.

61 Ezra Pound, *Collected Early Poems* (London: Faber & Faber, 1977), 226.

62 *The Cantos of Ezra Pound*, 485.

63 Pound, *Collected Early Poems*, 130; 149.

64 Pound, 'Cavalcanti', 205.

65 Donald Davie, 'Cavalcanti', in *Studies in Ezra Pound* (Manchester: Carcanet, 1991), 91.

66 'To Guido Cavalcanti' and 'Sonnet: Chi E Questa?' appeared in *Canzoni* (1911). See *Collected Early Poems*, 142–3, and David Anderson's introduction to *Pound's Cavalcanti*, xii. While working on Davie's Cavalcanti chapter, Prynne made his own version of the sonnet (published in *Prospect* 6 (1964), 35): 'the air lucid/with shaking/brightness'. There are echoes of Pound's 1934 translation of the *Canzone d'Amore* in Prynne's 1973 poem 'As grazing the light' in *Wound Response* (Cambridge: Street Editions, 1974). See J. H. Prynne, *Poems* (Edinburgh and London: Agneau 2, 1982), 227; *Poems* (Newcastle-upon-Tyne: Bloodaxe, 1999), 229.

67 Pound, 'Cavalcanti', 243. Likewise, Davie claims that 'the much heavier archaism' of Pound's revisions 'is not for the sake of loftiness and ornateness but, on the contrary, it serves to cleave more closely to the sense as Pound perceives it' (*Studies in Ezra Pound*, 96) The 'sense as Pound perceives it' means nothing, and the word 'cleave' can mean division as much as conjoining.

68 Pound, 'Cavalcanti', 210–11.

69 This line remains the same in both the 1932 *Rime* and 1934 Canto XXXVI translations. In the earlier version 'natural dimostramento' is 'nature's source', fitting into a rather flabby rendering of the first stanza of the canzone. In the later version it is simply 'natural demonstration'. I have taken Pound's texts as printed in Anderson's edition of Pound's Cavalcanti, 170–81. Since there are many variant editions of the canzone, I quote Pound's text when referring to his reading, and others as appropriate. When the first line of the poem is used as its title, *Donna me prega*, I follow the text in *Rime*, edited by Marcello Ciccuto (Milan: Rizzoli Editore, 1978).

70 Pound, 'Cavalcanti', 211.

71 Shaw, *Cavalcanti's Theory of Love*, 96. Shaw's detailed reading is torn between the claim that Cavalcanti gives a description of 'true love', realised in the 'complessione', 'which is neither ordinary carnal desire nor the anaemic, conventional, often fictitious devotion disingenuously celebrated by most of the poets' (89) and a negative account which finds this love to be in essence no more truthful than the courtly ideal: 'the active appetite of sense – the *irascibilis* that comes from Mars – is only aroused when a real woman becomes identified with the ideal woman cherished habitually in the mind of the lover ("perpetuale effetto"), and when that identity is destroyed, when, that is, the real woman ceases to be like the ideal, the passion abates, the darkness recedes' (88). Early commentators such as Egidio and del Garbo, with their lack of knowledge of Italian and Provençal verse, place too much emphasis on the sensual element in the canzone, so 'we should look in vain to either of them for an understanding of that permanent ideality, never destroyed even at the height of passion, which is the substratum of Guido's love' (156–7). Marc Cirigliano's interpretation is more resolutely pessimistic: 'One's face reveals nothing:/repressed/pallor overwhelming the victim/and, who hears well/sees nothing' (Guido Cavalcanti, *The Complete Poems*. Trans. Marc Cirigliano (New York: Italica Press, 1992), 67).

72 Shaw, *Cavalcanti's Theory of Love*, 88. Pound has 'compassion' (1932) and 'mercy' (1934); similarly, Cirigliano sticks with 'mercy'. In a translation appended to her *Guido Cavalcanti: The Other Middle Ages* (Toronto: Toronto University Press, 2002), Maria Luisa Ardizzone gives the more positive 'favour', which is just as inadequate but works with her heavily Pound-inflected interpretation.

73 Pound, 'Cavalcanti', 214. 'His definition of *l'accidente*, i.e. the whole poem, is a scholastic definition in form, it is as clear and definite as the prose treatises of the period, it shows an equal acuteness of thought.'

74 Line Henriksen, 'Chiaroscuro: Canto 36 and *Donna mi prega*', *Paideuma*, Vol. 29, No. 3 (winter 2000), 33.

75 Bernstein, *The Tale of the Tribe*, 44. Canto XXXVI has 'shineth out/Himself his own effect unendingly'.

76 Peter Nicholls, *Ezra Pound: Politics, Economics, and Writing* (London: Macmillan, 1984), 68.

77 Etienne Gilson, *History of Christian Philosophy in the Middle Ages* (London: Sheed and Ward, 1955), 264. See also James McEvoy, *The Philosophy of Robert Grosseteste* (Oxford: Clarendon Press, 1982), 507–8.

78 Pound, 'Cavalcanti', 206.

79 Pound, 'Cavalcanti', 210.

80 See Ardizzone, *Guido Cavalcanti*, 153; Cirigliano's introduction to Guido Cavalcanti, *The Complete Poems*, xxiii; Henriksen, 'Chiaroscuro', 41–2.

81 Etienne Gilson, review of of *Guido Cavalcanti Rime* (*Criterion*, October 1932, xii, 106–12), in Eric Homberger, ed., *Ezra Pound: The Critical Heritage* (London: Routledge, 1972), 277.

82 Pound, 'Cavalcanti', 215.

83 Surette, *A Light from Eleusis*, 72.

84 Shaw, *Guido Cavalcanti's Theory of Love*, 41. Cavalcanti's 'possibile intelletto' refers to the psyche's ability to receive the species of things. Grosseteste calls it the 'material intellect' (see Richard McKeon, trans., *Selections from Medieval Philosophers, vol. II: Roger Bacon to William of Ockham* (New York: Scribner's, 1930), 464. Pound changes 'latent intellect' (1932) to 'intellect possible' (1934) following Gilson's remark that 'latent' is too reminiscent of the Aquinian Passive Intellect, 'implying the materiality, possible, on the contrary, the immateriality of the intellect.' (Gilson,

review of *Rime*, 276.) He does not go on to hazard a guess as to how many angels can dance on a pinhead.

85 *The Cantos of Ezra Pound*, 480. Pound's *Rime* text has the noun-form not the verb, 'memora', used in Canto LXXVI.

86 Pound, 'Cavalcanti', 205.

87 Quoted in Terrell, *A Companion to* The Cantos of Ezra Pound, 277. Rabaté notes that 'Adams is aware of his passions, but transcends them, for he symbolizes both an impersonal memory and the acme of volition aimed at order and beauty.' (*Language, Sexuality, and Ideology in Ezra Pound's* Cantos, 125.)

88 *The Cantos of Ezra Pound*, 371.

89 Ezra Pound, *Jefferson and/or Mussolini* (1935) (New York: Liveright, 1970), 104.

90 Pound, 'Cavalcanti', 237.

91 Shaw, Guido *Cavalcanti's Theory of Love*, 213. Shaw's work has been all but ignored by Pound critics, probably because its otherwise exhaustive commentary on the canzone dismisses Pound's edition of the *Rime* out of hand: 'The translation in English verse is more obscure than the original in any version, and the "Partial Explanation" contributes no light on the meaning; nor do the desultory remarks entitled "The Vocabulary" and "Further Notes"' (213). Shaw is clearly put off by Pound's prose style, which typically withholds elucidation as much as offering it. This is odd, since much of his analysis is remarkably Poundian: 'The consideration of the ideal image in the imagination and memory is the shining of the Intellectual Light upon that image, Love in its first perfection, sensitive and intellectual, but not rational, for the logical faculty which forms syllogisms and reaches conclusions is not concerned' (115).

92 Pound, 'Cavalcanti', 211.

93 Makin, *Pound's Cantos*, 190.

94 Pound, 'Cavalcanti', 203; 210–11. (See note 23 on p. 000.)

95 Pound, 'Hell', in *Literary Essays*, 203.

96 Shaw, *Guido Cavalcanti's Theory of Love*, 105.

97 Pound, 'Terra Italica', 59.

98 Makin, *Provence and Pound*, 217ff.

99 Pound, 'Terra Italica', 58. (See the discussion of Canto LXXIV in the Introduction on p. 5 and Chapter 1, 38.)

100 Pound, 'Cavalcanti', 208.

101 Pound, 'Remy de Gourmont: A Distinction', in *Literary Essays*, 344.

102 *The Cantos of Ezra Pound*, 240.

3

MAXIMAL EXTENT: CHARLES OLSON AND C. G. JUNG

The city as a synonym for the self, for psychic totality, is an old and well-known image . . . There is a Coptic treatise in the Codex Brucianus in which we find the idea of the Monogenes or only son of God, who is also the Anthropos, Man. He is called the city with the four gates. The city with the four gates symbolizes the idea of totality; it is the individual who possesses the four gates to the world, the four psychological functions, and so is contained in the self. The city with the four gates is his indestructible wholeness – consciousness and the unconscious united. (C. G. Jung, *Analytical Psychology: Its Theory and Practice*)

In 1935, Walter Benjamin prefaced 'Some Motifs in Baudelaire' with a brief critique of the cult of *Lebensphilosophie*. Since the late nineteenth century, he argued, this atavistic tendency in German thought reacted to the 'denatured' condition of the civilised masses by rejecting concrete social life in favour of the submerged truths of nature, poetry and myth. What began as a desire to return the Central European bourgeoisie to the intuitive life exemplified by lyric poetry – as opposed to the mechanised perversions of mass culture – became grist to the mill of National Socialism's blood and soil political aesthetic: 'Dilthey's book *Das Erlebnis und die Dichtung* represents one of the earliest of these efforts which ends with Klages and Jung, who made common cause with Fascism.'[1] As he does not enlarge on this point, Benjamin must have considered the link between Jung's theory of mythic archetypes and the rise of National Socialism to be so self-evident as not to require further comment. Today the modernist equation of mass culture and a sterile bourgeois rationality with the loss of a spiritual identity at once noble and instinctual is seen as a crucial factor in the sublimation of nationalist and racist ideology. However, Jung's version of this myth has become so ingrained in Western culture that its roots in the theology of the Central European right have gone largely over-looked by academics, artists and psychotherapists alike, and if many intel-lectuals would see fit to question the political disingenuousness of Jung's ideas, few would go along with Benjamin in taking it as read that they ever made 'common cause' with Fascism. How could this be, as Jung was a Swiss citizen who as early as 1918 warned 'against the possibility of a breaking-out of a "blonde beast from an underworld prison" of the German spirit', and whose books were banned by the Nazis?[2] True, as even van der Post admits, Jung's anti-Semitic leanings were a 'mistake', but he did much to defend his Jewish colleagues against abuse by the Nazi regime.[3]

Benjamin's correspondence reveals that he had planned to write 'a critique of Jungian psychology, whose Fascist armature I had promised myself to expose', but the project was put off for an unspecified reason and he turned to the Baudelaire project.[4] A 1937 letter to Gershom Scholem shows that he was still grappling with the subject, but no further critique is to be found in his papers.[5] T. W. Adorno suggests that Benjamin's antipathy towards Jung was due to the fact that the theory of archetypes represents a false phylogeny because it denies cultural difference by reducing history to a set of static images. By contrast, 'Benjamin's images do not present invari-ant archetypes that are to be extracted from history; rather, they shoot together precisely by means of the force of history'.[6] Like Adorno and Lukacs, whose later work included a major repudiation of *Lebensphiloso-phie* and its Fascist exponents,[7] Benjamin was highly aware of a growing political climate in which cults of individuality, irrational life-forces and the substitution of myth for history were at one with the rhetoric of the 'German Spirit'. Such cults are pure products of ideology precisely because their rejection of political life in favour of a 'deeper', universal human iden-tity grounds and reifies the political agenda of a regime that seeks to reduce all difference to identity in the name of cultural unity. The ideas of the Frankfurt School Marxists derive from the need to critique this roman-tic–authoritarian tradition which, in fetishizing the primacy of 'instinct', 'Selfhood' and 'nature', equated knowledge with submission to mystical forces, self-identity with communal will, and the community with racial characteristics, exemplified by the term *Geschlechte*, which brings together 'race', 'sex', and 'type'. In its simplest formulation, the paradox here is that of the subject who seeks his or her 'freedom' and 'individuality' in the edicts of a guru. This is the basis of Benjamin's critique of cults; as Julian Roberts notes, the principle point in his rejection of Ludwig Klages' Vitalism and Jung's Analytic Psychology was that 'The personality was the organ of pure collectivity, and its manifestation was authority.'[8]

Benjamin's argument anticipates the recent work of Richard Noll, who shows that the formation of Jung's psychology was closely bound up with the ideas of various groups in Ascona, Switzerland and Munich around the beginning of the twentieth century who sought a 'long-lost Teutonic spirituality and a return to a Golden Age of paganism', and who predicted 'a mystical blood community of Volk' (*Volksgemeinschaft*) brought about by a revolution led by a spiritual and/or political elite.[9] Jung's version of psychoanalysis is essentially religious, and its key concepts, such as the collective unconscious, the archetypes, and individuation, have their origins in the mystical anthropology of Max Müller and J. J. Bachofen, whose theories of prehistorical utopianism greatly influenced groups such as the Schwabing and Munich based 'Cosmic Circle', which included the poet Stefan George and Klages. Jung's seminars on Nietzsche during the early 1930s refer to Klages, and his 1925 paper on psychological types, published in a journal edited by Klages, suggests links between the latter's idea of 'expression analysis' and Jung's typology.[10] While Klages introduced Bachofen's ideas to the *Georgekreis* in 1899, Jung came to them around 1908 through his friendship with the libertarian psychoanalyst Otto Gross, another Asconan devotee of pagan regeneration. Bachofen claimed to have discovered evidence in Greco-Roman culture of two phases of human society that preceded modern patriarchal organisation. The first of these was basically polygamous, nomadic, and communal but brutal, and was succeeded by an egalitarian, matriarchal culture that privileged body and earth over the rational mind and found sacredness in the chthonic. This phase, which Bachofen identifies with the Eleusinian Mysteries, gave way briefly to the cult of Dionysus and then declined into the Apollonian order of hierarchical law and patriarchy. The possibility of a return to the instinctual life symbolised by the phase of the Great Mother inspired Jung's first theory of a phylogenetic unconscious in 1911–12,[11] and formed the basis of his utopian desire for 'a natural analytic collectivity that . . . could transcend even "type and sex".'[12]

However, if the Eleusinian Mother is invested in Bachofen's scheme with guardianship of the pagan community organised by 'natural' right, she nevertheless comes to act only as handmaiden to male identity. Jung's theoretical sleight of hand gives the Mother nominal control, for the concept of spiritual rebirth here is ultimately patriarchal. The Hellenistic mysteries enact a scenario in which the (male) sun hero descends into the (female) earth, where he does battle with the forces of darkness and comes reborn into the light. For Jung, this symbolises the individual's confrontation with his own libidinal darkness, the passage through introversion towards Selfhood in the reconciliation of male and female principles (animus and anima).[13] Jung's humanist rhetoric makes radical claims for the overcoming of *Geschlecht*, but its reasoning is geared towards identifying and authorising the type of the phallic hero. Similarly, Jung's fascination with alchemy as a model for psychic transformation works as an analogue of individuation, where the instinctual or primitive aspects of the self are recognised and accepted, but in order to be spiritually sublated. The idea that the philosopher's stone might be found in base matter, that enlightenment involves passage through darkness, links Jung's history of consciousness with the racist element of the Romantic image of the primitive. Here, in an *apparent* reversal of the imperialist belief in the natural superiority of Western civilisation over the 'dark' regions of Africa and Asia, primitive cultures are privileged as remaining in touch with organic processes lost to Western society. But, like the feminine principle, they come to represent an ideal of instinctual being with which 'Western man' must be reconciled if he is to progress beyond the limits of the rational or mechanistic lifeworld. If the intention towards the primitive is utopian, it nevertheless regards its 'ethnic' object as a means to redemption, and therefore reinscribes imperialist destiny.[14]

In Erich Neumann's Jungian account of 'Mystical Man', the path to 'healthy' individuation can be achieved only by an 'heroic' facing-up to the 'repressed shadow and anima' and so reconciling the ego with the frightening realm of the symbolic 'outside' (i.e. the natal division), which has both brought the subject into being and resists him. The nihilistic 'uroboros mystic', on the other hand, denies the existence of this darkness and turns toward asceticism.[15] But if Neumann rejects an outrightly theological view of these symbols of human struggle with the not-self, he justifies their archetypal nature by treating them as authentic, hypostatised visions of reality at the very moment they are described as myths. The hero might be 'worldly' in taking a knowing, euhemeristic view of what influences him, but he remains a hero seeking his 'true self' in a word of questing romance, just as the anima remains part of the exterior world and the shadow remains black. The Jungian adept is moulded into a strong individual, initially by undergoing analysis that allows him an unashamedly Oedipal relationship with the mother (Neumann's best known work is *The Great Mother*), due to the fact that he no longer fears her prohibition; and then by building up his revised ego in deference to, but always in superiority to, other 'types' (*Geschlecht*). Neumann writes that 'paradoxical as it may sound . . . the ego must increase its charge of energy in order to make possible its own suspension and transposition'.[16] But if the old ego is suspended in favour of the new self, it is only because the archetypes that endorse the self give back a charge of egotistical energy. The typology proper to the archetypes stands in relation to *Geschlecht* as *Gestalt*; as Philippe Lacoue-Labarthe and Jean-Luc Nancy explain:

Rosenberg [Fascist author of *The Myth of the Twentieth Century*] declares: 'Freedom of the soul . . . is always *Gestalt*.' ('Gestalt' means form, figure, con-figuration, which is to say that this liberty has nothing abstract or general about it; it is the capacity to put-into-figure, to embody.) 'The *Gestalt* is always plastically limited.' (Its essence is to have a form, to differentiate itself; the 'limit', here, is the limit that detaches a figure from a background, which isolates and distinguishes a *type*.) 'This limitation is racially condi-tioned.' (Thus one attains the content of the myth: a race is the identity of *a* formative power, of a singular type; a race is the bearer of a myth.)[17]

The contradiction of Jungian 'humanism' – and its persuasive force – is that it offers transcendence of age-old divisions between race and gender even though the transcendent principle itself is presented through a set of timeless forms founded on such divisions. The Jungian attests to a 'whole-ness of being' beyond the politics of identity and difference but does not see that that wholeness is based on the reduction of difference to identity. When, for example, Laurens van der Post claims that 'After Jung's *Psycho-logical Types* we no longer have any valid excuse for not realising that we are all ultimately trying to say the same things and express the same long-ings in terms of our own unique natures',[18] he cannot describe the content of this difference-in-identity without collapsing it into a false unity: 'Man has a biological birth through woman of flesh and blood. He can have a spiritual or psychological rebirth within through his feminine self. Man's biological birth provides him with the base material for creating some-thing unique and individual of himself. The act of individual creation and recreation within is achieved through the feminine, but fathered within by man's male spirit.'[19] In the light of recent feminist and postcolonial theory, such 'humanist' claims look absurdly misconceived, but Jung's fusion of collective forms of occult knowledge with the promise of individual self-transformation has been central to the poetics of modernism and has had a radical influence on generations of Western artists and intellectuals seek-ing an alternative to official bourgeois Christian society.[20] Whereas for Benjamin, Lukacs and Adorno the atavism of analytic psychology was seen as collusive with political reaction, its later associations with the counter-culture of the United States in the 1950s and 1960s as well as with what Kristeva calls the second phase of feminism invested it with a politically liberal status. Jungian thought is rescued from the charge of Fascism by the fact that it is not *abject*; even if its deification of the feminine is merely an intermediate stage on the way to male individuation, this is a far cry from the deathly images of woman Klaus Theweleit describes as inhabit-ing the Nazi imaginary, which instead of treating the feminine as the organic well-spring of masculine culture, project it as a threat to phallic self-sufficiency that must be erased at all costs.[21]

At the same time, Jung's romance of the Self has helped to establish a modern orthodoxy of transcendent individualism, especially in North America, where psychoanalytic practice has tended to be aligned with a range of therapies designed to massage the ego. Motifs of heroic sublation of the (feminine, Eastern, 'underworld') shadow remain clichés of television drama and Hollywood cinema, and inform regenerative movements from New Age spiritualism to masculine wilderness cults. While the individual is seen as the creation of a 'higher' or 'deeper' impersonal power, this power reinforces the sanctity of the self, the self elevated through contact with the suprapersonal: 'Whoever speaks in primordial images speaks with a thousand voices; he enthrals and overpowers, while at the same time he lifts the idea he is seeking to express out of the occasional and transitory into the realm of the ever-enduring.'[22] The ideology of Jungianism, therefore, is not fascistic but works as a liberal humanist revision of romantic–authoritarian tradition, freeing the 'individual' from repressive obstacles to desire and self-development, while simultaneously disavowing and reifying the role of the Master.[23]

Of the many modern poets who have associated themselves with Jung's ideas, Charles Olson is significant in developing an entire poetic from the relationship between a transcendental self and its origins in the collective unsconscious filtered through world religion and arcane knowledge. Where Pound had looked to ancient China, Greece and Rome, and the European Renaissance for evidence of spiritual and political *virtú* lost to modern technocracy, Olson extended his inquiry to a massive study of human origins including prehistory, anthropology, cosmology, geography, genetics, shamanism and the occult. Everything from the early postglacial environment to quantum mechanics took on the potential for mythic synchronicity. Unlike Pound, however, Olson sought a localised complement to his cosmogony in America, and in particular the town of Gloucester on the Eastern seaboard.[24] Pound's historicising was to be fused with William Carlos Williams's demand for a specifically American poetic. And although he followed the example set by *The Cantos* and *Paterson* in reinventing the epic poem, Olson diverged from the perspectivism of these texts by centring his major work on the singular figure of Maximus, an extension of his own ego into the Jungian anthropos. Apart from Robert Duncan, no other poet has so eclectically taken up the modernist principle of a mythic method. But Olson's attack on the 'lyric ego' of Anglo-American writing meant that his own poetry was more discontinuous than Duncan's, and his cultivation of arcane material less systematic. But his theory of 'Projective Verse' coupled with his belief in 'finding out for oneself' has had a more radical influence on recent poetry in the United States and Britain, primarily because it has inspired a new freedom of objective form and allows

the poet to incorporate an ulimited range of material not normally associated with the poetic. The beauty of Olson's method is that, as a principle,
it goes far beyond his own prescriptions.

However, Olson's own prescriptions are the subject of the present
chapter, and I will argue that their dependence on the tenets of analytic
psychology leads to the same contradictions of archetypal selfhood found
in Jung's theories of consciousness. His historical practice attests to the
unity of experience as the prime matter for poetry, but it supports a phallic, egotistical ideology that is inconsistent with its universalist claims.

In 1950, Olson had read Jung's *Psychology and Religion* less than
enthusiastically: 'Mr Jung is, as I always hunched, a lazy fraud, in this
respect, a mere g.d. swiss soft pink hill of learning.' Two years later, he was
'full of total admiration (more than for any living man)' for the 'great doc-
tor'.[25] And by the time he was composing *Maximus Poems IV, V, VI* in the
mid-1960s, his entire poetic was dedicated to the heroic battle against the
shadow: 'Gloucester is a possible cosmos which threatens to dissolve into
the torpid condition of mass society, and Maximus regards himself as the
heroic ego that will attempt to drive the destructive uroboric forces of society back to a distant edge once more.'[26] As Tom Clark details in a recent
biography, 'Olson became during these years an intuitive dogmatist of private vision, a shamanic votary as committed to his own spiritual exercises
as the Greek poet-priests to the mysteries of the earth goddess they
guarded at Eleusis . . . The "voice of a sense of religion" which he had projected to student disciples at Black Mountain was now to find its ultimate
home in a fetishlike analogical poetry transmitted as runic spell, inaccessible to the point of incomprehensibility to the general public, but to a small
audience of acolytes nothing less than necessary data, the hermetic doctrines and protocols of "secret rites practiced by the initiates alone, just
like the mysteries."'[27]

Olson's poetics of the Self is directly opposed to the complacency and
pathos of the confessional 'I' of mid-century American verse. Charles
Altieri writes that for Olson, Creeley, and others associated with the Black
Mountain school, 'it seemed that poetry could be saved from decadence
only by shifting the basic unit of poetic intelligence from concerns for aesthetic complexity to concerns for emotional intensity and speculative
scope, even if the price had to be the rejection of traditional expectations
about craft and about coherent symbolic patterning as a structural principle.'[28] Robert Lowell's poetry represented the false consciousness of a self-
immolating personality, and needed to be overcome:

> Once one reduces the imagination to a surface of contingent details, the 'I'
> is likely to discover itself without grounds: 'I myself am hell;/nobody's here.'
> To place there somebody or something more powerful or less pathetic than

the anxious 'I' became the quest of most self-consciously post-modern poetry in the sixties – from Olson's myths, to O'Hara's glittering surfaces, to Ginsberg's blend of hipster and guru in search of alternative realities.[29]

That something was the reaffirmation of an originally expansive American selfhood, rejecting *ego* in favour of *ipse*.[30] Olson's 'pursuit of the deep image escaped the Freudian ego of confessional poetry only to rely on the equally problematic and theatrical Jungian self.'[31] Whereas the confessional poets worked in vexed reaction to Freud's denigration of the artist as a neurotic, those who embraced the ideas of Jung were projected into a vastly eclectic imaginary scene in which the figure of the artist stood for redemption from the dark night of Freudian identity. As far as Jung is concerned, Freud neglects the healing powers of the 'unconscious' by reducing the self to mere pathology: 'Ludwig Klages' saying that "the spirit is the adversary of the soul" might serve as a cautionary motto for the way Freud approached the possessed psyche. Whenever he could, he dethroned the "spirit" as the possessing and repressing agent by reducing it to a "psychological formula".'[32] Jung's own version of psychotherapy is dedicated to amplifying the creative aspects of phantasy as a way of exorcising the neuroses or 'demons' that take control when the unconscious self is enslaved by the conscious ego. The contents of the unconscious do not themselves spring from a private, inaccessible imaginary realm, but are objective and collective, and Jung seeks to answer the question of the origin of the 'I' by showing it to be informed by a symbolic *ur*text. Correspondingly, the work of art is not merely the product of the neurotic psyche but the concrete expression of primordial collective themes and images that speak through the self:

> I am assuming that the work of art we propose to analyze, as well as being symbolic, has its source not in the *personal unconscious* of the poet, but in a sphere of unconscious mythology whose primordial images are the common heritage of mankind. I have called this sphere the *collective unconscious*, to distinguish it from the personal unconscious. The latter I regard as the sum total of all those psychic processes and contents which are capable of becoming conscious and often do, but are then suppressed because of their incompatibility and kept subliminal. Art receives tributaries from this sphere too, but muddy ones; and their predominance, far from making the work of art a symbol, merely turns it into a symptom.[33]

The collective unconscious, on the other hand,

> is no more than a potentiality handed down to us from primordial times in the specific form of mnemonic images or inherited in the anatomical structure of the brain. There are no inborn possibilities of ideas that set bounds to even the boldest fantasy and keep our fantasy activity within certain

> categories: *a priori* ideas, as it were, the existence of which cannot be ascer-
> tained except from their effects . . . only by inferences drawn from the fin-
> ished work can we reconstruct the age-old original of the primordial image.[34]

Jung describes this image as both an archetype and a 'figure' which constitutes the 'psychic residua of innumerable experiences of the same type'.[35]
Possession is not restricted to that which can be classified as 'mine', but is
'ours'. Selfhood emerges via a return to an original pre-figural experience
that connects with timeless and essential human principles. The Freudian
ego is merely a front; to speak of either personal consciousness or uncon-
sciousness as primary would be mistaken, for the genuine principle is
situated in a hidden collective form or *chora*, the 'pre-conscious'.

If the archetypes remain prior to the division between conscious and
unconscious, but somehow, inexplicably, they are transmitted to the pit of
the unconscious. The demarcation of high and low orders preserves a
mythical value. Jacques Lacan has called into doubt the idea that the
unconscious 'speaks the truth'; why should it be any more true or false than
conscious thought? 'Every Jungian-style conception which makes of
the unconscious, under the name of archetype, the real locus of another
discourse, really does fall prey to this objection. These archetypes, these
reified symbols which reside in a permanent manner in a basement of the
human soul, how are they truer than what is allegedly at the surface? Is
what is in the cellar always truer than what is in the attic?'[36]

The alleged truth-value of each archetypal symbol is anterior to the
analytical process in that it disallows any specific economy of association
and reference: the analysand must conform to the edicts of mythology,
established as pre-subjective etymon but at the same time prescribing a
norm of selfhood to which the 'I' must attempt to return. Jung makes the
ego into a secondary feature in that it can only 'muddy' the pure source of
art, the *essentially* symbolic. The 'ego' comes to be 'self' in that it reverts
to the sameness of a spatialised collectivity, in turn authorised by a (non)
origin in myth. In order for a myth to contain its origin it must always manifest 'itself' in some sort of identity, and will therefore have to be purged
of any incidental or contextual details which emerge from a specific representation of its original symbolic constituents. The subject of the collective unconscious may only accede to the status of 'self' through the
ritual expurgation of anything not immediate to whatever is thought to
comprise an underlying reality. Moreover, Jung is clearly uncertain about
the means of transmission of archetypes to the unconscious; Elizabeth
Wright finds that Jung comes up with

> the dubious explanation that a *potentiality* for them [the archetypes] is
> anatomically transmitted. Hence he manages to avoid confronting the

nature-versus-culture dilemma: are the archetypes in the genes, that is naturally determined, or are they picked up in the course of experience? It is a non-explanation to speak of 'potentiality'; it is like Molière's joke, in which a 'dormative' property is attributed to opium ('What is the cause and reason for opium producing sleep?' Candidate: 'Because there is in opium a dormative property' – *La Malade Imaginaire*).[37]

Olson follows Jung in wishing to provide an essential distinction between ego and self. His work is conceived largely as a quest to find what he stridently asserts as 'THE ALTERNATIVE TO THE EGO POSITION'.[38] The further remark that 'the EGO AS BEAK is bent and busted' implies that *something* should replace the ego *as beak*, cancelling the thrust of the ego yet retaining its force.[39] This 'Maximal stance' is a strange contradiction, because although Olson's concept of Projective Verse is designed to transfer energy from objects 'with the minimal amount of ego-interference', in effect it resolves into an aggressively thetic rhetoric.[40] As James E. Miller points out, this sense of a moral imperative precludes objectivism – 'Olson clears the space for his own *Maximus Poems*, somewhere between Pound's ego-dominance and Williams' ego-submission' – becoming 'objectism'.[41]

I will return to the method of 'projective' composition later, but for now it is important to clarify what the self means for Olson as an alternative to the ego. Initially, it signifies everything that it does for Jung: preconscious, expansive, 'deep', centred, holistic, and male. Thomas Merrill notes that

> Those familiar with [Olson's] prose know how often he refers to Jung's expression that 'the self is not only the centre, but also the whole circumference which embraces both conscious and unconscious; it is the centre of this totality, just as the ego is the centre of consciousness'.[42]

The self is already a deeper identity than the ego, and is thus from the first a spatial concept. Olson is adamant that, in spite of appearances, his is not an ego-position, for he argues that the self he obeys is not 'ego'; it *is* a dependable object of obedience and devotion which is from the Jungian perspective decidedly 'other'.[43] That is, other to rationalism, Hellenism, Christianity, commodification; in short, everything that might come under the heading of what Olson termed 'pejorocracy'.[44] His research into early civilisations led him to posit them as organic precedents for overcoming the modern pejorocracy. Mayan, Sumerian, Hittite, Norse, Ancient Egyptian, and American Indian cultures gave him hope for a spiritually attuned form of writing, which like the Mayan hieroglyphs 'contain nature's force and testify that, indeed, "Man is no creature of his own discourse." To the contrary, he is a creature of Nature's force attuned to *his own* processes.'[45] The concept of writing here is at one with 'living breath', a manifestation of somatic purity:

Olson's recurring stress on the vital importance of breath stems from a conviction that breath liberates the 'self' from its traditional seat in the mind and reestablishes it in its proper place – the body. Thus, our knowledge of the world and our expression of that knowledge through speech comes from inside us. 'One's life,' says Olson, 'is informed from and by one's own literal body . . . the intermediary, the intervening thing, the interruptor, the resistor. The self.'[46]

The body, the proper place, man's own processes. Olson's primary concern is to effect a return to what he formulates as the truth of the 'literal'. The literal is an adjunct of the self; it is not personal, private or merely ontogenetic, but a preindividual beginning which according to Olson states the *true* name of the place. The implications of this truly literal place are ethnocentric. As Jung writes, 'it is not surprising that when an archetypal situation occurs we suddenly feel an extraordinary sense of release, as though transported, or caught up by an overwhelming power. At such moments we are no longer individuals, but the race; the voice of all mankind resounds in us.'[47] The linguistic aspect of this racial idea is the privileging of etymology as a scientific or imaginative foundation for human meaning, clearly embodied here in the notion of pejorocracy. Thus, the true literal is linked to the etymon as a return to things themselves, and entails a reactionary critique of capitalism:

> [Olson] attacks capitalism on the grounds that it fosters absentee ownership, which is an appropriation of objects with which the owner has had too little contact. Analogously, his attack on conventional syntax rests on the judgement that its patterns of word order are so worn that words lose their substance, nouns lose their referents, as they become mere signs in a too familiar pattern of thought.[48]

Possession by an original 'owner' is not called into question; just as language declines from its source, the materialism of Western civilisation represents a neglect of duty on the part of rightful owners towards the people and things in their dominion. Olson may have been following Veblen's critique of American capitalism, although he appears not to have read Veblen at first hand. In 'The Vinland Map Review' (1965), he quotes from Douglas Dowd's 1964 study of Thorstein Veblen, sketching a theory of 'waste' as originating from the 'new-mindedness' of Renaissance economic ideology.[49] In *Absentee Ownership* (1923), Veblen himself describes what he calls 'the craftsman's natural right grounded in workmanship' as having been superseded by new economic relations forged by the 'merchandising trade'.[50] This resulted in the wasteful exploitation of natural resources by the said absentee owners. Veblen's earlier critique of capitalism in the United States did not come from the left. He was influenced by both pragmatism and Social Darwinism, and was a lifelong supporter of free trade. Although highly critical of an economic order in which the captains of industry are able to manipulate the forces of production through the power of cartels and monopolies, he believed that radical change could only come from the members of the engineering class, who were less prone than the workers to emulating the wasteful consumption of their masters. By the time he came to write *Absentee Ownership*, however, he had become more pessimistic, arguing that the 'engineering class was too integrated into the business system to constitute a negation of it', and that 'the underlying populations would continue to put up with the "imbecilic institutions" of capitalism because they had absorbed its cultural ethic of individualism and materialism'.[51] Olson's jackdaw approach to history leaves his account of the economic origins of pejorocracy too abstract and sketchy for one to be able to say how far its politics coincide with Veblen's bourgeois pessimism. Nevertheless, what can be gleaned from Olson's theory of the conjunction of economic and linguistic decline is his implied remedy for a culture in which the hand of 'Man' is no longer in touch with nature's objects: the familiar modernist fantasy of a return to an authoritarian pastoralism based on the organic unity of an ideal *communitas*.

Olson's commentators have preferred to pass over the dodgy politics informing the poetics of organic unity in favour of a humanist reading of the integrated Self and its universalist projections. Joseph Riddel's essay 'Decentring the Image: the "Project" of "American" Poetics?' appears to go against this grain in arguing that Olson's work actually disrupts the organicist tradition. Riddel insists that Olson effectively counters Jungian symbolism because 'the mythopoeic is never inscribed in the power of some archetype, some universal centre, that governs the continuity between origin and image.' On the contrary, it is 'a place of violence . . . which underscores the need for creative discontinuity.'[52] Riddel makes an important gesture in questioning the relationship between Olson's authorial pronouncements and his fundamentally discontinuous poetic. However, he goes on to give a pseudo-deconstructive argument, which is legitimised by the force of of intentionalist reference. That is to say, the proper name Charles Olson becomes reclaimed as the master of his discontinuous products, defined against Jung's fallacies. Jungian symbolism is read here as possessing its own natural properties in order to be shattered by Olson's radical textuality, so that both the figure of Olson the poet and his figural writing become hypostatised. At one point, Riddel states that 'The "archaeologist of morning" . . . dismantles the myth of origins, only to construct another, a fiction of impure origins'.[53] And yet this 'fiction' continues to be seen as an origin, maintained by Olson's master discourse. There is no real recognition here of the ideological difference between intention and textual effect important to a deconstructive strategy. Moreover, this privileging of the poetic (figurative) discontinuity of association re-presents the rational versus post-rational dialogue essential to Jungian synchronicity, but now transferred to the language of deconstructive criticism. And throughout his essay, Riddel treats 'discontinuity' as being continuous with the concept of impurity as the mythical cure for 'essentialism'.

The project is complicated by the fact that Riddel's observations are actually based on a reading of Olson's 1950 essay 'Projective Verse' rather than the verse itself. This leads him to force Olson's logocentric pronouncements about the ontological status of 'breath' paradoxically into line with its 'deconstructive' other, writing, which in Riddel fails to escape the empiricism of which Jacques Derrida warns in the first part of *Of Grammatology*. In order to examine this problematic, it will be useful to outline Olson's formal method of poetic inscription/expression.

This formal method is one which Olson believes will voice 'cultural etymology', and is to be known variously as 'projective verse', 'composition by field', and 'field poetics'. 'Projective Verse' eloquently states Olson's objectives. Of particular relevance in this argument is the emphasis on breath and speech; as Riddel describes it, 'Speech . . . is the act which gives the poem "solidity" by breaking up the prescribed grammars, decentring the narrative line into the field of "elements", thereby restoring to the textual space the "play of their separate energies."'[54] The writing machine, the typewriter, paradoxically gives the poet a way of exceeding the limits of traditional writing, for it allows the text to be 'mapped' onto the page, allowing for the presentation of spatial elements in speech-patterning. For Olson, speech is the essential individual expressive medium through which preconscious energy is channelled. That is to say, his projective poetic shares with other twentieth-century artistic movements the desire to break down the *logical* grammatical structure of language in order to shake the rational belief in linguistic (and representational) order. Specifically, syntax is thought to hamper the production of pure, unalloyed semantemes. Composition by field frees the spacing of spoken language so that the words themselves may take place, as figures, on the page. Making a comparison with the musical score, Olson calls typescript 'the stave and the bar', indicating that written poetry is merely notation waiting for its realisation by the poet's voice.[55]

In connection with this notion of composition, Riddel invokes Derrida. In 'The Double Session', he notes, we find that 'Spacing suspends the semantic depth of the sign.'[56] Certainly, this can be applied critically to Olson's texts, in the place of the 'blanks' which disrupt the narrative line in many parts of *The Maximus Poems*:

> by the way into the woods

> Indian   otter
> 'Lake'   ponds   orient

>   show me   (exhibit
>   myself)[57]

Yet one would be hard pressed to see in this a Mallarméan poetic, which is the example Derrida gives.[58] The context of these moments in Olson's work is always one governed by a hectoring metalanguage which, even where it opens to a certain dissemination of meaning, still gestures toward discursive and imagistic coherence. By contrast, Derrida is less interested in the fact that coherence in language can be lost in poetry than in the resistance of Mallarmé's texts to thematic criticism, with the implication that the respective codes of 'literary criticism' and 'literature' (designated by philosophy) cannot emerge as a unity transcending both genres. This is because the site of unity could only be presented following an original difference between the concepts of literature and literary criticism always already inscribed by the latter as philosophical principle. In that case, unity would not arrive as the sublation of two 'things that are', but as the imaginary synthesis of self-identity.[59] Riddel, on the other hand, reaffirms the transgressive value of figural language while maintaining it under the name of the poet. To read the saga of Maximus, the endless lists and itineraries of Gloucester's maritime records, the mass of geochronological and anthropological material, and the range of mythical reference, as *Olson's project* to disrupt origins would be 'textually' valid but eventually pointless, since any 'spacing' is eventually brought back into the fold by the powerful metalanguage that asserts the egoic maximal stance:

> Hesiod said the outer man was the bond with which Zeus bound
> > > > > > > > > Prometheus

> > > the illusory
> > > is real enough

> the suffering
> is not suffered

> > > the foreknowledge
> > > is absolute

> > > > Okeanos
> > > > hangs in the father

> > > > the father
> > > > is before the beginning of bodily
> > > > > > things[60]

Riddel gives the impression that he wishes to vindicate a cherished poet, as well as the Whitmanian tradition he is heir to, under the aegis of American 'deconstruction'. He regards 'Olson' as the truth, but not Olson's intentions.

Finally, Riddel leaves out of the equation Derrida's remarks on the condition of syntax in order to centre his discussion firmly on Olson's spatial thesis.[61] Olson did not design his texts to overturn the tyranny of a logocentrism that subordinates syntactical spacing to semantic depth, but to bolster semantic substance in the myth of the proper name. Deconstruction does not verify the ideal status of the literary text, but poses the political questions of subject and inscription; as Derrida writes in response to John Searle's reading of 'Signature Event Context', 'What the text questions is not intention or intentionality but their *telos*, which orients and organizes the movement and the possibility of fulfilment, realization, and *actualization* in a plenitude that would be *present* to and identical with itself.'[62]

Space in the poetic line works as a metaphor to Olson's concern with the concepts of 'land', 'place', 'extension' and the 'local'. According to Don Byrd, 'Space, stance, and fact, are the first manifestations of Olson's secularized Trinity.'[63] Maximus, Jung's First Man or Anthropos as well as the Tyrian philosopher, is intended to stand firmly at the centre of being as the point where space is localised.[64] The spacing in projective verse discloses the placing of the noun, the proper name, which in turn reveals the literal fact of the Anthropos on earth which allows him to understand his place as locality. Olson's Herodotean notion of historical research ('finding out for oneself') works to this end, hence the wealth of documentary evidence of Gloucester's local history in *The Maximus Poems*. In 'Poetry and Truth' he attests to

> that sense of place in the same sense that I think names are almost always proper, of the earth, as sort of the place of our habitation, at least. But that that literal globe or orb is our lamp or clue to the whole of creation, and that only by obedience to it does one have a chance at heaven.[65]

Olson's emphasis on those things he calls literal and on his related notion of the essential, local place, is not stuck in the empirical world but attempts to reach some earthly 'substance', which in turn provides access to a higher, figural version of reality, idealised here as a version of the heavenly realm. Locality is given as a designation of *topos* in language, where 'local / relations are nominalized'.[66] The prime metric of the topological becomes a kind of mapping, and the locale Gloucester is presented as a synecdoche of the larger universe. The local symbolises, or projects, the universal as form. And the sum of the local lies in the poet's discovery of its history and origin. The land form of the local, along with the human events which have come to define it is for Olson structured like a language, and he finds the essential traits of ancient peoples in their traces, what is known of their language and material inscriptions: 'There is an effort to drive back to roots, both of Gloucester as the end of migrating Western man, and of man himself, back to the deglaciation and the sources of civilization.'[67] The vision is of nomadic cultures, settlements, and the specific societies emerging from those people who 'take place', place being defined here as *extension*, the 'proper' mode of historical existence. When a place comes into being, and when it is harmoniously ordered towards the unity of the collective unconscious, it is to be called 'polis'. In *The Special View of History* Olson rifles through the etymological meanings of the word (without paying particular attention to the question of synchrony, i.e., the signifiers 'publicus' and 'manipulate' are brought together by reading the latter as 'ample') to arrive at a synthetic definition: 'THE PURE PLACE is POLIS'.[68] As Merrill points out, 'The notion of "polis" is the moral centre of gravity of *The Maximus Poems*. "Polis" is a nucleus of true believers, an ideal, an obedience, an integrity and a prime of value.'[69] The concept is perhaps best clarified by taking it back to Jung's *Psychology and Alchemy* where, as Butterick notes, the term 'Monogene' is defined as

> the singlecelled genetic material from which the human species has evolved, originally from the sea (see *Maximus*, Pt. II, 72 and 147). Also, however, the 'only begotten' son of the Gnostic tradition ... 'This same is he [Μονογενεσ] who dwelleth in the Monad ... This same [the Monad] is the Mother-City [μετροπολισ] of the Only-begotten [μονογενεσ]'.[70]

So this *topos* is always in the position of an origin, pitted against the decadence of the modern city ('shitty'), and it represents a point from which true perception may be recovered, the destination of the poet's visionary quest.[71] It is 'the corporate spirit exhibited in the city, is literally a shared act of perceiving, and it is the poet's business to bring images back into the eye.'[72] Olson wants to bring poetry back in touch with the Real, by which he means a circuit in which the true literal becomes 'realised', along with the spiritual verities that are symbolised by the literal. In keeping with the drive towards origin, he claims that he is not interested in art as representation; the function of 'breath' in field poetics is described as allowing poetry to function as pure expression emanating from the body, 'Because breath allows *all* the speech-force of language back in (speech is the 'solid' of verse, is the secret of a poem's energy), because, now, a poem has, by speech, a solidity, everything in it can now be treated as solids, objects, things.'[73] Olson wants to reconfigure the ideality of poetic speech as physical, phallic energy, and he is constantly in search of scientific and mythical data that supports the 'hardness' of the Real, the vertical aspiration of the Maximal Self its quest to keep on growing like the Diorite Stone of Hurrian myth: 'this creature is nothing but a blue stone, and the stone grows . . . And the Diorite, for me, this Diorite figure is the vertical, the growth principle of the Earth.'[74] The history of stone becomes a primary medium for establishment of mythic space: 'Give me geology / then we don't have to worry about soft human history'.[75] That which is engraved in stone has original power; the glyphs of the Mayans are 'so clearly and densely chosen that, cut in stone, they retain the power of the objects of which they are images'.[76] The glyphs are the ground for the figuring of breath; without them the concepts of space, origin and etymology could not be realised. The principle of Projective Verse 'seeks a reincorporation of breath inside the textual economy as part of an extended tradition of representation (viz. the representation of the body in language and process)'.[77]

The figural dimensions of this textual economy are described in J. H. Prynne's 1968 review of *Maximus IV, V, VI*. Prynne was in a unique position to discuss this second volume of *Maximus* as he provided Olson with working material during the period of its composition – for example, the *Cambridge Ancient History* fascicles as they came out in the mid-1960s and 'Names of ships, their masters, cargoes and destinations, from the Weymouth Port Books' from the Public Record Office – and he had prepared the typescript for the volume at Cambridge in April/May 1964.[78] Olson had received a copy of the Prynne essay at the time of his *Paris Review* interview in 1968. Throughout the interview he refers Gerard Malanga's questions to him to Prynne, because Prynne 'takes care of everything I thought I was thinking myself, I mean, trying to think'; 'because Prynne is so – he's knowing, he's knowing like mad'.[79]

What does Prynne know? According to Prynne, to know the language of Olson's poetry is to know the composition of earth and history. On the relation of speech to 'hard' history, 'Traces of quite remote glottochronology fold into the diorite stone.'[80] Historical remains, the malleable tissue of the collective 'glottis', become one with the phallic properties of stone. Glottochronology is the statistical examination of vocabularies which, according to the *Cambridge Ancient History*, 'suffers from the naïvete of assuming discrete universals of perception and expression.'[81] Notwithstanding, Prynne invokes it in order to stress the primacy of voice, while the Diorite Stone as Olson figures it becomes 'outrightly phallic', from being 'a quasi-vegetation figure from Hurrian myth, which obeys Hesiod's growth principle in swelling to be "27,000 miles tall, so that it has to be severed with a meat cleaver."'[82] Prynne 'engenders' the geochronology of land-formation, making it continuous with the cytochronology of biochemical evolution, this transposed into the mythic. In turn, this is related to the ontological status of Olson's text: 'We should also be aware that the poetry is not secondary assemblage but primary writing'.[83] Poetry is the work of original inscription, imagination, and not fanciful *bricolage*. Writing becomes the necessary means to interpret the signs of the past, but although the (glyphic) signs themselves require an act of interpretation, hermeneutic indeterminacy is regarded as secondary to the expressive force of breath, as if the Maximal stance overrides problems of historical translation. *The Maximus Poems* 'persuade one all over again of the man speaking to men, the image of the most exact freedom to be gained, now, from the sustained sequence of full-grown speech, and from nowhere else.'[84]

Prynne concentrates on an implicit hierarchy of mythic and ontological value in *The Maximus Poems*. He begins by identifying the basic difference between the first volume and *Maximus, IV, V, VI*. 'In the previously published sections,' he writes, 'the literal founding of history and its local cadence into speech extend outwards by feeling into the sacral and divinized forms of presence upon the earth's surface.'[85] The land-forms of *basic* history inevitably extend towards urban settlement; essentially nomadic, human cultures leave their remains in momentary stases, the buildings on the surface of the earth. Knowledge itself, in its immediacy or non-temporal aspect, is decidedly pre-urban, so that while there is allegedly true movement over and across earth, knowledge is purely spatial. As Being, it leaves no trace, but can only be guaged from the marks left by beings. Prynne goes on to describe *Maximus IV, V, VI* as composed of a 'more variable euhemerism' leading to knowledge of 'the birth of the real'.[86] This indicates Olson's shift of attention towards an underlying mythic structure in *Maximus IV, V, VI*. As we have seen in the previous chapter, euhemerism is a method of interpretation that regards myths as accounts of real historical incidents, an attempt to make figural language literal. A myth becomes a way of describing actual events; its significance for a tribe or community is its ordering of those events into a narrative that transcends the chaos of temporal contingency. Mythic synchronicity, therefore, possesses for Olson (as for Jung) a greater reality than the contiguous 'facts' presented in Western historiography. This is why in Olson's terminology myth is the true 'literal'. However, identifying the Real as literal depends upon a further distinction between literal and figurative designations within the mythic narrative, which supposedly leads to a dialectical unity between the two qualities but in effect creates a hierarchy in which the figural is made secondary to the literal. This economy accounts for the contradictions of Jungian humanism; unity is achieved only by inscribing sexual division and then by eliding the submissive position allotted to the feminine. In Olson's pronouncements on the subject, the term 'literal' works much as the term 'Man' is meant to signify universal selfhood, but there can be little doubt that the figure of the Diorite Stone renders such ideals absurd. What Prynne calls 'a more variable euhemerism', then, is so variable that it ceases be euhemerism at all. 'Real' facts are always already mythic, so individual myths are allegories of a universal mythic-ness. In one of his Black Mountain College lectures, Olson insists that the originary power of primitive representation is its awareness of the mythic fusion of literal and abstract meanings. With the acquisition of language, feminised images of the real step up to masculine presence: 'Notice this doubleness, that man, from the beginning, took the real as at once literal and abstract, that both the cup-hole and the Venus could stand for the red-force as later man's phallus as language could stand likewise.'[87]

Prynne's essay likewise relies heavily upon a mythic disposal of qualities into essentially literal and figural categories, as for example Olson believes time to be abstract and space to be real.[88] The pretence to a dialectical argument is entirely governed by these assumptions: '*Land* is the abstract figure, sea the living face of the earth, teeming meadows for the new-comers perched on the edge of a continent.' This division between land and sea is organized into a wide structural topology which for Prynne is the core of *Maximus IV, V, VI*. The 'matrix' is already gendered: 'So with the sea constantly prying between Gloucester's legs, we rejoin the image of creative process in its originary genetic scope.'[89] 'Gloucester's legs' are visualised as a bay or port lapped by the waves of the sea, a metaphor taken to carry the truth as origin. As in I. A. Richards's understanding of metaphor, the vehicle is considered to be 'concrete' whereas the tenor becomes simultaneously 'abstract' and 'literal'. Literal land and sea are subordinate to the 'genetic scope' of 'the image of creative process'. Imagination is genetic and gendered. The myth of the earth as female principle, or anima, prevails throughout Olson's poetry ('The earth with a city in her hair / entangled of trees'[90]) and constantly requires its animus, the active, Dioritic, maximal self, who is realised as the one who creates: the poet. As Prynne defines it, the figure of the sea *generates* as 'the *living face* of the earth' in opposition to the land as '*abstract* figure' [my italics]; and just in case we are in any doubt, he continues: 'For Olson the earth as feminine and abstract gives him the perhaps unique process of charting the birth of the real . . . from the abstract of geological time.'[91] The choice is not between figural land and literal sea, for both are shown to be types of figures. It is therefore between 'abstract' and 'living' figures, the abstract associated with the form of literality and the living continuous with the flesh of mythical concretion. A curious distinction, because it must perplex the entire figural process. As we have seen throughout this chapter, Olson thinks of the Real as a return to a proper, literal body that would be indispensable to the reconstitution of self and polis. As a truth, the literal can no longer be held to be self-evident, but is in hiding. This is the only sense in which one can distinguish between a 'true' and a 'false' literal; language itself has fallen from the grace of the proper, so it follows that its present state, that of a pejorocracy, must be restored by the poet. Restoration may be achieved through the negative work of the figural, just as in Jung the properties of primary symbolism must be extricated from the corruptions of the signifier by endorsing a transcendent view of myth. But the moment figuration enters this scene, it ruins the chance of a return to the proper. For in order to escape the empirical naivety of the false literal, the inheritance of (pejorative) meaning must be lifted up to a figural plane, there to be 'concretised' and made truly real again. But then hasn't literality in any form been appropriated by metaphor, with the consequence that it can never be known as anything but a model, an appearance, rather than in its self-identity? Mere 'land' and 'sea' have to be sublated as genres, and their new figural status is presented as intermediate, gestatory. Therefore, something must be given back to the land, returning it to the essence of the true as opposed to the false literal. If everything is metaphorical, the literal is voided, in which case there would be no metaphor either. So it is significant that Prynne evaluates his figures in the way illustrated, as this forms the only way the return to the Real as the true literal can occur within the mythic field. Land as abstract figure valorises the image of the sea as a concrete, and therefore proper, figure, which would endow it with a supposedly higher literal status. It marks the 'literal founding of history ... upon ... the earth's surface', thus bringing it back to the original project of *The Maximus Poems*.

Prynne goes on to remark that Olson's source material fits into the overall scheme by illustrating 'how the causal presumptions of over-humanized history can be displaced, as they are in Olson's writing, where language is a mythic likeness resting on the earth, the mappemunde of man's being, and not by any means a "universe of *discourse* ."'[92] The last clause presumably means that this poetry moves beyond the anthropomorphic attitude, as well as being more than a purely linguistic construction. The gesture refers to the tradition of 'over-humanized' historicising, which myth should replace by restoring the originary force of pre-conscious space. But the achievement involves a rhetorical sleight of hand, by which 'the earth' has come to signify as a literal given, revealed by the statement that 'language is a mythic *likeness resting*' upon it. Language, then, is already in the position of myth, and not accidental to it, and 'the earth' escapes the category of myth in its literality. There is no sublation here, only the effect of a rhetorical turning. Myth works upon the earth through the principle of analogy, but it has already undercut the literal basis upon which it is said to rest. The fact of the earth's 'surface' (an excessive face, figure, and therefore always already anthropomorphically 'over-human') testifies to this.

The sea was born of the earth without sweet union of love Hesiod says

But that then she lay for heaven and she bare the thing which encloses
every thing, Okeanos the one which all things are and by which nothing
is anything but itself, measured so.

screwing earth, in whom love lies which unnerves the limbs and by its
heat floods the mind and all gods and men into further nature[93]

Because of his dependence on phallic mysticism, Olson had no worries
about the 'objective' validity of his mythifications: 'Olson's analogies are
usually more metaphoric than logical, his appropriation of scientific terminology dependent more upon parallels of resonance than upon any
objectively defined reference.'[94] Sanctioned by the rationalised irrationalism of the masculine desire for property and self-origination, and held in
place by the naive figural language of the archetypes, phallic literalness is
meant to resist all cuts and contradictions. It is thought to maintain its literal reality even when the real becomes a metaphor, and presented as
'hard' and 'concrete' even in its fundamental abstraction. In the passage
from *Maximus* quoted above, the geographic metaphor is used as an analogue of primary fatherhood, the father being the active participant in the
reproductive process. In the figural realm, however, the sea generates
itself, reproducing the father-figure in an act of pure self-identity. Tropo-
logically, the figure figures itself, creating itself as proper. It is only the
'mythical' account of this pre-Oedipal phantasy that gives it any credence
whatsoever. Only myth can make the poet into his own (erased) mother by
rationalising contradiction and confusion into seamless unity.

Notes

1 Walter Benjamin, *Charles Baudelaire: A Lyric Poet in the Era of High Capitalism.*
Trans. Harry Zohn. (London: Verso, 1985), 110.

2 Laurens van der Post, *Jung and the Story of Our Time* (Harmondsworth: Penguin,
1978), 195.

3 van der Post, *Jung and the Story of Our Time*, 197.

4 Benjamin, letter to Fritz Lieb, 9 July 1937, in *The Correspondence of Walter Ben-
jamin 1910–1940*. Ed. and annotated by Gershom Scholem and Theodor W. Adorno.
Trans. Manfred R. Jacobson and Evelyn M. Jacobson (Chicago: Chicago University
Press, 1994), 542.

5 Benjamin, letter to Gershom Scholem, August 5th, 1937, in *The Correspondence of
Walter Benjamin*, 544, and see editors' note on 545.

6 Adorno, 'Enleitung zu Benjamins "Schriften"', in *Gesammelte Schriften 11: Noten
zur Literatur*. Ed. Gretel Adorno and Rolf Tiedemann (Frankfurt am Main:
Suhrkamp, 1974); 574: 'Sie stellen nicht invariante Archetypen dar, die aus
Geschichte herauszuschälen wären, sondern schießen gerade durch die Kraft der
Geschichte zusammen.'

7 See especially the chapter on 'Pre-Fascist and Fascist Vitalism', in Georg Lukacs, *The Destruction of Reason*. Trans. Peter Palmer (London: The Merlin Press, 1980).

8 Julian Roberts, *Walter Benjamin* (London: Macmillan, 1982), 177. 'The organisational force of this ideology was its absolutising of the division of labour . . . an obsessive insistence on the cultic opposition between inspired creator and passive community' (193).

9 Noll, *The Jung Cult*, 261.

10 Noll, *The Jung Cult*, 162–9; 261. Klages' belief in handwriting analysis as a guide to personality traits 'formed the core of German psychology during the Nazi era and into the late 1950s. These techniques were used most prominently for the selection of German military officers during the Nazi era' (168). Although Noll bases too much on guilt by (sketchy) association here, the accumulation of evidence linking Jung's interests with *volkisch* gurus such as Klages and Keyserling reconstructs a social and intellectual network that to Benjamin was all too noticeable.

11 See Jung, *The Psychology of the Unconscious: The Evolution of Thought*. Trans. Beatrice M. Hinkle (London: Kegan Paul, Trench, Trubner and Co., 1933), and its revised version, *A Study of the Transformations and Symbolism of the Libido. A Contribution to the History of Symbols of Transformation: An Analysis of the Prelude to a Case of Schizophrenia*. Vol. 5 of *The Collected Works of C. G. Jung*. Trans. R. F. C. Hull (London: Routledge and Kegan Paul, 1956).

12 Noll, *The Jung Cult*, 261.

13 Noll, *The Jung Cult*, 173–4. Noll's exegesis oddly misses the crucial point that traditional gender roles are not transcended in Jung's theory but reinforced.

14 Edward Said describes this Romantic view as a revisionary structure of Orientalism: 'Friedrich Schlegel and Novalis, for example, urged upon their countrymen, and upon Europeans in general, a detailed study of India because, they said, it was Indian culture and religion that could defeat the materialism and mechanism (and republicanism) of Occidental culture. And from this defeat would arise a new, revitalized Europe: the Biblical imagery of death, rebirth, and redemption is evident in this prescription . . . what mattered was not Asia but Asia's *use to* modern Europe. Thus anyone who, like Schlegel or Franz Bopp, mastered an Oriental language, was a spiritual hero, a knight-errant bringing back to Europe a sense of the holy mission it had now lost.' *Orientalism* (London: Penguin, 1985), 115.

15 Erich Neumann, 'Mystical Man', in Joseph Campbell, ed., *The Mystic Vision: Papers from the Eranos Yearbooks*, Vol. 6 (London: Routledge and Kegan Paul, 1969), 397–9.

16 Neumann, 'Mystical Man', 404.

17 Philippe Lacoue-Labarthe and Jean-Luc Nancy, 'The Nazi Myth', *Critical Inquiry*, 16 (winter 1990), p. 307.

18 van der Post, *Jung and the Story of Our Time*, 193.

19 van der Post, *Jung and the Story of Our Time*, 235. Note the astonishing account of female discipleship at 223.

20 Among many other commentators on modern art, Evans Lansing Smith argues that 'the myth of the descent to the underworld can be seen as the Ur-myth of modernism': 'Descent to the Underworld: Jung and His Brothers', in Karin Barnaby and Pellegrino d'Acierno, eds, *C. G. Jung and the Humanities: Toward a Hermeneutics of Culture* (London: Routledge, 1990), 251 ff.

21 See Helga Geyer-Ryan's discussion of Theweleit in her *Fables of Desire: Studies in the Ethics of Art and Gender* (Cambridge and Oxford: Polity Press / Blackwell, 1994), 132–4. Ironically, Benjamin and Jung have much in common in their opposition to the pathology of abjection, as both were impressed by the Faustian myth of descent

to the realm of the Mothers, with its potential for reconfiguring identity through allegorised loss.

22 Jung, 'Of the Relation of Analytical Psychology to Poetry', in *The Spirit in Man, Art, and Literature*. Vol. 15 of *The Collected Works of C. G. Jung*. Trans. R. F. C. Hull (Princeton: Princeton University Press, 1972), 82. See also Elizabeth Wright, *Psychoanalytic Criticism: Theory in Practice* (London: Methuen, 1984), 72: 'Jung above all wants to save the work of art from the psychoanalyst's clinical scrutiny, from the equation of art and neurosis. He does this by exalting the creative process as such, as distinct from exalting the "poet as person". In this one might see the beginnings of the dethronement of the author from a central position. The effects of this are limited, however, because Jung replaces one idealization, a personal one, with another, a supra-personal one, in that the poet becomes a mouthpiece for a universal language of symbolism'.

23 Contributors to *C. G. Jung and the Humanities* grapple with the spectre of 'two Jungs': one fundamentalist, authoritarian, and hierarchical; the other deconstructive, paratactic, open to a continuous reappraisal of identity. The need to emphasise the second of these personae comes in response to what the authors call 'postmodernism'. In the awkward attempts to make analytic psychology relevant to the post-structuralist theories that follow, the first Jung gets pushed behind the scenes, while the second is thrust into the limelight as a founding father of postmodernism. Unfortunately, this gives the first Jung the rôle of the repressed waiting to return, while the second Jung's only claim to disruption of the symbolic is his religious desire to be 'unknowing'. See Edward S. Casey, 'Jung and the Postmodern Condition'; David L. Miller, 'An Other Jung and An Other . . .'; Edward S. Casey, et al., 'Jung and Postmodern Symposium', in Barnaby and d'Acierno, *C. G. Jung and the Humanities*, 319–40.

24 See Bernstein, *The Tale of the Tribe*: in 1919, Pound had begun 'to argue that the interpretation and narration of history must also proceed by the principles of assemblage and juxtaposition of particulars' (69). Olson took these principles back to his own place of origin: 'history is presented through the subjective, fragmentary responses of Olson's own daily reactions to Gloucester' (251).

25 See Maud, *Charles Olson's Reading*, 98.

26 Paul Christensen, *Charles Olson: Call Him Ishmael* (Austin: University of Texas Press, 1979), 147.

27 Clark, *Charles Olson*, 282.

28 Charles Altieri, *Self and Sensibility in Contemporary American Poetry* (Cambridge: Cambridge University Press, 1984), 39.

29 Altieri, *Self and Sensibility in Contemporary American Poetry*, 40–1.

30 'the expansionist impulse was reclassified as a romantic rite of passage, its aggressive makeshift ambitions glossed as a desire to begin again at the margin. Many thought that even after its closure in 1890 the frontier would continue to shape the American character; among them Charles Olson.' David Trotter, *The Making of the Reader: Language and Subjectivity in Modern American, English and Irish Poetry* (London: Macmillan, 1986), 175.

31 Altieri, *Self and Sensibility in Contemporary American Poetry*, 41.

32 Jung, 'In Memory of Sigmund Freud', in *The Spirit in Man, Art, and Literature*, 48.

33 Jung, 'Of the Relation of Analytical Psychology to Poetry', in *The Spirit in Man, Art, and Literature*, 80.

34 Jung, 'Of the Relation of Analytical Psychology to Poetry', 80.

35 Jung, 'Of the Relation of Analytical Psychology to Poetry', 81.

36 In *The Seminar of Jacques Lacan. Book I: Freud's Papers on Technique 1953–1956.* Ed. Jacques-Alain Miller. Trans. with notes by John Forrester (Cambridge: Cambridge University Press, 1988), 267.

37 Elizabeth Wright, *Psychoanalytic Criticism*, 72. See Jung, 'Of the Relation of Analystical Psychology to Poetry, 80–1.

38 Charles Olson, *Mayan Letters* (London: Jonathan Cape, 1968), 29. Don Byrd writes of the question Olson 'addresses again and again in his prose writings from 1951 through 1956. How can the poet establish some more reliable centre of attention than his own isolated ego?' (*Olson's Maximus Poems* (Urbana: University of Illinois Press, 1980), 22.)

39 Olson, *Mayan Letters*, 28.

40 James E. Miller, Jr, *The American Quest for a Supreme Fiction* (Cambridge: Cambridge University Press, 1979), 209. On 'thesis' in the work of Olson and Ed Dorn, see Trotter, *The Making of the Reader*, 167–70: 'Argument, decision, loyalty: these acts involve or imply a thesis (from the Greek word for "putting" or "placing"). In prosody the term "thesis" originally meant the stressed syllable in a foot or the stressed note in music. Your thesis is what positions you and holds you to a determinate identity; it bears your stress.' See also Butterick, *A Guide to* The Maximus Poems *of Charles Olson*, 686.

41 Miller, *The American Quest for a Supreme Fiction*, 205. See Charles Olson, *Projective Verse* (New York: Totem Press, 1959), 10: 'It is no accident that Pound and Williams both were involved variously in a movement which got called "objectivism". But that word was then used in some sort of necessary quarrel . . . with "subjectivism", It is now too late to be bothered with the latter. It has excellently done itself to death, even though we are all caught in its dying. What seems to me a more valid formulation for present use is "objectism", a word to be taken to stand for the kind of relation of man to experience which a poet might state as the necessity of a line or a work to be as wood is, to be as clean as wood is as it issues from the hand of nature, to be as shaped as wood can be when a man has his hand to it. Objectism is the getting rid of the lyrical interference of the individual as ego, of the "subject" and his soul, that peculiar presumption by which western man has interposed himself between what he is as a creature of nature (with certain instructions to carry out) and those other creatures of nature which we may, with no derogation, call objects. For a man himself is an object'.

42 Thomas Merrill, *The Poetry of Charles Olson* (Newark: University of Delaware Press, 1982), 207.

43 Merrill, *The Poetry of Charles Olson*, 211.

44 See Charles Olson, 'I, Maximus of Gloucester, to you', in *The Maximus Poems* (London: Cape Goliard Press, 1960). George Butterick notes that pejorocracy means 'Literally, "worse-rule" (Latin *pejor*, and -ocracy, as in democracy from the Greek *krateia*), a worsening form of government. Borrowed from Pound, Canto LXXIX of *The Pisan Cantos*; first used by Olson in "The Kingfishers".' (Butterick, *A Guide to* The Maximus Poems *of Charles Olson*, 13.)

45 Merrill, *The Poetry of Charles Olson*, 158. See also Ed Dorn's essay 'What I See in *The Maximus Poems*' (1960) in his *Views*. Ed. Donald Allen (San Francisco: Four Seasons Foundation, 1980), esp. 42.

46 Merrill, *The Poetry of Charles Olson*, 43.

47 Jung, 'Of the Relation of Analytical Psychology to Poetry', 82.

48 Robert von Hallberg, *Charles Olson: The Scholar's Art* (Cambridge, MA: Harvard University Press, 1978), 71–2.

49 Charles Olson, 'The Vinland Map Review', in *Additional Prose: A Bibliography on America, Proprioception, and Other Notes and Essays*. Ed. George Butterick (Bolinas: Four Seasons Foundation, 1974), 60.

50 Thorstein Veblen, *Absentee Ownership and Business Enterprise in Recent Times: The Case of America* (New York: Augustus M. Kelley, 1964), 55.

51 John P. Diggins, *The Bond of Savagery: Thorstein Veblen and Modern Social Theory* (Brighton, Harvester Press, 1978), 25.

52 Joseph Riddel, 'Decentring the Image: The "Project" of "American" Poetics?', in Josué V. Harari, ed., *Textual Strategies: Perspectives in Poststructuralist Criticism* (London: Methuen, 1980), 328.

53 Riddel, 'Decentring the Image', 327.

54 Riddel, 'Decentring the Image', 351.

55 Olson, *Projective Verse*, 8.

56 Riddel, 'Decentring the Image', 353.

57 Olson, 'Maximus, March 1961–2', in *The Maximus Poems IV, V, VI* (London: Cape Goliard Press, 1968).

58 Derrida, *Of Grammatology*. Trans. Gayatry Chakravorty Spivak. (Baltimore: Johns Hopkins University Press, 1984), 68: 'No intuition can be realized in the place where "the 'whites' indeed take on an importance" (Preface to *Coup de dés*)'; and *Dissemination*. Trans. Barbara Johnson (Chicago: Chicago University Press, 1981), 252–8.

59 See Derrida, 'The Double Session', in *Dissemination*, passim; and Rodolphe Gasché, *The Tain of the Mirror: Derrida and the Philosophy of Reflection* (Cambridge, MA: Harvard University Press, 1986), Chapter 10.

60 Charles Olson, 'HEPIT NAGA ATOSIS', in *The Maximus Poems IV, V, VI.*

61 Derrida is interested in what in language resists the reduction to either a purely semantic or a purely syntactic value; just as relations of contiguity are not determined by those of similarity, the spacing of syntax is not governed by the semantic field as is generally believed. See *Dissemination*, 221–2.

62 Derrida, 'Limited Inc. abc . . . ', *Glyph* 2 (1977), p. 193.

63 Byrd, *Charles Olson's Maximus Poems*, 57.

64 See in particular, Jung, *Alchemical Studies*. Vol. 13 of *The Collected Works of C. G. Jung*. Trans. R. F. C. Hull (London: Routledge and Kegan Paul, 1968), 139: 'The symbolical names of the *prima materia* all point to the *anima mundi*, Plato's Primordial Man, the Anthropos and mystic Adam, who is described as a sphere (= wholeness), consisting of four parts (uniting different aspects in itself), hermaphroditic (beyond division by sex), and damp (i.e., psychic). This paints a picture of the self, the indescribable totality of man.'

Jung goes on to discuss the Anthropos as *homo Maximus* at 169. The association of the Anthropos with hermaphrodites is odd, considering that it is pitched in opposition to the feminine anima. 'Man' is always the one who proceeds *from* the anima mundi, using the anima as a kind of stepping-stone to the intelligible plane.

See Butterick, *A Guide to* The Maximus Poems *of Charles Olson*, xxvii–xxviii. Tyre, the chief port of the Phoenicians, is an analogue for Gloucester.

65 Charles Olson, *Muthologos: The Collected Lectures and Interviews*. Ed. George Butterick. (Bolinas: Four Seasons Foundation, 1978), Vol. II, 34. See Steve McCaffery, *North of Intention: Critical Writings 1973–1986* (New York and Toronto: Roof / Nightwood Editions, 1986), 126: 'Document, in Olson (and perhaps more so in Pound), operates as a kind of syllable, a unit of unmediated plenitude, reconnecting it with a displaced present.'

66 Olson, 'John Burke', in *The Maximus Poems*. Olson gleans a concept of time as space and space as local from Benjamin Lee Whorf. See for example 'An American-Indian Model of the Universe', in *Language, Thought, and Reality: Selected Writings of Benjamin Lee Whorf*. Ed. with an introduction by John B. Carroll (Cambridge, MA: MIT Press, 1971).

67 Butterick, *A Guide to* The Maximus Poems *of Charles Olson*, xl.

68 Quoted in Merrill, *The Poetry of Charles Olson*, 173.

69 Merrill, *The Poetry of Charles Olson*, 173.

70 Butterick, *A Guide to* The Maximus Poems *of Charles Olson*, 255–6. See also 'Dogtown the dog town', in *The Maximus Poems IV, V, VI*: 'the mother city . . . METRO / POLIS.

71 See Olson, 'Maximus, from Dogtown – II', in *The Maximus Poems IV, V, VI*.

72 Gavin Selerie, *To Let Words Swim into the Soul: An Anniversary Tribute to the Art of Charles Olson* (London, 1980), 18 (referring to *The Maximus Poems*, 26).

73 Quoted in von Hallberg, *Charles Olson*, 178.

74 Olson, 'Causal Mythology' in *Muthologos*, Vol. 1, 73.

75 Olson, *Last Lectures*, quoted in von Hallberg, *Charles Olson*, 126.

76 Olson, *Human Universe and Other Essays*. Ed. Donald Allen (New York: Grove Press, 1967), 7.

77 McCaffery, *North of Intention*, 214.

78 Butterick, *A Guide to* The Maximus Poems *of Charles Olson*, xliii; 513; xliii.

79 Olson, *Muthologos*, Vol. II, 112; 106.

80 J. H. Prynne, 'Review of *Maximus, IV, V, VI*', *The Park*, nos. 4/5 (1969), p. 66.

81 W. F. Allbright and T. O. Lambdin, 'The Evidence of Language'. Fascicle 54 of the revised *Cambridge Ancient History* (Cambridge: Cambridge University Press, 1966), 127.

82 Andrew Ross, *The Failure of Modernism: Symptoms of American Poetry* (New York: Columbia University Press, 1986), 139.

83 Prynne, 'Review of *Maximus, IV, V, VI*', p. 66.

84 Prynne, 'Review of *Maximus, IV, V, VI*', p. 66.

85 Prynne, 'Review of *Maximus, IV, V, VI*', p. 64.

86 Prynne, 'Review of *Maximus, IV, V, VI*', p. 65.

87 Olson, lecture at Black Mountain College, quoted in Ross, *The Failure of Modernism*, 138.

See Olson, 'The Gate and the Center', in *Collected Prose*, 168: 'and are euhemerists like myself (so I am told ISHMAEL proves me) correct, that gods are men first? and how many generations does it take to turn a man into a god?'

88 In a transcription of a later exposition on *Maximus IV, V, VI*, Prynne discusses the importance for Olson of a recursive interpretative procedure based on the wholeness of the earth's curvature: 'It becomes the singular condition, so that everything we take is literal, and not an instance of something else. We escape the metaphor. We participate in the condition of being. And the condition of being is thankfully beyond the condition of meaning. Oh yes, the whole language has the vibrancy, that steady vibrancy of the singular curvature which is equivalent to what was anciently called nobility.' ('On *Maximus IV, V, & VI*: A Lecture Given at Simon Frazer University on July 27th 1971.' Transcribed by Tom McGauley (*Serious Iron* (*Iron* 12), 1971, unnumbered pages). When a version of this chapter was published in *fragmente 8: Psychoanalysis and Poetics* (summer 1998), pp. 67–90, I wrote: 'I have preferred not to concentrate on this lecture because it is only a transcription, and therefore not very dependable: unless Prynne was affecting Olsonian turns of phrase for a North Amer-

ican audience, MacCauley [*sic*] has put some very strange language into Prynne's mouth, replete with "wows" and "gees". However, the lecture does confirm the extent of Prynne's belief in the mythopoetic; for example: "'That circular, that curving rhythm, condition which you can finally reach to, is the condition of the cosmos where the cosmos becomes myth. That's true about the scientific condition as well – that there is no doubt in my mind at all that the limits of space and the limits, for example, of absolute temperature, the curvature to which they attain, is very closely isomorphic. So that, once that curvature is reached, the lyric concludes, and what takes over is the condition of myth.'" Since then, Tom MacGauley has shown that his transcription, from his own tape recording of the lecture (now in Special Collections at Simon Frazer University), is accurate, and that I was wrong to doubt it. ('Prynne's Simon Fraser Lecture', in *Minutes of the Charles Olson Society*, No. 28 (April 1999), p. 3. This issue also reprints the lecture itself.) In a letter to Ralph Maud of 26 November 1971 (unpublished), Prynne writes that 'the transcript has some great renderings (e.g. Pawson for Porson, long live the Classics; amor for aimant, long live French) but it catches the sense of that odd rush through time.'

89 Prynne, 'Review of *Maximus IV, V, VI*', p. 65.
90 Olson, *The Maximus Poems IV, V, VI*, part VI.
91 Prynne, 'Review of *Maximus IV, V, VI*', p. 65.
92 Prynne, 'Review of *Maximus IV, V, VI*', p. 66.
93 Olson, 'Maximus, From Dogtown – I', in *The Maximus Poems IV, V, VI*.
94 Bernstein, *The Tale of the Tribe*, 242.

SHAMANISM AND THE POETICS OF LATE MODERNISM: J. H. PRYNNE

So far, this study has moved from the context of Anglo-American modernism to that of mid-century late modernist poetics in the United States. Olson's work represents a major investment in the shift towards a distinctly North American modernist identity evinced by the 'Objectivism' of Williams, Zukofsky, Niedecker, Oppen and Reznikoff, and continued in various ways by poets associated with the San Francisco Renaissance (Robert Duncan, Robert Creeley, Jack Spicer, Diane Wakoski, Joanne Kyger and Gary Snyder, among others). Like Olson, these younger poets owe much of their sense of formal innovation and political commitment to the Objectivists and much of their interest in mythic consciousness to Pound. The Objectivists themselves made no investment in the 'mythic method' and pushed Imagism into new urban (Oppen, Reznikoff) and pastoral (Zukofsky, Niedecker) poetic forms without it. Their rejection of Anglo-American mores is to some extent more fully developed in the New York School of Frank O'Hara, John Ashbery, James Schuyler and John Wieners than in the enclaves of San Francisco and Black Mountain College. Olson himself tempered a strident commitment to the 'local' ('I take SPACE to be the central fact to man born in America, from Folsom cave to now. I spell it large because it comes large here. Large, and without mercy.'[1]) with a strong desire to forge new conceptual and geographic links between the old world and the new. His love–hate relationship with Pound's redemptive aesthetic made him a powerful if problematic magus for a generation of British poets seeking to revive Anglo-American modernism in the 1960s. London, Newcastle-upon-Tyne and Cambridge became important centres for fugitive groups and individuals opposed to the formal conservativism and little-Englandist sentiments of the post-war literary mainstream. Olson's big-Americanism, by contrast, appeared anything but provincial in scope, and the continued vitality of modernist experiment in the United States came to be seen as the fulcrum from which to spring an attack on the parochial values epitomised by New Lines verse.

The real and imaginary divisions between modernist and anti-modernist camps run very deep in British literary culture and have only recently begun to appear archaic. While in the final analysis the distinction between 'mainstream' and 'alternative' poetry is bogus, the view taken by the institutions and prize-giving bodies that have evolved since the 1950s has been one of pull-quote respect for the great modernists accompanied by unwavering contempt for 'foreign' experiments carried out by British poets. No-one doing the police in different voices is likely to pass muster with the judges of today's T. S. Eliot prize. But now that many of the small underground presses have emerged as significant publishers and the persistence of senior 'radical' poets has gained the respect of academics and younger poets unconcerned with old battles, the boundaries of aesthetic 'orthodoxy' and 'heresy' are changing, and new questions of what constitutes conservatism and the avant-garde arise. In concentrating on one of the British poets who embraced the Pound–Olson axis in the 1960s, J. H. Prynne, the following chapters offer a theoretical account of the rôle played by aesthetic mysticism in the formation of this second wave of Anglo-American modernism. Prynne is chosen because he engages directly with the the the occult poetics I have examined in the work of Pound and Olson, taking it to new levels of difficulty which cannot be approached without some understanding of the phenomenological basis of his writing. Prynne's staunch attachment to the modernist project, manifest in the impersonality, eclecticism, linguistic playfulness and Hermetic rigour of his poetry, has made him a legendary figure of Pound-like importance for the neo avant-garde *cognoscenti* and an absurd aberration for those poets and critics who regard modernism as a failed experiment. Until recently, his work was excluded from 'official' surveys of contemporary British poetry and regularly lampooned in journals such as *The Times Literary Supplement* and the now defunct *Quarto*. In the 1980s, its positive reception was limited to reviews by Alan Halsey and David Trotter in Michael Schmidt's catholic *P N Review* and scholarly essays in little magazines such as *The Grosseteste Review* (named after Pound's remarks on Grosseteste in 'Cavalcanti'), Peter Ackroyd's *Times* article 'Legislators of Language' being a notable exception:

> J. H. Prynne . . . is without doubt the most formidable and accomplished poet in England today, a writer who has single-handedly changed the vocabulary of expression, and who, through his teaching at Cambridge, has re-educated the sensibility of an entire generation of students.[2]

For his part, Prynne courted relative obscurity and coterie recognition. His first collection, *Force of Circumstance and other Poems* (1962), was published by Routledge under the auspices of his Cambridge mentor Donald Davie. The reserved yet oddly skewed Wordsworthian sentiments of these poems predate the Olson connection and were subsequently excluded from the collected *Poems* (1982). His next book, *Kitchen Poems* (1968), is a foray into Olson's maximal rhetoric verging on mimicry:

> The politics, therefore, is for one man,
> a question of skin, that he ask
> of his national point no more, in
> this instance, than brevity. The
> rest follows: so long regardful
>   of the rule, the decision
>   as knowledge and
>   above all, trust.[3]

Even so, Prynne successfully translates the Olsonian critique of 'pejoroc-racy' into his own 'Sketch For a Financial Theory of the Self', which turns away from consumerism (Pound's credit economy included) to relocate value in 'Fluff, grit, various / discarded bits & pieces', anything society cannot appropriate for use or exchange:

>   the splintered
> naming of wares creates targets for want
> like a glandular riot, and thus want
> is the most urgent condition (e.g. not
> enough credit).
>   I am interested instead in
> discretion: what I love and also the spread
> of indifferent qualities. Dust, objects of use
> broken by wear, by simply slowing too much
> to be retrieved as agents. Scrap; the old ones,
> the dead who sit daily at the feast. Each
> time I hesitate I think of them, loving what
> I know. The ground on which we pass,
> moving our feet, less excited by travel.
>   ('A Gold Ring Called Reluctance', 22–3)

This hostility towards commerce extends to the production of poetry itself. While the small press might not be entirely free from the process of exchange, it nevertheless represents an alternative to the market-led inter-ests of established publishing houses. *Kitchen Poems* was issued by Cape Goliard, significantly for Prynne because the Press brought out the Eng-lish editions of the first two volumes of *The Maximus Poems*. Ironically, Tom Raworth's Goliard Press had joined up with Jonathan Cape, compro-mising the alternative economy before it had really got under way. Prynne's response was to move increasingly further away from mainstream production, publishing his next book, *The White Stones* (1969) with Tim Longville's Grosseteste Press, and other collections with a variety of DIY imprints run by fellow poets such as Andrew Crozier, Wendy Mulford, Barry MacSweeney and Iain Sinclair. At times, Prynne appeared like an Elizabethan poet, discreetly circulating texts to a select group of friends and initiates; *Into the Day* (1972), *High Pink on Chrome* (1975), *The Oval Window* (1983), and *Bands Around the Throat* (1987) are marked simply 'Cambridge' or 'Cambridge, privately printed'. Where other poets hoped to work their way up from little magazines and presses to gain greater recognition with Faber, Cape, Oxford University Press, and other major publishers, Prynne reversed the process, placing higher value on small-scale enterprises.

All this changed with the arrival of the Bloodaxe edition of the collected *Poems* in 1999 (an earlier *Poems*, composed of works written between 1968 and 1979, was published by Anthony Barnett and Fiona Allardyce in 1982). Prynne's about-turn was due in part to the patronage of John Kinsella, a prolific Australian poet equally at home with the narrative verse of Les Murray and the postmodern *écriture* of the LANGUAGE poets, whose grant money got the project going. But it may also have had something to do with a general awareness that once-small presses such as Carcanet and Bloodaxe were taking over from many of the big publishers – who were abandoning their 'uneconomic' poetry lists – and were opening their doors to the 'new British poetry'.[4] The old rules had ceased to apply. However Prynne squared this new four-colour profile with his self-abnegating ethics, the result was instant attention from the papers and journals that had hitherto dismissed his work as crank material. Welcoming what they mistakenly see as Prynne's rejection of the 'esoteric small presses', critics now admit that he is a force to be reckoned with, although with the caveat that his more 'impenetrable' texts remain lost to poetry's right reason.[5] For Michael Glover, Prynne's work 'seems to strive after two things simultaneously: the need to define, and to pin down, the nature of the relationship between language and actuality and the need to let some thwarted inner sweetness flow, which might have flowed all the more easily had he not followed the road of experimentation with quite such ruthless single-mindedness.'[6]

There is a clear parallel here between the politics of poetic form and the occult trajectory of late modernism I have described in earlier chapters. The 'esoteric' small presses are not simply low-status, low-budget imitations of genuine publications, they are 'underground', chthonic forces disseminating the coded texts of poetry kabbals. Underground production goes hand-in-hand with obscurantist verse pitted against orthodox media and revealed modes of artistic expression. This politics of suspicion works both ways, as can be seen from Davie's claim that a 'silent conspiracy' has tried to suppress British modernist writing.[7] At its most basic, the contin- ued hostility towards 'experimentalism' in British poetry stems from the belief that the function of poetry is to crystallise thoughts and feelings in a language accessible to all and that the modernist obsession with 'difficulty' violates this contract between poet and audience. It is bad enough, there- fore, that the mandarin rhetoric and dialectical argumentation of *Kitchen Poems* and *The White Stones* keep 'inner sweetness' at bay, but when from *Brass* (1971) onwards Prynne's work comes into its own violent lyricism, both thought and feeling are threatened with incoherence:

> A limit spark under water
> makes you see briefly
> how patience is wasted
>
> that deep sadness is a perk
> of the iron will; no sound
> catches the binding dark
>
> side of this relish, head-on
> in thermite lock. Each one
> bound to wait, the other
>
> blunders to see it and suffer
> the play at choking
> or not turning away.

> (*Down Where Changed*, 306)

The terse little poem has an almost overwhelming sense of pathos, of long- ing and regret. Yet the more one tries to explain that sense in the text, the more it retreats into an uncanny and even ludicrous reflection on motives. 'Deep sadness' and 'iron will' are reassuringly clichéd expressions, but why is deep sadness a 'perk' of the iron will? Something 'perky'? Hardly conducive to *gravitas*. Or the sentimental bonus of stoical reserve? An absurd reward. 'Relish' is a pun like 'Mr Leopold Bloom ate with relish the inner organs of beasts and fowls'. What is a 'thermite lock'? How does its heated embrace result from the 'limit spark under water' which allows you to glimpse what is inchoate, blundering, subterfuge? Perhaps painful feel- ings are as clouded and resistant to expression as this poem. You search for reason but 'suffer / the play at choking / or not turning away.' You turn away in despair, but is that really turning away? The poem has a strong enough basis in emotive idiom to lure the reader into wanting to make sense of it, yet it returns the demand for meaning back on itself. The painful recogni- tion that emotions, like lyrics, tend to be rationalised into an 'image' that mirrors the desire for subjective certainty is bound to cause perplexity and even disgust. Prynne does not thwart an 'inner sweetness' by enclosing it in a hard shell of depersonalised, dissonant language, but plays off tonal against atonal elements to expand the emotional range of the lyric into areas not covered by the simple appeal to experience, empathy, and identity. It is hardly surprising, therefore, that since his poetry radically assaults the concept of meaning*ful*ness it gets condemned as 'meaningless'. Hence, even in its most minimal forms, it 'remains' charged with love for detritus, everything which cannot be redeemed for what Pound calls 'immediate consumption':

> at all
> anyway
> whatever
>
> even so
>
> rubbish

(Down Where Changed, 307)[8]

'Have / you had enough? Do have a little more? / It's very good but, no, perhaps I won't.' ('A Gold Ring Called Reluctance', 24.) While the final chapter of this book argues that Prynne's poetry of the late 1960s and early 1970s clearly derives from a late modernist sensibility, it suggests that its aesthetic of lessness takes late modernism to the verge of deconstruction, since its resistance to hermeneutic appropriation leaves all readings radically uncertain, *including those which lay claim to an unsayable poetic essence or Heideggerian Saying.* That this effect can be contextualised as the culmination of late modernist ambivalence and/or as the foundation of postmodern conceptualism shows that the distinction between modernist and postmodern poetics at the end of the twentieth century is far from being cut and dried.

We have seen that Prynne was a dedicated explicator of Olson's poetics and that his early poetry is stylistically close to Olson's. Yet Prynne tempers Olson's thrusting campaign for the revival of the heavenly city on earth ('Polis') with what he calls 'discretion': the attention to what cannot be assimilated by any programme for civic totality. In Prynne's cautious assessment, the Polis is an agreeable utopian dream which cannot reconcile the conflicting human desires for settlement and nomadic wandering. All we can see are the 'few / outer lights of the city, burning on the horizon' ('Numbers in Time of Trouble', 19); the light by which we see and with which we mark territory is already enmeshed in the process of consumption ('burning'), so that the 'light' of our 'most familiar need, / to love without being stopped for some im- / mediate bargain, to be warm and tired / without some impossible flame in the heart' is itself a utopian fantasy, and perhaps a suburban one at that:

> In any street the pattern
> of inheritance is laid down, the truth is for our
> time in cat's-eyes, white markings, gravel
> left from the last fall of snow. We proceed
> down it in dreams, from house to house which
> spill nothing on to the track, only light on the
> edge of the garden.

('The Common Gain, Reverted', 88)

There is nothing derisory about this; the poet is genuinely attracted to the security of 'home', but he is also drawn by the need to 'wander' in less comfortable environments, identifying with other outsider figures, the monks and Siberian shamans who populate *The White Stones*. Throughout these poems of the late 1960s, identificatory positions are offered but suspended. When Prynne writes in 'Thoughts on the Esterhazy Court Uniform' that 'home is easily our / idea of it, the music of decent and proper order' (98) he doesn't make it easy to decide whether this ease should be rejected or affirmed. The plea for 'worked self-transcendence' in 'Questions for the Time Being' (112) is not necessarily incompatible with being 'warm and tired / without some impossible flame in the heart'. The desire for some form of transcendence, whether pastoral, political or spiritual, is a necessary condition for moving forward, but it is also prone to misrecognition as a hope for imaginary plenitude, the filling of lack promised by the commodity form, nationalism, the family, etc., which, being impossible, inevitably results in splenetic, passive acceptance of the damaged lifeworld. The sanguine 'recognition' of this 'deep, blunting damage of hope' ('In the Long Run, to be Stranded', 47) checks the longing which both inspires progress and stifles it:

> The consequence of this
> pastoral desire is prolonged
> as our condition, but
> I know there is more than the mere wish to
> wander at large, since the wish itself diffuses
> beyond this and will never end

('Moon Poem', 54)

If the poet goes on to assert that 'the wish is gift to the / spirit, is where we may dwell' (a dwelling that is Sisyphean, accepting the beyond of mere wish as more wish), his songs and/or psalms shine in the night, a night of 'negligence and still passion' (54). In these poems, assertions of spiritual illumination vie with stoical reserve. The moment of epiphany is also the moment of error; vigilance or watchfulness is everything: 'There is a tradition, derived from Christ's unassisted watch in the garden, of regarding sleep as a weakness on a pilgrim's part, a slackening-off from the clear march to the trusted home'.[9] 'we carry ourselves by ritual / observance, even sleeping in the library' ('First Notes on Daylight'); 'But sleep may also be a necessary nourishment from which good may emerge, if identity is reconstituted on waking',[10] and Prynne does defer to what he calls 'that extremity of false vigilance' ('Questions for the Time Being', 112), with which he checks even the stoic response.

Whether you want to call this dialectic or mere equivocation depends on how you are disposed towards the rigours of Prynne's poetic. In this dark light, 'Questions for the Time Being' should perhaps be taken literally as an indication of Prynne's intent. The text is a blatant contradiction: more prose manifesto than poem, it is a splenetic diatribe against splenetic tendencies in late 1960s political postures, a 'defence' of stoicism that infringes the decorum of its own ethics. The indignant opening line, 'All right then *no* stoic composure' (111) says as much, declaring the thetic speaker's foray into the very rhetoric he would prefer to avoid. The outburst that follows takes a Nietzschean view on the relation of grammar to will, insisting on caution regarding problems of mastery and transgression. The current 'masters' of language may be 'self-styled', but they do 'own and / control the means of production', a fact that has escaped those who assume a revolutionary stance without any understanding of *realpolitik*:

> so much talk
> about the underground is silly when it would re-
> quire a constant effort to keep below the surface,
> when almost everything is exactly that, the
> mirror of a would-be alien who won't see how
> much he is at home.
>
> ('Questions for the Time Being', 111)

Modish talk of an underground masks the lack of action on the part of what Prynne describes sceptically as 'any discrete / class with an envisaged part in the social process'. The idea of revolution is thus no more than fashion, the 'idea of change is briskly seasonal' and 'scout-camp' militants are so bound by their (and our) separate desires that any possibly genuine action is interminably delayed, being 'not part of any mode or con- / dition except language & there they rest on / the false mantelpiece, like ornaments of style.' The 'historic shift' is in actuality subject to forces outside telic fantasies ('hope', once again, here reviled as 'Micawberish') and any response to a 'really crucial moment' must be able to reject the blind world of wish: 'the wheel is permanently / red-hot, no one on a new course sits back and / switches on the automatic pilot' (112). Prynne remains stoical because he resists the sleep of desire while ultimately seeing no escape from it. Nevertheless, he makes a claim for overcoming the self and its narcotic fantasy politics: 'What goes on in a / language is the corporate & prolonged action / of worked self-transcendence' (112). Whatever this means – the dodgy authority of its abstraction should not blind us to its lack of qualification, for if it is a case of 'language speaks, not man', where is the ground for agency? – it stands opposed to the culture of teeming *ressentiment* in which even this text is enmeshed: 'No one has any right / to mere idle discontent, even in conditions of most / extreme privation, since such a state of arrested / insight is actively counter-productive' (112). Nor does it follow that the alternative is a state of Epicurean disregard: 'Contentment or sceptical calm will produce instant death'. But the poet is on the ropes, and he knows it; the whole diatribe is just, well, *too personal*. As a last despondent snipe suggests that 'luminous take-off' is merely another pose, the poem sinks into nihilistic pathos: 'in a given con- / dition such as now not even elegance will come / of the contemporary nothing in which life goes on' (113).

In *The White Stones*, then, Prynne appears to be struggling to overcome his residual allegiance to the Olsonian ethic of *Kitchen Poems*, for which the 'politics . . . is for one man', and 'the true literal has very few names', but he is stuck oscillating wildly between sceptical spleen and cosmic ideal: 'Where we go is a loved side of the temple, / a place for repose, a concrete path' ('The Holy City', 43). Civic virtue is a desirable but impossible aim, and the turmoil produced in trying to achieve it is contrasted with projections of *ataraxia* in the 'thereness' of 'love' and 'the world', an oxymoronic concreteness in abstraction. In a sharply critical essay drawing attention to what he calls Prynne's 'neo-Stoical, Senecan *consolatio* of argument', D. S. Marriott has described this as 'The world as sacred object subjectively intuited in the sound of the sentient as immutable and timeless as contrasted to the privacy of individual time as a form of knowing within terrestrial process.'[11] Davie's contention that Prynne's peculiarly English modernism is influenced by Hardy is not without credence: 'Prynne's emphasis is frequently on patience, on lowering the sights, settling for limited objectives.'[12] But it misses the existential complexity of the poetry, which calls for discretion but avoids complacency:

> The English condition is now so abstract that
> it sounds like an old record; the hiss and
> crackle suborns the music, so that the
> true literal has very few names.
>
> ('A Gold Ring Called Reluctance', 23)

Constantly wrong-footing interpretation, Prynne's work is primarily nomadic, not ruling out the possibility of a resting place but insisting that identity is never at home to itself, never more than a contingent point from which we must move on, being 'this we must leave in some quite / specific place if we are not to carry it / everywhere with us ('Thoughts on the Ester-hazy Court Uniform', 98). The strategy is to create the heuristic conditions for a reading subject attentive to the paradox of the *Unheimliche* in the way Heidegger describes as *Dasein*, 'Primordial, thrown Being-in-the-world as the "not-at-home" – the bare "that it is" in the nothing of the world . . . it is something like an *alien* voice.'[13] Prynne's own take on the uncanny in the 1971 Olson lecture is filtered through a reassuringly pat description of one of Heidegger's later essays:

> We have to go to the exactness and completeness of poetry to tell us what such a condition of home would be like. And if we want it in its largest sense, you have to go to the largest distance from it in order to come right back round to take it in at one sweep. That condition of home, as I say, is quite stunning. When the German metaphysician Heidegger was trying to get himself straight with the poems of Hölderlin . . . he seized onto the phrase 'poetically man dwells on this earth': and he ponders it, and he turns it round, and he's asking himself what is the condition of being that makes it possible for man to be at home on the earth.[14]

The White Stones, however, is much more troubling in its assessment and reassessment of the determination of being. While the essay finesses Olson's mythic method into Heidegger's poetic dwelling, the poetry disrupts Olson's conflation of history with myth. This is achieved by portraying the moments of Heideggerian *Dasein* and their contingent mythic dimensions as ontic determinations in the history of Being, opposing the Jungian archetypes of Olson's Maximus poems. Rendering myth historical forms the anthropological basis for interpretation in the minor epic 'Aristeas, In Seven Years' (1968). Nevertheless, as I will show, although the radical contingency of Prynne's poems disturbs Olson's archetypal appropriation of Being, it is underlaid by a desire for sacred origins and ritual space in the form of a 'divine insistence', as it is called in 'Aristeas' (89). If the shamanic 'spirit excursion', which is used in that poem and throughout the book as a figure of knowledge, is literalised as 'no more than the need and will of the flesh' (91), the wish for mystical transcendence takes precedence over materiality, and Prynne's emphasis on 'desire', 'longing' and 'hope' carries with it a deep sense of nostalgia for a 'time' of ritual 'multeity in unity'.

Heidegger is an ambivalent thinker in terms of how his philosophy influences modernist poetics. His quest for an ontology freed from meta-physics can be read as proffering both a theology of transcendent Being and an hermeneutic refusal of the transcendent by showing that Being is never present to itself and can only be thought in the ontic realm of his-torical determinations, or beings. The indeterminacies and contingencies of modernist poetry become the site both of the mystically unsayable (the pastoral) and a radical openness to ideological construction (the avant-garde). A reading of *The White Stones* in the light of this doubleness shows Prynne to be a poet concerned with the conflicting demands of the modernist tradition. Thus, the temporal horizon in *The White Stones* belongs to what Prynne calls 'a quality of man and his becoming' meeting 'the divine family of ends' ('Frost and Snow, Falling', 69). An implicit figural order allows this conjunction of the divine and the ideological to come 'to light': 'Luminous / take-off shows through in language forced into any / compact with the historic shift' ('Questions For the Time Being', 113). To understand it we need to examine the the rôle played by shamanism in Prynne's work.

The shaman is a mark of the doubleness of Hedeggerian poetics in combining the romantic mythification of the poet as visionary outsider with a primitivist dislocation of western priorities of history, knowledge, and religion. If the figure of the shaman serves to reify the western romance of myth, it also allows for a critique of the discourse of reason and its occulted yet rationally coherent other, the irrational. Anthropological studies of shamanism have tended to mystify the conditions of 'magic' in so-called primitive society by importing western ideals of spiritual unity into their accounts of heterogeneous cultural events. Prynne's own use of anthropological evidence in *The White Stones* is complex, because it works to bracket the mythic while sustaining sacred intention. Prynne's poetry embodies a mystical and mythic enquiry which implies that poetry moves towards a reinscription of the sacred, even when access to a 'mystic moment' is denied in favour of an historical and hermeneutic account of human becoming. However, I want to show that this is achieved not simply because Prynne invokes magical reference – this would be contradicted by every point in the text at which the magical references are undermined – it is achieved on one plane by the rhetorical 'magic' of the *ordine inverso*, that is to say, the 'inexplicable' coming-into-its-own of the negative familiar in Rilke's poetic, and on another by Prynne's residual dependence on Olson's Jungian claims for a 'special view of history', which argues for the universal and spiritually transcendent while insisting on supposedly specific and 'literal' facts about the origins of man.

In *Kitchen Poems*, Prynne contrasted the pejorocracy of technocratic culture with the transcendent act of naming: 'The first essential is to take knowledge / back to the springs' ('Die A Millionaire', 13) in order to purify language, for 'The fact is that right / from the *springs* this water is no longer fit / for the stones it washes: the water of life / is all in bottles & ready for invoice' (15–16). The stones it washes are white: the 'classic' modernist call for purification is echoed by the late modernist obsession with archetypal knowledge, the psychologised mystification of the primitive offered against a stale yet manipulative rationality. Prynne's philology owes something to the mystifying theories of the origins of language which were a counter-current of the Enlightenment, and which empiricists such as Locke abhorred as mystical forms of meaning 'springing' from etymology.[15] Criticising this philological tradition, Jacques Derrida has argued that all attempts to secure the origin of meaning through etymology are by nature empirical. Drawing on Heidegger's ontology, Derrida argues that to assume the earliest meaning of a word and its cognates would appear to mark it as a proper name, which escapes metaphor and is thus the name of Being. But Heidegger says that to name Being is to use an ontic metaphor, and this must differ from the ontological basis of being (itself). Therefore, the history of Being will be the history of metaphorical positions for Being. To describe Being in terms of its own philology, as 'respiration', as do Renan and Nietzsche, merely sets up a positive definition that denies its always-already other term, 'non-respiration':

> Empiricism is thinking by metaphor without thinking the metaphor as such . . . Supposing that the word 'Being' is derived from a word meaning 'respiration' (or any other determined thing), no etymology or philology – as such, and as determined sciences – will be able to account for the thought for which 'respiration' (or any other determined thing) becomes a determination of Being among others.[16]

In essence, Being escapes these determinations, but

> because Being is nothing outside the existent, and because the opening amounts to the ontico-ontological difference, it is impossible to avoid the ontic metaphor in order to articulate Being in language, in order to let Being circulate in language . . . At one and the same time language illuminates and hides Being itself. Nevertheless, Being itself is *alone* in its absolute resistance to *every metaphor*. Every philology which allegedly reduces the *meaning* of Being to the metaphorical origin of the *word* 'Being' . . . misses the history of the meaning of Being.[17]

In spite of his Heideggerian persuasion, Prynne's position seems to be much closer to that of Renan and Nietzsche. But Heidegger too, as a reader of Nietzsche, sets great store by philology and continually determines the Call of Being (if not Being itself), in its presencing-withdrawing structure, through this method. Names remain 'the tricks we / trust' ('Numbers in Time of Trouble', 21). It is not the statements *about* magic that should be regarded as indicating Prynne's belief, but rather the 'magic' of the literal (itself) in its resistance to figures. In 'Aristeas', Prynne presents the reader with dense analyses of the history of economic and mythic determinations, for which, he asserts, 'The literal is *not* magic, for the most part' ('A Note On Metal', 129). Could some small part of the literal still be invested with magical power? This would seem to remain questionable, just as the shamanic figure of flight at the close of 'Aristeas', and the historical, economic and anthropological 'facts' on which it focuses the poet's attention, remain at the close of the poem no more than questions asked. Except that as long as the literal is maintained as such, and is therefore thought as 'coming before' metaphor, it continues to be invested with the magic of a Being that *presents itself*, instead of coming to light through the act of poetic Saying (which is neither ontological nor ontic, neither literal nor metaphorical).[18]

The academic, highly discursive argumentation of 'Aristeas' calls for careful explication in the context of the wide range of its source material, classical, archaeological, philological, geographical, geomorphological and mythological (bibliography supplied by Prynne). The sifting of this material provides only the starting point from which interpretation begins. For the argument is hardly restricted to the rationally discursive; its Olsonian composition by field works to bracket the frame of reference. 'Aristeas' meets Barthes's requirements for the status of a text: 'the activity of associations, contiguities, carryings-over coincides with a liberation of symbolic energy'.[19] Narrative structure is not sequential but recursive; definition of statement is constantly promised but usually elided; sentences frequently change course, hopping from referent to referent without regard for continuity; scholarly quotations hang in the text without qualification; demonstratives create a strong referential effect, but their exact referents all too often cannot be located (e.g., 'Aristeas took up it / seems with the / singular as the larch / tree, the / Greek sufficient / for that. From Marmora // And sprang with that double twist into the / middle world and thence took flight over the / Scythian hordes and to the Hyperborean, / touch of the north wind / carrying with him Apollo'). Or cannot be located, it would seem, without the master key that the bibliography offers but cannot disclose, because it can only supply the reference and not the sense. Through its description of a shamanic journey, a mythical account of actual historical events in Greek, Siberian, and Central Asian prehistory, 'Aristeas' is an elided epic poem that draws attention to the Orphic origins of narrative.[20] Beyond this, it is a poem *about* reference. Like the study of ancient history itself, the text is based on the fragments of lost civilisations, and Prynne chooses to make this fact into an hermeneutic exercise, playing off forensic and mythic findings against one another and ensuring that the reader pursues the Olsonian imperative of 'finding out for oneself'. (Olson got this principle from Herodotus who, in Book 4 of the *History*, provides the initial 'historical' account of Aristeas's journey from the Pontic region to Scythia.[21])

Prynne may have intended Aristeas to represent his own version of Olson's mythical persona, Maximus. P. L. Henry's study of the early English and Celtic lyric, which Prynne cites in his philological collage 'A Pedantic Note in Two Parts' links the figure of Aristeas with *The Seafarer* and *The Wanderer*: 'The acquisition of wisdom is of outstanding importance for the journeys of Aristeas, as appears from a . . . passage in Maximus of Tyre'.[22] E. D. Phillips goes into more detail. First, by summarising Herodotus:

> Aristeas, a citizen of Proconnesus on the island now called Marmora, and an epic poet, claimed in his poem [the *Arimaspeia*] that once he became *phoibolumptos*, that is, 'seized or possessed by Phoebus Apollo', and in that state reached the people called Issedones beyond Scythia. Beyond the Issedones lived the Arimaspeians, one-eyed men, and beyond these the griffins from whom they snatched the guarded gold.

and then by going to Maximus:

> Maximus of Tyre, a Platonist writer of the second century A.D., adds important details, interesting to him as a believer in the soul which can leave the body and survive it. He says that the soul of Aristeas left his body, as it lay still breathing just enough to maintain life, and wandered in the upper air like a bird, looking down on everything from above . . . it then entered his body again and roused it to its feet, using it like an instrument, and recited all that it had seen and heard.[23]

Many of these elements of the legend are present in Prynne's text; the details of Aristeas's origin, shamanic transformation, and flight of discovery are clearly documented, and the poem's narrative closes with a description of the griffins' gold, which 'reposed as the divine brilliance' (94). Prynne ends the poem by reaffirming the divine value of gold prior to its being wrested from the griffins by the Arimaspeians. Phillips notes that 'gold found anywhere may have been regarded by the Scythians, as by other Asiatic nomads, as a heavenly and so a sacred metal. The office of the Scythian kings who had to stay awake guarding the sacred gold implements fallen from heaven also takes on a heightened significance'.[24] This divine status of gold, 'guarded' from use- and exchange-value and the 'plural' greed of imperial tribes, is linked to the shaman's 'singular' condition:

                    it was
        himself as the singular that he knew and
        could outlast in the long walk by the
        underground sea. Where he was as
                        the singular
                location so completely portable
                that with the merest black
                wings he could survey the

> stones and rills in their
> complete mountain courses,
> *in name the displacement*
>   Scythic.

('Aristeas', 90)

In turn, he is identified with the nomadic culture for which 'the / vantage is singular/as the clan is without centre' (92). Only the decentred individual or group has access to the realm of the sacred. Although Prynne is drawing on spiritual experience to attack the kind of group rationale that ends in 'massive slaughter as the / obverse politics of claim' (94), he nevertheless buys into the political evasion of mythic 'centres' (and the elite bands of 'adepts' maintaining them) which are believed to exist outside all economic determination. In fact, this configuration is akin to (and, indeed, allegorises) the contemporary function of art in capitalist society, which can be prized by the market precisely because its value has been idealised, made 'priceless'.[25] The shaman is an aesthetic figure, identifying the romantic predicament of the poet; aestheticised also by representing the ideal antithesis of commodification.

But what exactly is a shaman? Maximus depicts the shamanic experience as one of extasis, a spiritual movement that gives access to knowledge. The word itself comes from the Tungus language of central Siberia, and has corresponding terms in the Central and North Asian tongues; thus Prynne's particular interest in types of shamanism deriving from the Siberian region (95–6).[26] Mythically, the shaman is a tribal 'magician' and keeper of secrets. Usually male, his lore and practice are Hermetic, his arcane knowledge gained from precisely that ability to take spiritual flight and undertake a 'mantic journey' to the farthest reaches of the earth through any of the four elements, or to visit the gods or the dead, and return to his native land with messages (having been, so to speak, informed by the Other). The mythical shaman takes many cultural forms throughout subsequent history, including the figure of Orpheus.

The word 'mantis' means etymologically one who is summoned by madness, so from an anthropological point of view it becomes clear that the shaman is a member of a tribe or society who has been 'touched by the hand of God' (hence the term 'touched' to describe mental instability), marked by the trace of the other, and is therefore invested with uncanny powers.[27] Rather than casting out these 'madmen' or simply shunning them, the tribe will *make sense* of them by converting its collective fear of difference (madness, death, castration) into something positive and unifying.[28] As a kind of witch-doctor, the shaman is regarded as a healer of spiritual (i.e., psychological) and psychosomatic disorders. Through a version of sympathetic magic his ritual dances and schizoid songs (often drug-induced) seem to exorcise the 'evil' lodged in the minds and bodies of 'normal' members of the community. His 'spiritual excursions' are realised in states of trance, which are seen by the group as having cathartic power. It is as if by embodying the external evil that 'subjects' the group the shaman contains its psychic indetermination by giving it a face. Mircea Eliade writes that 'Shamans are of the "elect" and as such they have access to a region of the sacred inaccessible to other members of the community'.[29] And the shaman himself is made worthy as an individual by having been imbued with this liminal role: 'were it not for the transformative powers of community and ritual, the shaman would remain an isolated neurotic. The shaman must be *recognized*.'[30]

Already in this account of the shaman's role, which conflates scholarly material from both comparative religion and anthropology, we can see a problem emerging in terms of providing an adequate description of what shamanism means, for both 'primitive' and modern cultures. The vision of the mystic can be regarded as the incarnation of sacred values in the group, or as an allegory of the group's socio-psychological condition. These positions, represented by Eliade in the first case and by the social anthropologist I. M. Lewis in the second, both tend towards an organic concept of symbolic unity in the group, which creates its marginal figures in order to reverse the pathological threat of chaos into a state of order and homogeneity. The other becomes hypostatised as transcendental Other, and the fear of radical difference is presented as an essential human trait. It will form an ideal, reified concept of difference that, programmed into the theory of the literary text, makes the text into the fetishised site of pure difference which is a negative version of romantic redemption through art.

Being themselves caught up in western myths of the primitive other as giving access to a realm of healing spiritual unity lost to 'modern man', many anthropological commentators on shamanic identity reify both the mystical and the psychological sides of the evidence as well as making them continuous. And their analyses do not take up the socio-political conditions of the shamanic experience itself. This is largely due to theological and humanist traditions that see the shaman as a variety of pilgrim, whose liminal position with regard to the socius necessarily sets him apart from political, juridical and economic concerns.[31] From this point of view, the 'mystic' subject gains a sense of fundamental subjectivity through his or her marginalised position, and so is able to prescribe a kind of 'unacknowledged legislation' to the community. This view maintains transgression within a theocentric and individualistic ideology. For Western Man, the shaman becomes a catch-all figure for the individuation process, the heroic quest to unify the self with what is external to it: 'In order to experience the paradoxical reality which is present before, outside of, or behind the polarization of world and self, the personality must – temporarily at least – transform itself and assume an attitude which leaves open the possibility of a union between ego and non-ego.'[32]

In Michael Taussig's book *Shamanism, Colonialism, and The Wild Man*, this tradition is made problematic by the inclusion of political referents for fear and alterity. Taussig's research among the Indians of the Putamayan region of Colombia leads to a reassessment of the entire notion of mystical and psychological order when applied to 'primitive' cultures in both its poetic and scholarly configurations. His account is so attentive to the complex of factors involved within and without the divided community, which is the object of his study, that it is difficult to describe this reassessment without falling into the generalisations against which the book works. But, broadly speaking, Taussig is concerned with the differential nature of the discourses of magic and rationality, and the power relations that put them to work. In the case of shamanism, he shows that Western concepts of order and unity, which are used to misrepresent foreign policies based on coercion and domination, consistently recreate the figure of the shaman as an image of harmony. Instead of this idealised cosmology that comprises mystical flight, the organic absorption of the individual into the tribe, the charisma of ritual leaders, and so forth, the shaman tends to be a member of the community who, having survived his own physical and/or mental illness, seeks to cure the ills of others. His tasks may range from curing a swollen stomach to attempting to exorcise the various 'evil spirits' that inhabit the social symbolic of the culture. However we might want to take the real or imaginary nature of 'magic' in the ritual confrontations between healer and patient, they are not bound to the *communitas* model of ritual subscribed to by academic commentators. On the contrary, the shaman's 'wild' behaviour, pitched into chaos, is designed to break up the symbolic order that 'subjects' the patient to the evil *magia* of desires, envies and fears, whether these are imposed from within by what festers in the community or from without by forces such as imperialism. For if the colonists imagined in the 'savages' they encountered the worst excesses of their own mythologised and demonised view of primitive cultures (which they then had to 'suppress'), the alien technology of the white man possessed its own terrifying magic for the native inhabitants, a magic continued into the present through the mythologies of commodity culture. Taussig articulates a chiasmic structure of terror that has at its crux the ambiguous, mythologised and mythologising figure of the shaman whose symbolic anarchy acts on colonizer and colonised alike. Shamans are the shock-absorbers of history. In following the cross-currents of these relationships with otherness, the important thing is, he writes, 'To see the myth in the natural and the real in magic, to demythologize history and to reenchant its reified representation; that is a first step.

To reproduce the natural and the real without this recognition may be to fasten ever more firmly the hold of the mythic.'[33]

To narrow the subject down to the question of poetics, Taussig rules out the idea (put forward by Lévi-Strauss, among others) that the shaman's song amounts to an ordering of internal chaos, for the song itself is unintelligible, 'part of a baroque mosaic of discourses woven through stories, jokes, interjections, and hummings taking place not only through and on top of one another during the actual séance but before and after it as well.'[34] The song is a form of burlesque, which squeezes out 'the magic implicit in the discourse of ruling reason', achieved through a process Taussig likens to montage:

> The 'mystical insights' given by visions and tumbling fragments of memory pictures oscillating in a polyphonic discursive room full of leaping shadows and sensory pandemonium are not insights granted by depths mysterious and other. Rather, they are made, not granted, in the ability of montage to provoke sudden and infinite connections between dissimilars in an endless or almost endless process of connection-making and connection-breaking.[35]

Taussig finds similarities here with the theories of Benjamin and Brecht. This fact already makes his theory of shamanism problematic because it ultimately depends as much on western models of (re)presentation as do the archetypal theories he rejects. But the important point here is that, as a coherent alternative description of shamanic practice, it explodes the western myth of organic order connecting shamanic song with modern poetry. Deleuze and Guattari, as well as Barthes, have produced theories of the radical symbolic disorder produced by overdetermined (or schizoid) acts, which are relevant to Taussig's description of shamanic practice.[36] However, it is questionable whether their versions are not merely indeterminate as well as overdeterminate, as they lack a sufficient understanding of the role of context in *determining* the ideological direction of the shamanic effect. As Taussig shows, the shamanic ritual is an *event*, and its meaning cannot be divorced from the specific dynamics of its production.

Returning to Prynne: does his poetry squeeze out the magic in the discourse of ruling reason, or does it merely oppose the 'dark light' of magic to rationality in a way that represents it as a higher order of being? According to my reading so far, the answer goes towards the latter, for the emphasis on originality, cultural and intellectual unity, and mystical resistance to technocracy converge with a politics based on Coleridgean principles of the elect, where the reiteration of the singular 'one' stands for divine unity as well as the charismatic singularity of self-transcendence. But in *The White Stones* the increasing tendency towards a poetic that displays non-identical forms of reference, which means that the emphasis is on the conditions of being rather than on a transcendentally determined Being, implies that the divine has already been divested of its univocal nature. Here, it is *Dichtung*'s 'letting-be' of Being that is important, and not the determination of Being as essence. In 'Aristeas', the following lines on the shamanic condition could thematise a reading of this kind: 'the spirit demanded the orphic metaphor / *as fact* / that they did migrate and the spirit excursion / was no more than the need and will of the / flesh' (91). It is possible that the 'orphic metaphor' here, being a kind of 'ontic metaphor', is reduced to the raw contingency of its determination. '*The* spirit' remains the subject of the statement, but we might go so far as to draw out an intertextual irony in 'the spirit demanded' as a reversal of Pound's haughty 'The age demanded an image / of its accelerated grimace'.[37] What the spirit *demands* is not necessarily what it needs. Yet the 'no more' refers to an earlier poem in the collection, 'First Notes On Daylight', where 'the whole sequence of person as his own / history is no *more* than ceremonial' (69). Ritual may be necessary to the spirit, but it does not transcend the ontic metaphor, and cannot be construed as being Being (itself). It is on the 'concrete path' where 'no mystic moment' ('The Holy City', 43) is involved. This is the philosophy of limit and *Dasein*. Moving farther back to another direct shamanic reference, we have what looks to be the now familiar site of contradiction: 'for / the door', Prynne writes, 'we must / have the divine sense, / of entrance' ('Just So', 59). The 'divine sense' of entrance is of course en*trance*, where we go 'in at the back door' to the plane of the mystic.

But this is precisely the point at which contradiction is annulled: we must have the divine *sense*; that is to say, *even* if we cannot claim the divine as literal truth. For Prynne, 'hope', damaging or not, is 'truly' our condition, which is first and foremostly spiritual in intent. 'That this could / really be so & of use is my present politics, / burning like smoke, before the setting of fire.' ('First Notes On Daylight', 69.) Smoke being the index of fire, we reach toward the transcendent flame of spirit. This appropriation brings a particular insistence to the pastoral nouns that circulate abstractly through these poems, governed by the tropes 'day', 'light', 'sky'.[38] Through a syntax which leaves them detached yet multiply connective, the words function talismanically:

> the sky is our eternal
> city and the whole beautiful and luminous trance
> of it is the smoke spreading
> > across into the upper air.
> > ('Charm Against Too Many Apples', 68)

It would be hard to read lines such as these without the 'divine sense' recommending itself. If the luminous figure of flight attested to in 'Questions

For the Time Being' were to succeed, it might reinstate the universal love signified by 'home'; but this ethic must take place on an ideal 'plane', that is, not the 'false literal' of flight made possible by the aeroplane ('the plane skids off / with an easy hopeless departure.' ('Airport Poem: Ethics of Survival', 38.)), but via the 'heart', which will 'journey / over any desert and through the air, making / the turn and stop undreamed of: / love is, always, the / flight back / to where / we are' (38–9). Prynne's critique of modern economic materialism, which is perhaps most powerfully (and 'economically') expressed in the short poem 'Starvation / Dream', rests in the refusal of ends-governed ritual:

> By any
> ritual of purpose we extend the idea
> of loan and we dream of it, the
> payment of all our debts. But we
> never shall, we have no single gain
> apart from the disguise of how far
> we earn.

> ('Starvation / Dream', 113–14)

For speculative, capital gain, 'the case / of fire rests in a flicker, just / short of silence' (113).

Obversely, the poetic is concerned with another extremity, affecting those poems where the land rather than the air is the centre of attention: 'Prynne's poems are not only severe; their intransigence rises to effects of sharp beauty, a kind of cool aesthetic which draws on imagery of ice, tundra, human extremity'.[39] Again, no contradiction, but a *complementary* order. The poem 'Frost and Snow, Falling' deals with the earthly matter of pilgrimage, the way of the nomad, offering 'along the way' a commentary on 'The Holy City', for

> Gregory did not
> believe in the pilgrimage of place: Jerusalem,
> he says, is too full of rapine and lust to be
> a direction of the spirit. The rest is some kind
> of flame, the pilgrim is again quality, and
> his extension is the way he goes across the crust
> that will bear him.

> ('Frost and Snow, Falling', 70)

Calling home 'Ierusalem' would not be enough; keeping on the move in the 'cold light of day' is a worldly priority, the infinite process of 'becoming'. The title, 'Frost and Snow, Falling', is a translation of lines from the OE poem *The Wanderer*, and the pilgrims, the marginal figures in the poem who 'cannot be identified and so identify us',[40] are represented by the figure of snow, which is denied the usual negative connotations:

> 'We travelled throughout the winter, often
> sleeping in the desert on the snow except when
> we were able to clear a place with our feet.
> When there were no trees but only open country
> we found ourselves many a time completely
> covered with snow driven by the wind.' That
> sounds to me a rare privilege, watching
> the descent down over the rim. Each man
> has his own corner, that question which
> he turns. It's his nature, the quality he
> extends into the world, just as his stature is
> his 'royal dignity'.
>
> ('Frost and Snow, Falling', 70)

The frozen land is identified as a 'crust', affording spiritual nourishment.[41]
As something elemental, ice bears a differential but complementary relation to fire. And the wanderer's relation to the nuclear group is necessary,
like the relation of beings to Being, figure to literal. Prynne leaves us with
little doubt as to the 'politics' of this relationship. Like Wordsworth's 'The
Old Cumberland Beggar' the wanderer *is* identified as being 'over there',
a tolerable but secondary feature in the order of things:

> The wanderer with his
> thick staff: who cares whether he's an illiterate
> scrounger – he is our only rival. Without this
> the divine family is a simple mockery, the
> whole pleistocene exchange will come to
> melt like the snow, driven into the ground.
>
> ('Frost and Snow, Falling', 71)

The wanderer is secondary because he exists in order to be set against
the 'divine family', and by remaining outside of it, to verify its sacred
quality. Prynne's terms are deprecating: 'who cares whether he's an illiterate / scrounger', where the addition of 'scrounger' modifies 'illiterate'
so that the language slips into the bourgeois rhetoric of responsibility and
blame. 'Without this / the divine family is a simple mockery'; it is clear
that whatever Prynne means by the 'divine family' it represents the primary quality of order and spiritual culmination, and must be preserved at
all costs ('The / preservative of advice, keeping to some kind of order, /
within the divine family of ends', as earlier the poem states it).[42] Prynne's
privileging of the 'singular' (represented by the wanderer) is here contradicted, for the real source of value, while it may be a singular group (the
family), nevertheless stands against the 'one'. Similarly, the poem's
reserved affirmation of 'royal dignity' works against the critique of the
imperium in 'Aristeas'.

The 'pleistocene exchange' refers to the epoch that is the theme of 'The Glacial Question, Unsolved', one of Prynne's most crystalline poems:

> In the matter of ice, the invasions
> were partial, so that the frost
> was a beautiful head
>   the sky cloudy
> and the day packed into the crystal

('The Glacial Question, Unsolved', 64)

Incorporating a mass of geographical and archaeological evidence, Prynne reworks the subject-matter of one of Olson's mentors, the American geographer Carl Ortwin Sauer, who proposed an Herodotean synergy of man and environment.[43] Sauer paid special attention to the Pleistocene epoch, significant because the deglaciation gave birth to human settlement: 'The time of the great deglaciation lies on the steeply ascending part of the curve of cultural innovation.'[44] Only with the deglaciation could settlement be achieved; for Olson this means origin, the beginnings of 'place'. For Prynne, too, 'man' is inseparable from the environment which informs him. The Glacial Question of the title is of the kind scientists use to demonstrate the relatively inconsequential 'time' of man on earth:

> Our climate is maritime, and
> 'it is questionable whether there has yet been
> sufficient change in the marine faunas
> to justify a claim that
>   the Pleistocene Epoch itself
> has come to end.' We live in that
> question, it is a condition of fact

('The Glacial Question, Unsolved', 65)

The quotation incorporated here comes from a paper on geological history by W. B. R. King.[45] In Prynne's hands, it takes on a sublime insistence that links it to the entire configuration of 'hope' ('the striations are part of the heart's desire' (64)). In this hard history of 'literal fact', man is the debris of glacial extent:

> We know where the north
> is, the ice is an evening whiteness.
> We know this, we are what it leaves:
> the Pleistocene is our current sense, and
> what in sentiment we are, we
> are, the coast, a line or sequence, the
> cut back down, to the shore.

('The Glacial Question, Unsolved', 65–6)

'Ice' has now shifted to the position of ontological fact, becoming the 'whiteness' from which both day and night originate ('The monk / Dicuil records that at the summer solstice / in Iceland a man could see right through the / night, as of course he could.' ('Frost and Snow', 70). We can no longer say whether it is fire or ice that gives meaning, for both have appropriated the place of origin. It follows that the distinction between spiritual and material qualities has been destroyed. Therefore, we return to the crossings of rhetorical inversion, which, 'called into being' by the neither/nor structure of *Dichtung*, uproot the literal origin of Being. Rather, *Dichtung* has spoken being from outside the ontological divide.

But what has been instituted on the way to that presencing? The moment we lay claim to any of the thematic statements made in the text, including the signifier 'hope' as soon as it comes to *signify* in terms of 'spirit', 'land', etc., they effect a withdrawal from being. If we can say *both* spirit and non-spirit, we must also acknowledge neither of them. The mystical reading appears to explode, then, not through Prynne's 'own' materialist practice but because no distinction can be upheld by a commentary on the text. But this does not mean that the text is now, miraculously, open, in the sense of a Heideggerian opening that allows the letting-be of Being, for what exactly is *being* let-be? The divine family? The sublime 'voiding' of man? Certainly not the 'visionary', 'pastoral', 'hopeful', 'originary', or 'spiritual' content attested to by the poet:

> With so little water
> the land creates a curved &
> muted extension
> the whole power is
> just that, fantasy of control
> the dispersion, in such
> level sky
> of each pulse the sliding
> fade-through of hills
> 'a noble evasion of privacy'
> ('If There Is A Stationmaster at Stamford S. D. Hardly So', 45)

If the rhetoric of inversion grounds a metaphysic which leaves references to 'spiritual flight' intact in their 'own Saying', ignorant of the differential structure which gives positional and political meaning to that saying, the 'fantasy of control' involves mysticism itself, a less than noble evasion of policies implemented in the name of the Other. In *The White Stones*, Prynne's double presentation of the sacred and profane, which invites the reader to understand them as contraries without hierarchy, finally reinstates the hierarchical terms of opposition by submitting the temporalised, materialist interpretation of mythic value to the transcendent order of the sacred. By doing so, his poetic valorises the sacred as an aesthetic and anthropological principle which is intended to stand against the profane world of economic exploitation but which actually reifies its contemporary mythic 'order'.

Notes

1 Charles Olson, *Call Me Ishmael* (New York: Grove Press, 1947), 11.
2 Peter Ackroyd, 'Legislators of Language', review of Andrew Crozier and Tim Longville, eds, *A Various Art* (Manchester: Carcanet, 1987), in *The Times*, Thursday, 3 December 1987. Aside from French translations of his work included in Pierre Joris and Paul Buck, eds, *Matières d'Angleterre: anthologie bilingue de la nouvelle poésie anglaise* (Amiens: Trois Cailloux (Maison de la Culture d'Amiens), 1984) and the strange inclusion of an early, disowned poem 'Along Almost Any River' in Angela King and Susan Clifford, eds, *The River's Voice: An Anthology of Poetry* (Dartington: Green Books, 2000), Prynne has refused to appear in anthologies.
3 Prynne, 'The Numbers', in *Poems* 1982), 10. Quotations from individual poems in the main text will be followed by page references to this edition, except when indicated otherwise.
4 Prynne, *Poems* (1999). Kinsella is editor of the journal *Salt* and the rapidly expanding Salt Publishing. The anthology *The New British Poetry*, edited by Gillian Allnutt, Fred D'Aguiar, Ken Edwards and Eric Mottram (London: Paladin, 1988), was one of the results of an ill-fated liaison between Grafton Books and the poets Iain Sinclair and John Muckle. The rot began to set in when an anthology of poetry by Thomas A. Clark, Barry MacSweeney and Chris Torrance was unexpectedly pulped due to Grafton's fears that it was unsellable. This event did not prevent the publication of Iain Sinclair's proselytising anthology *Conductors of Chaos* (London: Paladin, 1996).
5 Roger Caldwell, 'The flight back to where we are', review of J. H. Prynne, *Poems*, in *The Times Literary Supplement*, 23 April 1999, p. 27.
6 Michael Glover, 'Not a recluse in the pub', review of J. H. Prynne, *Poems*, in *The Independent on Sunday*, 22 August 1999, p. 13.
7 Donald Davie, 'See, and Believe', in *The Poet in the Imaginary Museum*, 67.
8 The editors of *Quarto* offered a year's subscription to anyone who could spot the difference between parts of *Down Where Changed* and a poem 'written in forty-five seconds by someone who was sitting in the office with nothing better to do' (*Quarto*, No. 9, August 1980, p. 1). Rubbish is, after all, merely rubbish.
9 N. H. Reeve and Richard Kerridge, *Nearly Too Much: The Poetry of J. H. Prynne* (Liverpool: Liverpool University Press, 1995), 82. See my review article on this book. 'Toy of Thought: Prynne and the Dialectics of Reading', *Salt* 11: In the Mix: International Regionalism and Hypermodernism 1 (1999), pp. 55–68.
10 Reeve and Kerridge, *Nearly Too Much*, 82.
11 D. S. Marriott, 'Contemporary British Poetry and Resistance: Reading J. H. Prynne', *Parataxis: Modernism and Modern Writing*, 8/9 (1996), p. 170.
12 Donald Davie, *Thomas Hardy and British Poetry* (London: Routledge and Kegan Paul, 1973), 113.
13 Martin Heidegger, *Being and Time*. Trans. John MacQuarrie and Edward Robinson (Oxford: Basil Blackwell, 1962), 321 (§ 277).
14 Prynne, 'On *Maximus IV, V, & VI* (no page no.).

15 Although Locke took little interest in etymology and, according to Hans Aarsleff, never used the word itself (*From Locke to Saussure: Essays on the Study of Language and Intellectual History* (Minneapolis: Univesity of Minnesota Press, 1982), 66). Nevertheless, Aarsleff points out that Locke's rejection of 'innate notions' meant that his theory of language contrasted with that of Leibniz, for whom sound is linked to sense and thus to nature, and worked against the etymological approach to meaning exemplified by a work such as John Webster's *Abacademiarum Examen* (1654) in which naming signifies the naming of nature itself, the original and Adamic language (*From Locke to Saussure*, 61).

16 Jacques Derrida, 'Violence and Metaphysics', in *Writing and Difference*, 139.

17 Derrida, 'Violence and Metaphysics', 138–9.

18 See Derrida, 'Violence and Metaphysics', 22.

19 Roland Barthes, 'From Work To Text', in *Image – Music – Text*, essays selected and translated by Stephen Heath (London: Fontana, 1982), 158. Barthes's emphasis on non-identity treats experience in a strikingly similar way to other poems in *The White Stones*. As he writes, what the 'passably empty subject . . . perceives is multiple, irreducible, coming fom a disconnected, hetergeneous variety of substances and perspectives: light, colours, vegetation, heat, air, slender explosions of noises, scant cries of birds, children's voices' (159).

20 As Donald Davie writes, 'Aristeas' 'seems to make significant play with the profound difference in spatial relations which we encounter when we move into understanding the shamanic religions from those we are more used to, such as Christianity. For in fact it seems to be the case that the shaman's dream journey is not up or down a vertical axis as in Dante, or even in Homer, but along the level. At most, the shaman's soul, when it is conceived of as having left the body, moves up or down only in the sense of upstream or downstream – a habit of spatial perception natural enough to the hunting or pastoral nomadic cultures in which shamanism, whether is Asia or America, has been chiefly practised. (Accordingly, Prynne is right to take as his fable the epic journey of the Pontic Greek Aristeas into the Asian hinterland of Scythian and other tribes. For whereas C. M. Bowra in *Heroic Song* persuasively saw the Western epic as emerging from and superseding shamanism, the epic journey of Aristeas represents a reversal of this.)' (*Thomas Hardy and British Poetry*, 128–9.)

21 E. D. Phillips notes the euhemeristic method in Herodotus in 'The Legend of Aristeas: Fact and Fancy in Early Greek Notions of East Russia, Siberia, and Inner Asia', *Artibus Asiae*, XVIII, 2 (1955), pp. 161–77. Phillips himself employs this method of using 'fable for discovering unexpected facts about history'(161).

22 P. L. Henry, *The Early English and Celtic Lyric* (London: Allen and Unwin, 1966), 138. Henry writes of *The Seafarer* that the poem organises 'a loose juxtaposition of ideas which the modern reader seeks – and is at a loss – to relate to one another', and that it suggests that 'We should think of our real home and devise how to reach it' (152). See Prynne, 'A Pedantic Note in Two Parts', in *The English Intelligencer*, Series 2, Part I (1966/67), pp. 346–51.

23 Phillips, 'The Legend of Aristeas', pp. 161–2.

24 Phillips, 'The Legend of Aristeas', p. 174.

25 Pierre Bourdieu, *Outline of a Theory of Practice*. Trans. R. Nice (Cambridge: Cambridge University Press, 1977), 197 (my italics): 'The denial of economy and of economic interest, which in pre-capitalist societies at first took place on a ground from which it had to be expelled in order for economy to be constituted as such, thus finds its favourite refuge in the domain of art and culture, the site of pure consumption – of money, of course, but also of time convertible into money. The world of art, a sacred

island systematically and ostentatiously opposed to the profane, everyday world of production, a sanctuary for gratuitous, disinterested activity in a universe given over to money and self-interest, offers, *like theology in a past epoch, an imaginary anthropology obtained by denial of all the negations really brought about by the economy.'*

26 See also M. L. West, *The Orphic Poems* (Oxford: Clarendon Press, 1983) esp. 5; Mircea Eliade, *Shamanism: Archaic Techniques of Ecstasy*, Trans. Willard R. Trask (Princeton: Princeton University Press, 1972), 4ff.

27 The implications for a romantic (viz. ro-mantic) ideology are legion. Defending his poem 'The Idiot Boy', for example, Wordsworth declared that he had always considered idiots (the mentally subnormal) to be exceptional and otherworldly people: 'I have often applied to Idiots, in my own mind, that sublime expression of scripture that *"their life is hidden with God"*. They are worshipped, probably from a feeling of this sort, in several parts of the East.' (Letter to John Wilson, 7 June 1807, in *The Letters of William and Dorothy Wordsworth*, Vol. I, The Early Years 1787–1805. Arranged and edited by Ernest de Selincourt, revised by Chester L. Shaver (Oxford: Clarendon Press, 1967), 257.) The status of marginal figures in romantic and post-romantic poetry has been explored by David Trotter. The romantic pilgrim, he writes, 'hoped to enter at the margin into a generic human bond. But who now could tell him when he had arrived at the margin? Who could tell him where to look? Such was the predicament of those Romantic poets who, as Heidegger said of Hölderlin, lived during the time between the departure and the return of the gods.' (*The Making of the Reader*, 8.)

28 See I. M. Lewis, *Ecstatic Religion: An Anthropological Study of Spirit Possession and Shamanism* (Harmondsworth: Penguin, 1971), esp. 179ff.

29 Eliade, *Shamanism*, 7.

30 Eliade, *Shamanism*, 14.

31 See Victor Turner, *The Ritual Process* (Harmondsworth: Penguin, 1974), passim, and Trotter's discussion in *The Making of the Reader*, 6–8. Trotter manages to elide the somewhat less innocent side of Turner's anthropology, as in this passage from *Image and Pilgrimage in Christian Culture*: 'In flow and communities what is sought is unity, not the unity which represents a sum of fractions and is susceptible of division and subtraction, but an indivisible unity, "white", "pure", "primary", "seamless".' (Quoted in Michael Taussig, *Shamanism, colonialism, and the Wild Man: A Study in Terror and Healing* (Chicago: Chicago University Press, 1987), 442.)

32 Erich Neumann, 'Mystical Man', in Campbell, ed., *The Mystic Vision*, 380. This speculative project, which lets go of the ego in order to get it back with interest, requires the 'experience of a "creative void" which leads man to form an image of creation from nothingness [which] is called "the self" in analytical psychology. In dealing with himself, man is a *homo-mysticus* (383).

33 Taussig, *Shamanism, Colonialism, and the Wild Man*, 10. 'Officialdom strives to create a magical reality' (4). Elsewhere, 'the word "magic" magically contains both the art and the politics involved in representation, in the rendering of objecthood' (134). For Taussig, the term 'shaman' is itself something of a misrepresentation; he calls it 'that Western projection of a Siberian name [which] finds life in a language of heroic restraint generally awfully male, poetic, originary, and so on' (448).

34 Taussig, *Shamanism, Colonialism, and the Wild Man*, 460.

35 Taussig, *Shamanism, Colonialism, and the Wild Man*, 279; 441.

36 Gilles Deleuze and Félix Guattari, *Anti-Oedipus: Capitalism and Schizophrenia*, Trans. Robert Hurley, Mark Seem and Helen R. Lane. Preface by Michel Foucault (New York: Viking, 1983); Roland Barthes, 'From Work To Text'.

37 Pound, 'Hugh Selwyn Mauberley', in *Selected Poems 1908–1959* (London: Faber, 1981), 98.

38 In one of Prynne's sources for 'Aristeas', G. S. Hopkins sets out to discover the semantic history of the Indo-European word **Deiwos* before it came to mean 'divine', 'god'. She finds a complex etymology involving words for 'day', 'noon', 'shine', 'light', 'sky' ('Father Sky') and 'Zeus'. Prynne slips the Latin phrase 'sub divo columine' into the poem (93), which Hopkins glosses as 'beneath the open sky'. The 'divo' indicated an obscure usage, 'as it stood in a religious context and was therefore felt to have some mystic significance. ('Indo-European **Deiwos* and Related Words', *Language Dissertations Published by the Linguistic Society of America* (Supplement to *Language*), XII (1932), pp. 60–1) See Colin Renfrew, *Archaeology and Language: The Puzzle of Indo-European Origins* (London: Johnathan Cape, 1987), 259–60.

39 Nigel Wheale, 'J. H. Prynne', in James Vinson and D. Kirkpatrick, *Contemporary Poets* (London: St James Press, 1985), 774.

40 Trotter, *The Making of the Reader*, 223.

41 Compare Walter Pater, *Marius the Epicurean: His Sensations and Ideas* (London: Macmillan, 1937), 351: 'In the moment of his extreme helplessness their mystic bread had been placed, had descended like a snowflake from the sky, between his lips.'

42 To take some words on rivalry from another context – Christopher Fynsk and Avital Ronell on the concept of the Other in Heidegger's early philosophy – '"The hero and friend may be rivals, but any encouter or any *agon* with them is finally, or also, an encounter with an Other, the Other – call it the spirit of history if you wish.' (Ronell, *The Telephone Book*, 71, drawing on Fynsk's essay 'The Self and Its Witness: On Heidegger's *Being and Time'*, *Boundary* 2, 10, No. 3 (spring 1982).) This may be a point from which a more positive reading of what Prynne means by 'who cares' could be undertaken, but the question is too large to go into in the present chapter.

43 See, for example, Olson's comments in *Additional Prose*, 13.

44 C. O. Sauer, *Land and Life: A Selection from the Writings of Carl Ortwin Sauer* (Berkeley: University of California Press, 1983), 269.

45 W. B. R. King, 'The Pleistocene Epoch in England', *The Quarterly Journal of the Geographical Society*, CXI (1955), p. 207.

5

THE SPIRIT OF POETRY: HEIDEGGER, TRAKL, DERRIDA AND PRYNNE

> The poetic work speaks out of an ambiguous unambiguousness. Yet this multiple ambiguousness of the poetic saying does not scatter in vague equivocations. The ambiguous tone of Trakl's poetry arises out of a gathering, that is, out of a unison which, meant for itself alone, always remains unsayable. The ambiguity of this poetic saying is not lax imprecision, but rather the rigour of him who leaves what is as it is, who has entered into the 'righteous vision' and now submits to it. (Heidegger, 'Language in the Poem' (1953))

So far in this study, I have tried to balance two kinds of disavowal in contemporary British and American poetry. One is fairly straightforward: the tendency to condemn modernist writing after 1940 as pointless and anachronistic, the remains of an elitist experiment long since superseded by what Simon Armitage and Robert Crawford call 'the democratic voice'.[1] The other is more complex and contentious: late modernist writing continues to invest in modernism's esoteric and organicist project of cultural redemption while disavowing its reactionary politics. As far as the first goes, I argued that reports of the death of modernism are based on misconceptions of literary periodisation and an institutional resistance to formal experiment in poetry which has never applied to music and the plastic arts. As for the second, I suggested that late modernism should be seen as a vital link between the high modernist aesthetic and its development into the materialist, critical forms of cultural practice known as postmodernism. My examples, Olson and Prynne, attempt in their different ways to transform Pound's mythic method into a new conception of civic virtue, yet their splenetic critiques of consumerism remain caught up in a nostalgic opposition between the forces of modernity (as technocratic alienation) and nature (as the origin of the human and sacred). In the second half of the twentieth century this residual attachment to the modernist distinction between political economies, which dissolve the true properties of things into exchangeable commodities, and organic cultures, which maintain their practical and symbolic use-value, becomes a pervasive countercultural fantasy of socio-economic relations. This binary opposition between sacred use and secular exchange has little to do with Marxism, with which it is frequently associated, and slips effortlessly into a romantic jeremiad on the loss of spiritual destiny: 'The combined reification and mystification that result from equating nature with use-value are hallmarks of the bourgeois concept.'[2]

Prynne's apparent rejection of use-value as well as exchange-value shows a radical distrust of both Pound's credit economy and Olson's Polis, yet his spiritual attention to what is 'beyond use' threatens to be nothing more than a form of Stoic consolation. Modernity, for Prynne, represents a world in which value inheres exclusively in the circulation of material resources that are used until they are used-up. In the commodity system, the 'immaterial', e.g., love, poetry, death, is shorn of social significance and left to its own devices in the private realm. Community is channelled entirely through the rituals of mimetic desire ('The public / is no more than the sign on the outside of the / shopping-bag; we are what it entails and / we remain its precondition' ('A Gold Ring Called Reluctance', 22–3)) leaving no place for the expression of 'difficult matter' ('The Numbers', 10) except solitary fantasy. When death, for example, means only that a body is worn-out and refused, painful feelings arising from the sense of loss become reduced to a kind of false consciousness, as if they are merely the lingering sentiments of a culture which once exalted the spirit. At such moments, individuals experience loss, but they have no shared ground for expressing negative emotion. That is to say, the erosion of the primitive belief in the soul (the existence of the immaterial) means that they cannot be certain about what they are grieving for. In a later defence of lyric poetry against György Lukacs' claim that it hypostatises the subject as 'the sole carrier of meaning, the only true reality', Prynne argues that 'in the hands of writers with powerful creative intelligence, the calling up of such exclamatory powers in the language of passion is a form of acknowledgement and dialectical holding to the locus of a demanding but possible truth, at least as much as simply the expression of some feeling about a moment particularly stressed by the pressures of experience.' Far from merely representing 'the trailing remnants of a discredited sacral destiny' as 'figments of unregenerate self-isolation' and 'private sentimentalism', the lyric's 'self-conscious and genre-governed shaping of contexts' merge 'public and private modes' to 'locate a dialectic convergence of outward and inward sense'. When properly achieved, its potential to objectify moments of private anguish or joy is anything but a form of subjective resistance to historical reality; but to be achieved, it must be reflexive enough to 'fully admit false consciousness if the moment of stress is to locate the possibility of more true and completed forms of culmination'.[3]

It is not clear to me what Prynne means by these 'more true and completed forms of culmination', but they must entail some process of healing the division in modern society between 'public and private modes' of expression, the overcoming of 'private sentimentalism' by reinstating the spiritual power of 'sacral destiny'. Prynne's own poetry holds out the possibility of such a return to the sacred, but it systematically checks its own 'hope' for redemption, knowing that 'interest' and 'value' all too easily become privatised fantasies of cultural absolution. *Kitchen Poems* and *The White Stones* are full of gnomic, recursive propositions designed to wrong-foot any sentimental appropriation of their 'difficult matter', yet they are haunted by the secular apparitions of sacral destiny:

> So that the dead are a necessity to us,
> keeping our interest from being too much
> about birth. The end is a carpet on
> which we walk: they are our most formal
> pursuit and we have our private matters
> by this allowance.
>
> ('A Gold Ring Called Reluctance', 23)

Who or what are these *revenants*, these discarded remains of consumption which persist in the modern 'age' as 'the dead who sit daily at the feast' (24)? What is the 'spirit' of poetry?

Modernism was always caught up in the problem of what it means to conceptualise the present in relation to the past, and in particular to restitute the occult, *unheimlich* aspect of the spiritual while clinging to the desire for spiritual transcendence. In this chapter I describe Prynne's work as an example of late modernism with the sense that it is late simply in terms of linear time, but late also in the sense of living an afterlife, whether you want to call that condition of the undead sacred or secular, neither-nor, or both-and.

Although they are not typical of Prynne's hermetic writing, some passages in *The White Stones* declare a nostalgic wish to return the self to a moment of ritual 'multeity in unity', as in these lines from 'The Wound, Day and Night':

> I am born back there, the plaintive chanting
> under the Atlantic and the unison of forms.
> It may all flow again if we suppress the
> breaks, as I long to do
>
> ('The Wound, Day and Night', 63)

The possibility of a temporal return to mythic origins, the 'unison of forms', may only be achieved by cancelling historical discontinuity, The poet 'longs' to suppress those conflicts of interest and ideology that make up historical change and subvert the idea of a continuous, monolithic cultural tradition. For the high modernist, when 'temporality' goes unchecked by the timeless imperative of myth or religion, it is merely an hypostatisation of history experienced as endless, meaningless conflict; it has become an an-arche, a falling-off without direction from human and divine origins (which are never so much temporal origins as origins of value). Against this, the spatial unity embodied by myth and ritual offers images of undisturbed and unbroken community. The temporal horizon belongs to what Prynne calls in another poem, 'Frost and Snow, Falling', 'a quality of man and his becoming' meeting 'the divine family of ends'.

Already, Prynne's atavistic leanings appear to coincide with a more orthodox theological insistence. Throughout *The White Stones* Christian themes of pilgrimage, longing, revelation and perfection coincide with the darker rituals of the shamanic journey and are played off against the phenomenological consciousness of limits for which the apprehension of a 'horizon' may mean 'closure' as much as it means the broadening of desire. However, the concept of 'limit' undercuts these Christian themes so that the historical theology to which they attest is foreclosed. To this extent Prynne displays mystic iconology in a way that maximises interpretative pressure: the white stones of the title carry theological reference through allusion to the Book of Revelation. John says: 'To him who conquers I will give some of the hidden manna, and I will give him a white stone with a new name written on the stone which no one knows except him who receives it' (2:17). But the plural 'stones' would appear to have more to do with symbols of loss: the white stones of 'Hansel and Gretel that failed to show them the way home, and the stones of Mandel'shtam's first volume of poetry'.[4] So, because they make iconic certainty indeterminate, these poems work against a strictly typological reading. Prynne constantly plays on the allusiveness of words and themes which can be read as having mystical importance and yet take on other, secular, connotations, so that there is no fixed sense of the loss or gain of the significant. Ultimately, Prynne wants to get rid of 'meaning' altogether, and replace it with a formal significance, which, through the indeterminate contingencies of poetic Saying, moves beyond them to reaffirm a hidden agenda of mystical return. It is in this 'light' that we might regard one of the most obscure poems in *The White Stones*, 'John in the Blooded Phoenix', the title of which both governs and perplexes the response to the textual *bricolage* that follows it:

We could pace in our own fluids, we speak
in celestial parlance, our chemistry is
reduced to transfusion. Who would for-
bid fair Cleopatra smiling/on his poor
soul, for her sweet sake still dying? If
he were he is, the condition of prompt
dilatancy is exactly this: the palest
single spark in all the Pleiades.

('John in the Blooded Phoenix', 119–20)

The title invokes the gnostic *Secret Book of John* as well as the Book of
Revelation, although the figure of the phoenix, with its positive incarnation of 'hope' in the Resurrection, comes from the Old English poem in the
Exeter Book (which has a Hermetic source in Lactantius), a text on which
Prynne comments in 1967 in, 'A Pedantic Note in Two Parts'. He writes
that 'the phoenix is venerated as the icon of Christ and is not superseded
by any crude assumptive fiction under the title of "meaning"'.[5] If the
phoenix *is* venerated as the icon of Christ, it is within the terms of a particular structure of belief, and not because Prynne appears to be emphatic
in wanting an iconic poetry so integrated into the ritual naming sanctioned
by tradition that it escapes the contingencies of interpretation. Unless, that
is, the hermeneutic resides in our being able to *recognise* the figure of the
phoenix as an iconic symbol rather than as merely a metaphor, 'significant'
rather than simply having meaning. Prynne doesn't necessarily accept a
Christian version of reality, as we shall see, but he wants the iconic certainty from which it springs, the literal condition as an article of faith. This
is why his poem both resists and bolsters sacred interpretation. Like many
of Prynne's poems, 'John in the Blooded Phoenix' deals tentatively with
the interiority of somatic experience and mundane personal ritual
('sodium in dreams of all the body / drawn into one transcendent muscle';
'the gas-fire we sit by, the sharp smell of burning / orange-peel.' (119)), and
links these to an ontology based on the vast span of geomorphic change
('The axis of land form runs / through each muted interchange' (119)), and,
inchoately, to a larger mythic realm of ancient summits, omens and side-
real influence. Our actions are always determined by one form of ritual
observance or another, and we are always reaching for the stars, whether
we use this 'celestial parlance' (120) as a handy metaphor or as divine insistence. The two levels coexist because, in the modern age, 'Days are uncertain' (119) and the ambiguities are symptomatic of that fact. The poems
play out these symptoms, maintaining the condition with some degree of
detached irony. Their 'saying' forms the condition of being. Prynne's
essays, on the other hand, tend to be more determinate, privileging the
'concrete' figural level, with its imputed access to the 'true literal', over the

falsely literal abstractions of an empirical rationalism that 'uses' metaphor as a convenient fictional tool for expressing the ordinary. But beyond this, Prynne's writing demands sacred certainty while holding any systematic theology at bay: the phoenix *is* venerated as the icon of Christ, but the emphasis is on the veneration rather than the Christianity. For in 'A Pedantic Note', Prynne reaches back to a literal origin that he clearly regards as being more 'primitive' and more significant than Christianity. This does not mean that he simply rejects the Christian 'myth' upon discovering a more original sacred alternative, but it is as if he wants to say that here is the genuine origin, the ontological point (Being) upon which all ontic determinations (beings), depend, and yet, at the same time, this Being is determined as the true literal, in which case all the subsequent ('newer') determinations are false. Being, properly that which escapes all ontic determination, gets determined as soon as a specific (ontic) point of determination is attributed to it. Whereas we might have said that all ontic determinations of Being are equally true in terms of their temporal *Dasein*, and therefore the Christian icon could take an *is*-form as Prynne says that it does, or the temporally original origin, vouched-for by the philogical method, represents the Being of beings and renders the other manifestations untenable. Prynne's essay equivocates between these two positions, whereas his poetry suggests that both positions may be the case.

'A Pedantic Note in Two Parts' charts the pastoral extent of the runic *wynn* into the constellation 'bliss', 'joy' and 'longing'. The redemptive teleology of Christianity is subjected to a purely diachronic reading of desire and attainment. According to this view, the runic sign 'was the *name* for "bliss"; it was a *proper* name, reaching right across Germania and back before the division of the Indo-European peoples.'[6] Prynne describes this quality of naming as taking us back 'to the sounds of our proper selves'.[7] 'Proper selves' are evinced by the word's archaeology, which includes the tropes of 'paradise' ('"garden of bliss", "field of the (immortal) happy ones", "the elysian fields"') that feature in Old English (OE) Christian poetry, but Prynne is at pains to show that its frame of reference has a specifically literal entailment, which proves the Christian meaning to be an abstraction. 'Wynn', 'winsome', 'bliss', extends by way of 'meadow', 'pasture', to agrarian references including work, getting in the harvest, taking pleasure in the prospect of a harvestable crop, and, according to Prynne, these pastoral images display a fundamental distanciation between nomadic and settled forms of existence, situated in the temporal signifier 'longing':

> The connection suggested here between 'to long for, longing' and 'long, extended on length (of space or time)' is not accidental; it sets out the spatial or historical metaphor, in 'desire' separated by exile from 'fulfilment', as a *literal* component of the land; the ground of being and the dimension of

spiritual travel (hence the recurrent pilgrim-motive in OE exilic or elegiac poems)[8]

In 'Moon Poem', this is translated into the emotional predicament of 'our' modern condition:

> The consequence of this
> pastoral desire is prolonged
> as our condition, but
> I know there is more than the mere wish to
> wander at large, since the wish itself diffuses
> beyond this and will never end: these are songs
> in the night under no affliction, knowing that
> the wish is gift to the
> spirit, is where we may
> dwell

('Moon Poem', 54)

The 'spiritual' invocation would appear to keep the argument in line with Christian redemption, but in fact it denotes a problematic correlation between the materiality of 'pastoral desire' and ontic existence, which arrests Christian determination. If we are in any doubt, Prynne concludes that

> The runic concentration is in each case the power of longing to include its desired end, to traverse the field without moral debate or transcendent abstraction; joy as the complete ground gathered underfoot. Without commitment (before Milton) to the Christian projection into time as redemption, the quality is held by the *extent* between longing and love; desire, wish, and the attainment of paradise.[9]

Prynne uses philology to promote an affirmative Saying of Being, a 'spiritual' quality 'without moral debate or transcendent abstraction'. The 'paradise' of which he writes apparently 'predates' Christian inflection just as an archaic culture founded on runic lore and cyclical (pastoral) cosmogony preceded the linear time perspective of Judaic and Christian historicity. And yet we are not being invited simply to accept the 'magical' stasis of the primitive 'diurnal round' as a radical alternative to the fall into history. On the contrary, Prynne's emphasis on 'extent' and his maintenance of Christian themes as tropes necessitates the temporal condition as the horizon of Being: 'This level sequence of history / is . . . our total'. How, then, is the 'spiritual' not dependent on theological 'abstraction', not imbued with Judaic–Christian redemptive transcendentalism?

Mircea Eliade's classic text of archetypal anthropology *The Myth of the Eternal Return* provides one answer to the tension between spatial and temporal conditions. Eliade claims that archaic societies achieve a state of being, as opposed to the historical condition of 'becoming', through a cyclical or mythical 'time' founded on ritual observance that is 'sacred': 'insofar as an act (or an object) acquires a certain reality through the repetition of certain paradigmatic gestures, and acquires it through that alone, there is an implicit abolition of profane time, of duration, of "history".[10] This *Lebensraum* effectively gives form to chaos, changing it into a cosmogony; the ritualised act allows it to acquire a definite meaning' within the culture that 'in some way participates in the sacred'. Although the ritual cycle takes place in a certain 'time' (e.g., the waxing and waning of the Great Year, in which the symbolised slip into chaos must be continually, formally, restored), its 'paradise of archetypes' signifies the annulment of time itself. But with the coming of a historical time based on Messianism or redemption, Eliade claims, there is a growing anxiety that the eternal repetition of archaic culture traps humanity in a negative space-time. 'History', therefore, begins from the premise that 'earthly' time will be transcended by accession to the heavenly 'beyond' (announced by the trump sounding the end of time). From a Christian perspective, the meaning of history is ahistorical.

Eliade accounts for what he considers to be the unfortunate but necessary demise of the archaic-archetypal by pointing out a dysfunctional aspect of its 'being'. The man of these traditional societies, he says, needs to refuse history and to confine himself to repetition because his thirst for the real involves a 'terror of "losing" himself by letting himself be overwhelmed by the meaninglessness of profane existence'.[11] Anything heterogeneous to the cycle is liable to cause purely negative moments within it that must be overcome by the community. Yet, presumably, the consciousness required to deal with such gaps (or 'chaos') falls out of step with the sublime paradise of the purely repetitious, purely sacred, state of being.

Eliade's theory deconstructs by positing an *a priori* consciousness of historicity within an archetypal or pre-historic world picture. This occurs because, in spite of a romantic allegiance to the idea of an organic and autotelic cultural formation, its '*Dasein*' is based on a theological model of reality. Thus, the dismissal of Heidegger's 'materialist' theory of historicity later in the book comes about because it cannot give credence to *Being and Time*'s foreclosure of redemption. Heidegger's insistence on the structure(s) of temporality itself as the transcendental horizon of Being for beings (which refuses to make time into an entity) destroys both the cyclical ('spatial') archetype of time and the teleological and redemptive 'historical' programme. In Part Two of *The Basic Problems of Phenomenology* he states: '*Time is earlier than any possible earlier* of whatever sort, because it is the basic condition for an earlier as such.'[12] This does not mean that time is ontically the first being, nor that it is eternal and 'timeless'. As such, the German word for 'history', *Geschichte*, is reduced to its derivation from the verb *geschehen*, which means simply to occur, to happen. The consequence for Eliade's thesis is to rule out the properly sacred determination of time-as-space that it supports. Unless one accepts a rigorously anthropological point of view in which the sacred emerges as the result of particular ideological structures and which cannot therefore be claimed to represent transcendent truth. And Eliade does not accept this.

In Prynne's case, the response to the archaic (or the originary) and to Heidegger's place in the argument is more complex. In 'A Pedantic Note', Prynne endorses the ritual, 'magical', canny (the occult past is our 'home'), and originary designation of pre-Christian culture, except that he finds it to be compatible with, and not antithetical to, Heidegger's temporal horizon. The primary significance of 'wynn' is its linguistic subversion of 'history'; it discloses that the 'winsome land' refers to the *Dasein* of a territory 'bounded' or 'enclosed' by a temporality signifying *no more than* the radical time of what Heidegger calls the 'ecstatic' horizon (ek-stasis).[13] This is to say that the spiritual essence of any place or state of being derives from its significant coming into presence for those beings who recognise the diachronic underpinnings of their earthly condition (e.g., the clerisy of poet-philologists). For Prynne this means through the act of intellection, as his concluding quotation from Blake's *A Vision of the Last Judgement* makes clear: 'Men are admitted into Heaven not because they have curbed & govern'd their Passions or have no Passions, but because they have Cultivated their Understandings. The Treasures of Heaven are not Negations of Passion, but Realities of Intellect, from which all the Passions Emanate Uncurbed in their Eternal Glory.'[14] The word 'cultivate' has a special resonance in this context, for it binds 'culture' to the pastoral (and temporal) imperative of 'working the land' and 'traversing the field' that Prynne finds crucial to the etymology of 'wynn' (and which he also finds crucial to identifying the select group of 'pastoral' poets who keep alive the promise of home).

The idea of a 'Heaven on earth', of building Jerusalem in England's green and pleasant land, appears as a straightforward answer to the problem of why Prynne maintains Christian tropes as appropriate fictions. Certainly, it makes sense in terms of the poem 'The Holy City', where although 'Where we go is a loved side of the temple, / a place for repose, a concrete path', which 'you could call . . . Ierusalem', paradoxically 'There's no mystic moment involved' (43). But to see this as a conclusion would be to glide over the larger question of how spiritual qualities can be claimed to have relevance in a demystified universe. 'The poem incorporates this fact in its careful placing of the word 'could' ('you *could* call it Ierusalem'), which introduces a 'suspension of belief' into the pastoral meditation. Therefore, the problem centres on what it means to subvert a set of theological presuppositions while at the same time retaining their language in the name of an 'alternative' described as being both *not* sacred and *yet* sacred. While 'The Holy City' denies mystic involvement, other poems affirm it: the deferred promise of the Holy City is what Prynne terms a 'divine insistence' ('Aristeas, in Seven Years', 89), so that 'we must / have the divine sense' ('Just So', 59).

The notion of 'spirit' has often been used in broadly secular contexts ('fighting spirit', 'the spirit of place', 'the spirit of a nation', and so forth). But the words 'divine' and 'holy' have no such ambiguity unless they are placed ironically within archaic culture, which offers the ritual cycle as site of the 'sacred' against the 'corrupt' linearity of Christian history. Even so, the spiritual itself can never be divested of 'the semantics which regulates the use of this term', as Jacques Derrida puts it in *Of Spirit: Heidegger and the Question*, which shows how pervasive (or ghostly) its theological meaning remains in Heidegger's thought.[15] And this brings us back to the connection between Heideggerian 'destruction' and Prynne's philology. For Heidegger constantly invokes the spiritual in his texts (especially the later essays on *Dichtung* in Hölderlin, Rilke and Trakl) and, like Prynne, he claims to have undercut Christian (and Platonic) appropriations of the term by returning to a prior or original temporality: 'In its most proper essence, as the poet and thinker allow it to be approached, *Geist is neither* Christian *Geistlichkeit* nor Platonic-metaphysical *Geistigkeit*.[16]

According to Derrida, Heidegger is most forthcoming on the 'real origin' of spirit in his 1953 essay on Trakl. In his poetry, Trakl locates the meaning of spirit in 'flame', that which 'inflames', 'flares up', in an act that gives birth to the traditional concept of the informing *pneuma* or breath (as in 'respiration', 'inspiration'; Heidegger presumably has in mind the physical fact of air deriving from fire). Because flame itself simply in-flames, spontaneously combusts in an act of what Heidegger calls 'auto-affective spontaneity', which 'has need of no exteriority to catch fire or set fire, to pass ecstatically outside itself', it gives to '*Geist*' a 'thrownness' (through the cognate *gheis*) that is ontologically prior to the breath of Platonic and Christian spirituality. 'It is because *Geist* is flame that there is *pneuma* and *spiritus*.'[17]

Derrida's point is that Heidegger transfers the 'original' meaning from the Greek or Latin to the German language. Rather than belonging to some state of philological and ontological neutrality, the concept of the origin is dependent on the politics of the *Geschlecht* ('race'). As Edward Said notes, 'It is too often forgotten that modern Western philology, which begins in the early nineteenth century, undertook to reverse commonly accepted ideas about language and its divine origins. That revision tried first to determine which was the first language and then, failing to achieve that ambition, proceeded thereafter to reduce language to specific circumstances: language-groups, historical and racial theories, geographical and anthropological theses.'[18] The arcane pursuit of etymological value arises as a justification for, as well as a sublimation of, crude beliefs in national, racial and sexual superiority. Imagined nostalgia for a displaced ritual hegemony conforms to this order, as the primitivism of Yeats, Eliot, Pound and Olson – and Prynne – confirms. Furthermore, the case of Eliot shows that the Christian tradition is perfectly capable of fitting in with such a scheme, for it is as if that spirit could maintain itself through all the overdeterminations and revisions carried out in the *epoché* of its name.

Marking the origin of the transcendent, but without embracing the theology it fans into being, the flame of the Trakl essay leads on to a reappraisal of the archaic and cyclical 'closure' of time. Essentially, as in Prynne's essay, we are dealing with the cultural programme of defining and returning to our 'proper home', in a neat dovetailing of Indo-European linguistic origins with the philosophy and poetics of temporality. In *Kitchen Poems*, Prynne had poured scorn on 'those sickening and / greasy sureties' of home ('Numbers in Time of Trouble', 17–18). This is a moment of pure spleen directed against the consumer society, which wants 'home' to be something that can be attained by mere material purchase, whereas Prynne regards home as something that may be attained only through the most rigorous intellectual and spiritual work. And in 'Thoughts on the Esterházy Court Uniform'

> home is easily our
> idea of it, the music of decent and proper
> order, it's this we must leave in some quite
> specific place if we are not to carry it
> everywhere with us.
>
> ('Thoughts on the Esterházy Court Uniform', 98)

Prynne infers that there is something irreducibly nomadic about being-in-the-world, and if we are ever to feel 'at home' in the world we must accept the paradox that the *heimlich* is also the *umheimlich*. In that case the 'proper' can never be 'our place'. On the other hand, 'A Pedantic Note' is clearly an attempt to 'take us back, to the sounds of our proper selves'.[19] In *The White Stones*, too, 'return' acts as both theme and figure, pre-figured by the 'archaicism' of Heidegger's 'listening' to romantic *Dichtung*. The constellation of signifiers around 'spirit' drawn attention to by Derrida are of considerable relevance here. For Heidegger, the poet speaks momentously of a 'fire of heaven': 'Hölderlin is he who has been struck by the God of light. "He is," says Heidegger, "on the return path (*auf der Rühkehr*) from his walk towards the fire" . . . We are always dealing with a thought not of the circle but of the return, of a turning of the *Rühkehr* towards the home (*Heimat, heimisch, "nemlich zu Hauss"*). It belongs to the essence of spirit that it only *is* properly (*eigentlich*) if it is close to itself'.[20] In spite of its standing outside the subject, spirit conforms to the property of a certain self-identity, an auto-erotism. As flame, thrownness, return, it corresponds to the category, now familiar in Derrida's work, of the transcendental sig-nified, desiring (in a moment of blind anthropomorphism) its own Being beyond any supplement or trace of difference. This is perhaps why it is necessary for Heidegger to return to the myth of return: spirit, as the spirit of man, comes close to Eliade's 'man of traditional societies' whose terror of losing himself 'dooms' him to the indefinite repetition of archetypes. The stage is already set for historical salvation, requiring an additional spirit, one that would not be proper to itself but would 'be' ineffably and unspeakably other. This sublimation, far removed from ontophenomeno-logical principles (for which it is the world itself that is transcendent), inaugurates the negative moment of mysticism, the fall into history Eliade regards as necessary, and the point from which Heidegger and Prynne draw back while 'presenting' in spite of themselves.

The constituent terms of Heidegger's return come from Trakl's use of *Geist*. If we translate this 'spirit' into its secular form of 'ghost', the *unheim-lich* resonance of return as a 'haunting' becomes apparent. A line from Trakl's *Frühling der Seele* becomes the starting point for Heidegger's read-ing against the grain of Platonic and Christian exegetical traditions: 'Yes, the soul is a stranger upon the earth.' Heidegger's interpretation, in which the soul as 'stranger' 'does not signify that one must take it to be impris-oned, exiled, tumbled into the terrestrial here below, fallen into a body doomed to the corruption . . . of what is lacking in Being and in truth is not' involves an inversion of meaning in terms of this generally accepted Pla-tonic inference: instead of being a stranger on the earth, the soul is 'prop-erly', that is, from the German philology of the word *fram*, on the way *towards* earth as a destination. 'The soul is a stranger because it does not yet inhabit the earth – rather as the word 'fremd' is strange because its meaning does not yet inhabit, because it no longer inhabits, its proper . . . place.'[21] Moving through related poems by Trakl, Heidegger comes to the formulation that the soul's spiritual journey follows the course of the year and even the day as a return from night to morning in the diurnal sense, rather than through a linear and finite movement corresponding to meta-physico-Christian 'decadence'. The stranger does not plunge towards death but is already in the position of being estranged, solitary, de-ceased, and by dint of this already-deadness his condition is one of in-nateness, of what is as yet un-born. The connotation is of a kind of 'haunting' (Derrida uses the word '*revenant*'), by which we can assume 'the coming and going of this dead man as a coming back [*revenir*], from night to dawn, and finally as the returning [*revenir*] of a spirit'.[22] Death comes before birth, the end precedes the beginning, and thus we arrive at a more originary account of time. But this essence is veiled by the Aristotelian *representation* of time, which depends on the notion of succession.

My reading here is that Heidegger gives a positive value to the 'ghostliness' implied in the idea of spirit; the 'haunting' is not intended to have anything *unheimlich* about it, it stands as an affirmation of Home, of 'coming home', a reversion from the speculative metaphysics of Platonism and Christianity to the mythical time of the diurnal sequence. In sharp contrast to the negativity signified by movement towards a single, extinguishing night, the crepuscular becomes (already) a path towards the matutinal and vernal, its joy culminating in Trakl's 'Springtime of the Soul'. As Prynne writes in 'A Pedantic Note', it is 'joy as the complete ground gathered underfoot.'[23]

However, as I have suggested, Prynne does not accept the notion of a return to mythical time without reservation. The poem 'Thoughts on the Esterházy Court Uniform' represents his most protracted meditation on the subject of return. The preoccupation with linguistic origins is what motivates Prynne's poetic argument and not some discreetly psychological impulse, although the effect of 'wanting to know' produced by the text comes about as the result of this linguistic insistence being combined with Prynne's characteristically personal and didactic tone:

> *Again* is the sacred
> word, the profane sequence suddenly, graced, by
> coming back. More & more as we go deeper
> I realise this aspect of hope, in the sense of
> the future cashed in, the letter returned to sender.
> ('Thoughts on the Esterházy Court Uniform', 98)

The stress on 'again' is there to bring attention to the word's linguistic 'turn' in that the reader is made aware of its meaning to 'repeat' and 'return'. Signifying the sacred time of the cosmological cycle, which in Prynne's lexicon links it to 'hope', it nevertheless cannot be separated from another aspect, that of the *speculative*: to 'come back' means also 'to profit' (a gain), which also refers to the spiritual 'gain' of 'rebirth'. Here indeed is hope, whether we prefer to think of it in terms of re-cycling or an afterlife. And yet, as soon as Prynne has reached this point, as soon as he has 'gone deeper', he is presented with a 'significance' that is thoroughly profane, and which quickly checks the positive gleam of hope: gain *is* profit, in the secular sense, and 'cashes in' the future. If there appears to be some equivocation over accepting a Christian or archaic interpretation of the cosmos, the real problem lies in the impossibility of reclaiming a sacred and spiritual warmth from the iniquities of capital (or 'materialist' culture in general) when the language we use cannot help but have become secularised. We cannot easily rely on philology to extract the ore of sacred meaning from the *scoriae* of current parlance. The words we use in sequence are lodged between 'heaven' and 'earth', and the hope we entertain is that some interpretative *communitas* may make sacred meanings inhere, 'we' being the projection of Prynne's own hope. If we long to return to the sacred, we must recognize *loss* as a constituent part of that dream, 'Since each time what / we have is increasingly the recall, not / the subject to which we come' (98).

Temporality, then, is the condition of the sacred, even though it is thought to reserve itself as an unspeakable 'entity' ('the subject', death 'itself'). But this must entail a belief in the pejorative slide from sacred to profane, for the poem does not merely speak of a division between the idea of death or the memory of loss and the 'thing itself'. What we have is *increasingly* the recall, so that correspondingly there must be a falling-off from the original sense. If the notion of falling were not there, there would be no way of making a distinction between sacred meaning as a primary quality and profane meaning as the secondary, debased form of experience that the poem presupposes in its very use of these words. For what is profanity if not that which literally lies outside the temple, the ritually unclean and common? As Derrida says of Heidegger's maintenance of the *geistlich*, it can never be divested of the semantics which regulates the use of the term. Even though the poem will question our easy observances of these words, it never loses its grip on the quest to reinstate them as durable qualities, following the Heideggerian project of 'destruction' that attempts to clear away metaphysical abstractions from supposedly original properties.

Prynne's ambiguity' is actually a more rigorous and belated exploration of the problem of image and time found in Basil Bunting's *Briggflatts*, which, as Andrew Lawson writes, 'is a poem that revises its own tropes. The moment of fullness and restoration at the close of *Briggflatts* is a knowing conceit that admits its provisional nature.'[24] This is why in 'Thoughts on the Esterházy Court Uniform' Prynne draws on the musical analogue that is a constituent part of Bunting's poetic:

> I walk on up the hill, in the warm
> sun and we do not return, the place is
> entirely musical.
>
> ('Thoughts on the Esterházy Court Uniform', 97)

The musical idiom used by Bunting supposedly transcends the barren instrumentality of ordinary language. Indeed music, according to J. Hillis Miller, is 'the very model of the use of time to transcend time. It proceeds by repetition, with variation, echo, reverberation. Music constantly circles back on itself. Its aim is not to go in a straight line, from place to place, but to achieve the most complete exploration of its primitive germ. The listener is diffused throughout the musical space and copresent to all parts of it at once, and all these parts interpenetrate one another in the closest intimacy.'[25] At the beginning of 'Thoughts', the abstraction of the musical conceit is immediately confronted as to its promise of universal harmony: *I walk on up the hill and we do not return*. For Prynne, to begin any phenomenological journey is to refuse to leap to bland assumptions about the *polis*. That his texts so often go on to dictate the terms of assimilating 'who we are' is an indication of the mandarin impulse supporting this quest, the point being that it is the profane, the 'uninitiated', who jump to conclusions about public identity, as opposed to the clerisy of interpreters of the world who can seriously claim to speak for 'us'. Thus the poem can shift in this way from one position to another with startling rapidity:

> I refer directly to my
> own need, since to advance in the now fresh &
> sprouting world must take on some musical
> sense. Literally, the grace & hesitation of
> modal descent, the rhyme unbearable, the
> coming down through the prepared delay and
> once again we are there, beholding the
> complete elation of our end.

> ('Thoughts on the Esterházy Court Uniform', 97)

The 'musical sense' is a necessity, and yet 'rhyme' is described as being 'unbearable'. Not to be borne, perhaps, because the 'dying fall' signifies the 'complete *elation* of our end' in a neat inversion of the adage that 'what goes up must come down': falling, or 'coming down', leads to a kind of joy, a 'lifting-up of the spirits' that counters the emotional 'resonance' of 'dying'. As a result, the text complicates empirical experience by displacing it into the variety of rhetorical gestures centred on it, and holds these to their 'face' value. The chiasmic movement forms the ground from which a certain revaluation of experience may be achieved. As soon as the reader of the poem has registered the 'elation of our end', it is described as 'that same loss', so that 'joy' and 'loss' no longer carry the stability of the emotive meanings conventionally attached to them. The crucial sense of loss becomes the starting point for appropriation by the aesthetic: 'my life slips into music', 'The end cadence deferred like breathing, the / birthplace of the poet'. The following lines draw attention to the poem's gnomic title: 'all put out their lights / and take their instruments away with them' refers to Haydn's time at the Esterháza Court, when he composed the 'Farewell' symphony, with its gradual bowing-out of the players in the final movement (each blowing out a candle before leaving), as a polite way of freeing his company from the over-extended patronage of Prince Esterházy.[26] If these lines are to some extent reminiscent of Eliot's 'they all go into the dark' from *East Coker*, the more arresting and ironic sense is not only that of the musicians' 'having their lights put out', but of the origin of the metaphor 'bowing-out' for dying. Likewise, the poem's concluding lines will play on vernacular metaphors in order to 'bring home the pastoral aptness of its topography: 'We think we have / it & we must, for the sacred resides in this; / once more falling into the hour of my birth, going / down the hill and then in at the back door.' If death is a matter of decline, of 'going downhill', then the rebirth figured by the detour of rhetoric takes us 'in at the back door', as if to say that spiritual rebirth must be approached by way of conceits or ruses (albeit ones that are taken very seriously by the poet).

Following the near-pathos of the 'farewell', the poem poses its central question:

How can we sustain such constant loss.
I ask myself this, knowing that the world
is my pretext for this return through it, and
that we go more slowly as we come back
more often to the feeling that rejoins the whole.
('Thoughts on the Esterházy Court Uniform', 98)

It is easy to slip from the 'question' itself to the avowal of self-knowledge that comes after it. However, the 'asking' has been forestalled – the lack of a question mark alone testifies to this, but, more importantly, the syntactic position of the word 'sustain' makes the sentence ambiguous. The text goes a step further than diffusing the traditional pathos of 'loss' by keeping it unclear as to whether it is something 'we' must 'hold out under' or something we would wish to prolong. In other words, does 'sustenance' consist in enduring loss, or in indulging in it? The poem's notion of loss does not elicit pathos, but destroys it in an act of sovereignty that takes the poem to the limits of available sense. Even so, 'soon one would live in a sovereign point and / *still* we don't return, not really, we look back / and our motives have more courage in / structure than in what we take them to be' (98). If 'the world converges on the idea / of return', if it 'is my pretext for this return through it', the motives that would have the 'self' rejoin 'the whole' in some kind of organic consummation are at least suspect; further than that, they may be self-deceptive. Instead, the world converges to 'our unspeakable loss; we make / sacred what we cannot see without coming / back to where we were' (98). Whatever it is we make sacred, it remains invisible until it is sanctified by ritual; as in an earlier poem in the collection, 'First Notes on Daylight', 'we carry ourselves by ritual / observance, even sleeping in the library' (68). But it is not enough to affirm the "'ceremonial use of the things described'" (68), however arcane they may be.[27] Because ritual depends on being able to 'recall' and repeat, it is inevitably caught up in the entropic memorialising process that makes hope into little more than a doomed attempt to resist death (the proper emerging as a 'prop'), and thus the future is merely 'cashed in':

> Our chief
> loss is ourselves; that's where I am, the
> sacral link in a profane world, we each do
> this by the pantheon of hallowed times.
> Our music the past tense
>
> ('Thoughts on the Esterházy Court Uniform', 98)

This 'personal loss' is a constituent part of all the manifestations of the self Prynne describes in *The White Stones*. Through the pastoral ontology of 'A Pedantic Note', we can see how it has been included in the notion of 'extension':

> How
> to extend, anyway to decline the rhetoric
> of *occasion*, by which the sequence back
> from some end is clearly predictive. We
> owe that in theory to the history of person
> as an entire condition of landscape – *that*
> kind of extension, for a start.
>
> ('First Notes on Daylight', 68)

The 'field is more extended than the garden, since it *includes* the whole range of love, desire, the pursuit of happiness; it is the nomadic or excursive condition of *longing* fulfilled and completed . . . it sets out the spatial & historic metaphor, in "desire" separated by exile from "fulfilment", as a *literal* component of the land; the ground of being and the dimension of spiritual travel'.[28] Extension requires an approach to the world that is less comfortable, less 'contained' than the habit of the occasional; that regaining a true home entails a certain nomadism in its reaching out means that the loss is necessarily exilic, the flame of desire and estrangement: 'That this could / really be so & of use is my present politics, / burning like smoke, before the setting of fire' (69).

Prynne invokes the OE *Wanderer* as an archetype of the spiritual traveller, but he is also indebted to the poetics of Trakl's 'stranger', who must leave in order to be born into the world. Prynne states in his 1971 lecture on Charles Olson:

> There was that unbelievable close photograph of the earth taken across the surface of the moon, which is now in all the soap ads, which was supposedly the first picture of earth as home . . . We have to go to the exactness and

completeness of poetry to tell us what such a condition of home would be like. *And if you want it in its largest sense, you have to go to the largest distance from it in order to come right back round to take it in at one sweep.*[29]

In 'Thoughts on the Esterházy Court Uniform', if music

> would only
> level out into some complete migration of
> sound. I could then leave unnoticed, bring nothing
> with me, allow the world free of its displace-
> ment. Then I myself would be the
> complete stranger, not watching jealously
> over names. And yet home is easily our
> idea of it, the music of decent and proper
> order, it's this we must leave in some quite
> specific place if we are not to carry it
> everywhere with us.
>
> ('Thoughts on the Esterházy Court Uniform', 98)

Leaving in order to return – the logic is almost ridiculously simple, and yet for Prynne the proposition carries an enormous weight of metaphysical baggage in need of de-struction. The extent of the paradox is great, entailing the neither/nor resolution that one reject both the proper idea of home and a permanent exile. But only so that an inexplicable 'proper proper' may be reached.

> I know I will go back
> down & that it will not be the same though
> I shall be sure it is so. And I shall be even
> deeper by rhyme and cadence, more held
> to what isn't mine.
>
> ('Thoughts on the Esterházy Court Uniform', 99)

Thus, living in a state of misrecognition, the subject radically displaced by the word 'free of its displace- / ment' and by language, allows the text to reaffirm its aesthetic and ethical categories. The 'music of decent and proper order' has been rejected, leaving it the property of the im-proper:

> Music is truly the
> sound of our time, since it is how we most
> deeply recognize the home we may not
> have: the loss is trust and you could
> reverse that without change.
>
> ('Thoughts on the Esterházy Court Uniform', 99)

'We' gain the recognition, trusting in the tricks of naming and the paradox of loss 'itself' (reversal) in a total expenditure of the self, 'without change'. Through this 'clearing' the poem as *Dichtung* claims its transcendental moment, one in which 'again' comes back to gainfulness without cashing-in the future:

> With such
> patience maybe we can listen to the rain
> without always thinking about rain, we
> trifle with rhyme and again is the
> sound of immortality. We think we have
> it & we must, for the sacred resides in this
>> ('Thoughts on the Esterházy Court Uniform', 99)

The upshot is that we get a sense of 'the true / limit to *size*' ('First Notes on Daylight', 68); we are 'small / in the rain' ('The Numbers', 10), but can move beyond such restriction through the intellect and imagination.

Prynne's poetic, then, remains true to the Poundian spirit even through its deflation of Pound's politics of the ego, aiming to provide that 'sudden sense of liberation' from time and space limits. But Prynne's rhetorical strategy is only coherent if the reader is willing to accept its presumed relation to the real, and if the 'facts of death and insufferable loss' which remain fixed and finally insurmountable in *Briggflatts* can be made amenable to a process of supersession in this way. Certainly, Prynne challenges the pathos that has come to be attached to these apprehensions, both as concepts and 'experiences', but the mystical 'redemption' claimed by the poem threatens this project by its Heideggerian reinscription of the 'sacred' and 'spiritual'. Prynne's text is true to the 'no ascertainable result', where even loss (itself) is questionable, and the certainties of faith cannot be reclaimed even through inverse pressure. Immanently, the baffling play on 'property' and 'home' ruins even the philological links it lays claim to in terms of a 'sacral convergence' without a 'mystic moment':

> it really is dark and the knowledge
> of the unseen is a warmth which spreads into
> the level ceremony of diffusion . . .

>> the wish is gift to the
>> spirit, is where we may
>> dwell

>>> ('Moon Poem', 53–4)

>> the sound
>> in a great arc for the
> world, it is an open fire, a hearth
> stone for the condition of trust . . .

>> love in the air
> we breathe. Fire on the hearth.

>>> ('Just So', 59–60)

> The street that is the
> sequence of man
> is the light of his
> most familiar need,
> to love without being stopped for some im-
> mediate bargain, to be warm and tired
> without some impossible flame in the heart.
>
> ('The Common Gain, Reverted', 88)

The Heideggerian prescription that spirit 'is *flame*' appears to be maintained by many of these poems, where it is attached to the soul and to declarations of universal love. Yet their sequence shows that it too, as origin and property, cannot remain free from scrutiny. The passage from 'The Common Gain, Reverted' quoted above destroys any promise of access to the transcendental, not simply as the secular myth of a 'real' bargain (stressed by the line-break in 'im- / mediate'), but by substituting the literal and limited 'warm and tired' for the trope 'flame in the heart'. Spirit, here, is revealed 'again' as being hopelessly mediated, in the gap between language and the real, and as a concept that cannot be wrested from the actual flame of consumerism. Unlike T. S. Eliot, who could not see that the drive to mythic order was already a constituent of the capitalist dissociation of sensibility and not an alternative to it, Prynne is aware that a poetic of mythic synchronicities without complication will only buy into the rhetoric of the market and the advertising executive.

Notes

1 Simon Armitage and Robert Crawford, 'Introduction: The Democratic Voice', in *The Penguin Book of Poetry from Britain and Ireland Since 1945* (London: Penguin, 1998). See Anthony Mellors and Robert Smith, 'Call for Papers', in *Poets on the Verge. Angelaki: Journal of the Theoretical Humanities*, Vol. 5, No. 1 (April 2000), pp. 5–7.

2 Neil Smith, *Uneven Development: Nature, Capital, and the Production of Space* (Oxford: Basil Blackwell, 1984), 27. Marx's mature economic theory critiques the 'ideology of nature': 'One and the same relation appears sometimes in the form of use-value and sometimes in that of exchange-value, but at different stages and with a different meaning. To use is to consume, whether for production or consumption. Exchange is the mediation of this act through a social process. Use can be posited as, and be, a mere consequence of exchange; then again, exchange can appear as merely a moment of use, etc.' (*Grundrisse: Foundations of the Critique of Political Economy*. Trans. Martin Nicolaus (Harmondsworth: Penguin, 1973), 647.)

3 Prynne, 'English Poetry and Emphatical Language', *Proceedings of the British Academy*, Vol. LXXIV (1988), pp. 139; 149–50; 167; 169.

4 Werner Hamacher, 'The Second of Inversion: Movements of a Figure through Celan's Poetry', *Yale French Studies*, No. 69: *The Lesson of Paul de Man*, p. 306.

5 Prynne, 'A Pedantic Note in Two Parts', p. 350. See Albert Stamborough Cook, ed., *The Old English* Elene, Phoenix, *and Physiologus* (New Haven: Yale University Press, 1919), xlivff.

6   Prynne, 'A Pedantic Note in Two Parts', p. 346.
7   Prynne, 'A Pedantic Note in Two Parts', p. 348.
8   Prynne, 'A Pedantic Note in Two Parts', p. 350.
9   Prynne, 'A Pedantic Note in Two Parts', p. 351.
10 Eliade, *The Myth of the Eternal Return*, 35.
11 Eliade, *The Myth of the Eternal Return*, 91–2.
12 Martin Heidegger, *The Basic Problems of Phenomenology*. Trans. Alfred Hofstadter. (Bloomington: Indiana University Press, 1982), 325.
13 See Heidegger, *The Basic Problems of Phenomenology*, 266–267 and 299–300. Ontic being, in the sense of the 'self', is not immanent, but transcendent – it is always already constituted by its being-in-the-world, outside itself. To this extent, its structure is that of a 'stepping-beyond' the classical determinations of subject and object: 'This transcending does not only and not primarily mean a self-relating of a subject to an object; rather, transcendence means *to understand oneself from a world* . . . The *selfhood* of the Dasein *is founded on its transcendence*, and the Dasein is not first an ego-self which then oversteps something or other. The "towards-itself" and the "out-from-itself" are implicit in the concept of selfhood.'(Heidegger, *The Basic Problems of Phenomenology*, 299–300.) Earlier, Heidegger has written: 'The essence of the future lies in *coming-toward-oneself*; that of the past [having-been-ness] lies in *going-back-to*; and that of the present in *staying-with*, *dwelling-with*, that is, being-with. These characters of the *toward*, *back-to*, *with* reveal the basic constitution of temporality . . . Temporality as union of future, past, and present does not carry the Dasein away just at times and occasionally; instead, as *temporality*, it is itself the *original outside-itself*, the ekstatikon . . . future is carried away intrinsically as toward – it is ecstatic. The same holds for past and present' (266–7). As Herbert Spiegelberg explains, this futural aspect is linked to the idea of hermeneutics, which 'as Heidegger now uses the term [in *Being and Time*] . . . no longer refers to documents or symbolic expressions, but to non-symbolic facts of the real world, to human being or *Dasein*.' (*The Phenomenological Movement: An Historical Introduction* (The Hague: Martinus Nijhoff, 1969), Vol. 1, 324.) Such 'facts' are apprehended in their reaching-out toward what is 'at stake' for the *Dasein*: 'Thus every interpretation of ordinary items in daily life is related to a frame of relevance (*Bewandtnisganzheit*) which embraces it (*Vorhabe*), implies a preview (*Vorsicht*) looking toward anticipated meanings, and requires conceptual patterns for it (*Vorgriff*).' Although interpretation is not free from presuppositions, Heidegger maintains that 'the anticipations of hermeneutic interpretation are not determined by chance ideas or popular conceptions but by the "things themselves."' (*The Basic Problems of Phenomenology*, 324.) Prynne's use of 'hope' and 'extent' are perhaps best understood at this point as versions of the radical 'toward'.
    Heidegger's analysis provides one key to the question of the self in Objectivist poetics. Heidegger writes that 'The *Dasein* does not need a special kind of observation, nor does it need to conduct a sort of espionage on the ego in order to have the self; rather, as the *Dasein* gives itself over immediately and passionately to the world itself, its own self is reflected to it from things. This is not mysticism and does not presuppose the assigning of soul to things.' (Quoted in Ronell, *The Telephone Book*, 431.) 'No ideas but in things', William Carlos Williams wrote (in *Spring & All*, 1923); with the density of *Dasein*'s objective reflection of 'its own self', Olson's self-ish 'proprioception' and 'objectism' is played out.
14 Prynne, 'A Pedantic Note in Two Parts', p. 351.
15 Jacques Derrida, *Of Spirit: Heidegger and the Question*. Trans. Geoff Bennington and Rachel Bowlby (Chicago: University of Chicago Press, 1987), 55. Because Derrida's

argument proceeds by way of a careful translation (or negotiation) of Heidegger's German, I cannot claim to do more than provide a schematic account of the 'logic' guiding the tropes with which it deals. Derrida writes of being unable 'to translate these words without lengthy formalities', and that in any case 'Nothing is more foreign to Heidegger than commentary in its ordinary sense . . . Heidegger's statements let themselves be *carried, conducted, initiated* here by lines of Trakl's which they seem in turn to *precede* or *attract*, guide in their turn'(85). Without similar 'lengthy formalities', the material culled from Derrida will remain somewhat thematic, but the purpose is to show that Prynne's thinking, like that of Heidegger, contains vestiges of the Christian teleology he attempts to overcome by a return to 'origins', and not to read Prynne exclusively through Heidegger. See also J. Hillis Miller's remarks in *Topographies* (Stanford: Stanford University Press, 1995), esp. 220.

16 Derrida, *Of Spirit*, 96.

17 Derrida, *Of Spirit*, 97.

18 Said, 'The World, the Text, and the Critic', in Harari, ed., *Textual Strategies*, 179. In *Orientalism*, Said writes that philology 'embodies a peculiar condition of being modern and European, since neither of those two categories has true meaning without being related to an earlier alien culture and time. What Nietzsche also sees is philology as something *born, made* in the Viconian sense as a sign of human enterprise, created as a category of human discovery, self-discovery, and originality. Philology is a way of historically setting oneself off, as great artists do, from one's time and an immediate past even as, paradoxically and antinomically, one actually characterizes one's modernity in so doing' (132). See Prynne's 'A Letter to Andrew Duncan', *The Grosseteste Review*, Vol. 15 (1983–84), p. 111: 'In the matter of the defensive historicism of philology in his day Nietzsche alleged as a paradox . . . "Dies ist die Antinomie der Philologie: man hat das *Altertum* tatsächlich immer nur *aus der Gegenwart* verstanden – und soll nun die *Gegenwart aus dem Altertum* verstehen?" ("Wir Philologen").'

19 Prynne, 'A Pedantic Note in Two Parts', p. 348.

20 Derrida, *Of Spirit*, 96.

21 Derrida, *Of Spirit*, 87; 88.

22 Derrida, *Of Spirit*, 91; see also note 39 of Derrida's *Spectres of Marx: The State of the Debt, the Work of Mourning, and the New International*. Trans. Peggy Kamuf (London: Routledge, 1994), 196: 'Given that a *revenant* is always called upon to come and to come back, the thinking of the spectre, contrary to what good sense leads us to believe, signals toward the future. It is the thinking of the past, a legacy that can only come from that which has not yet arrived – from the *arrivant* itself.'

23 Prynne, 'A Pedantic Note in Two Parts', 351. Prynne' exploits the philology of 'Day' in a set of small volumes of lyrics that comprises a 'diurnal sequence': *Day Light Songs* (Pampisford: R. Books, 1968); *Fire Lizard* (Barnet: Blacksuede Boot Press, 1970); *A Night Square* (London: Albion Village Press, 1971); *Into the Day* (Cambridge: privately printed, 1972); *Vernal Aspects* (*The Grosseteste Review*, Vol. 10, 1–4 (summer 1977), pp. 37–40).

24 Andrew Lawson, 'Basil Bunting and English Modernism', *Sagetrieb*, Vol. 9:1/2 (spring and fall, 1990), p. 118.

25 Quoted in Charles Tomlinson, 'Experience into Music: The Poetry of Basil Bunting', *Agenda*, Vol. 4, Nos. 5–6 (1996), pp. 11–16; see Lawson, 'Basil Bunting and English Modernism', pp. 115–16.

26 The anecdote is recounted in Karl Geiringer, *Haydn: A Creative Life in Music* (Berkeley: University of California Press, 1983), 44–5.

27 '"The ceremonial use of the things described", / the *cinar* trees or the white-metal mirror, forms / of patience, oh yes, and each time I even / move, the strophic muscular pattern is *use*, in / no other sense. The common world, how far we / go, the practical limits of daylight. And as I / even think of the base-line the vibration is / strong, the whole sequence of person as his / own history is no *more* than ceremonial' ('First Notes on Daylight', 68–9).

In *The Making of the Reader*, David Trotter writes of this passage, 'Ritual observance would seem to be the answer to our problems. But it is not proposed glibly. Prynne knows how exotic the "ceremonial use" he refers to must appear, how remote from our common world; rather, he knows how powerful the conviction must be – "forms of patience, oh yes, and each time I . . ." – which would pull ceremony and world together.' Furthermore, on a lighter note, '(One can imagine Larkin endorsing the emphasis on ceremony, but not the white-metal mirror and the trees with a funny name.)' (222–3). Although I agree with Trotter that Prynne is searching for forms of mythic affirmation, which are by definition ritualistic, and that the problem of conviction is crucial to this affirmation, my own reading suggests that these texts are much more de-structive and circumspect in their response to ritual than Trotter supposes.

28 Prynne, 'A Pedantic Note in Two Parts', p. 350.

29 Prynne, 'On *Maximus IV, V, & VI* (my italics; no page no.).

OBSCURITY, FRAGMENTATION AND THE UNCANNY IN PRYNNE AND CELAN

J. H. Prynne's poetry represents the most serious engagement with the modernist poetics of impersonality, Hermetism and fragmentation in postwar British poetry. The relatively unified, even didactic, style of his work through the 1960s gave way to an uncompromising textuality in which the personal voice or lyric ego of the poet ceases to be an organising principle and gets dispersed in the mêlée of mutually exclusive utterances which now make up the poem. Through these dense sheets of text, semantically opaque but teeming with strange images, doggerel verse, sententious remarks, theoretical propositions and quotations from technical manuals, Prynne never quite gives up the claim to an authorial presence that might unify the fragmented text, but, from *Brass* onwards such a 'presence' becomes increasingly contingent, haunting the poem as a call to a unity that fails to materialise. The prospect of meaningfulness is always shadowed by the spectre of meaninglessness. To be sure, this could be said to be the hermeneutic experience attending any difficult literary work. But Prynne's poetry is notable for the reflexive pressure it exerts on the act of interpretation, so that conceptualisations such as the 'fullness' and 'lessness' of meaning are placed in a dialectical relationship that forces the reader to question the presuppositions on which any interpretation is based. Furthermore, by luring the reader into an engagement with the poetic subject as an effect of rhetoric rather than as the arbiter of meaning, Prynne's poetry stages reading as an uncanny encounter with the limits of reflexion. As an example here are the first lines of the poem that begins *Brass*, 'The Bee Target On His Shoulder':

Gratefully they evade the halflight
rising for me, on the frosty abyss.
Rub your fingers with chalk and

grass, linctus over the ankle, now TV with
the sound off & frame hold in
reason beyond that. Paste. Thereby take
the foretaste of style, going naked
wherever commanded, by
>   the father struck
>   in the plain. His
>   wavy boots glow
>   as he matches
>   the headboard.
Do not love this man. He makes
Fridays unbearable, with the
ominous dullness of the gateway
to the Spanish garden. His
herb-set teeth are impossible,
tropic to R.E.M. and the white doll.

                    ('The Bee Target On His Shoulder', 148)

This poem begins by evoking a scenario that is both beneficent and anxi-
ety-ridden, leading to a sense of equivocation and absurdity with the figure of 'the father' as its fulcrum. Tension is created by the sense of vague
expectancy surrounding the initial positing of a 'they', a 'me', and a 'you',
coupled with the text's urgent exhortations to 'take / the foretaste of style',
to go 'naked / wherever commanded', to 'not love this man'. Such terms of
reference imply a world outside of the immediate text, yet there is no way
of making sense of these directions and the rituals they denote except by
rationalising the text into a message by attempting to edit out its 'noise'. By
producing a cybernetic fiction, finding a thematic message from within the
crackle of semi-random signifying gestures, the 'frame hold[s] in / reasons
beyond that'. Switching to a visual metaphor, it may be like 'TV with / the
sound off'. The contingency of the framing process makes the text end-
lessly re-markable, 'on the frosty abyss', to the extent that even the 'enacting' or seemingly self-referential lexias I have singled out must be
regarded as contingent, provisional. Are we to regard the poetic then as
meaning something to do with chance, noise, foiled expectations? These
negative and non-sensical elements are rather the hermeneutic condition
of meaning and non-meaning through which the poem appeals to the
response of the reading subject. In his earlier collection, *The White Stones*
(1969), Prynne presents loss and waste as important 'matter' for poetry. In
Brass, too,

                    Rubbish is
>   pertinent; essential; the
>   most intricate presence in
>   our entire culture; the

> ultimate sexual point of the whole place turned
>> into a model question.

('L'Extase de M. Poher', 161)

Readers are faced with a truly questionable and questioning poetic that draws attention to the least recoverable aspects of language and meaning in the modernist project and its attempt to distance itself from the threat of the coercive parlance of the State:

>> Crush tread trample distinguish
> put your choice in the hands of the town
> clerk, the army stuffing its drum.

('L'Extase de M. Poher', 161)

Poems in *The White Stones* focus on questions of symbolic and referential coherence and figural determination. The ventriloquised, cacophonic texts of *Brass* lead to different, although not unrelated, questions: are there limits to poetic language? Is poetic language radically heterogeneous, and if so, what is left of the form (or *gestalt*) of art? Does poetry void reference or is it on the contrary multi-referential? Does poetry give access to a hidden order of meaning, or is it simply a play of surfaces? Is poetry finally anything more than a series of utterances collected under the heading 'poetry'? From Mallarmé onwards, the 'obscurity' of modernist writing challenges tacit assumptions about the nature and function of poetry, eliciting ontological questions about the purity or impurity of the poem in relation to other modes of discourse. In Prynne's poetry, obscurity is combined with excess: there is always more language, more reference, more signification in an expenditure which may or may not be concerned to recuperate some core of meaning from its riot of utterances. Prynne's poems mime the signs of readability only to withdraw them at the moment the reader believes intellectual purchase has been gained. As Nigel Wheale argues, the reader

> has to construct a meaning which can only be called fragmentary, and beyond this a beguiling lure remains, indicating that there is much more still to be known, in terms of the formal beauty and ethical purchase which the lines offer and withdraw. This is to say that Prynne's poetry requires its reader continuously to consider how any meaning is derived at any point during the process of interpretation, and further, that whatever meaning is temporarily entertained, be then subject to rigorous question . . . references to economic pressure or to arguments within the life sciences are intrinsic to many of his poems, and the central strategy of putting into question the nature of our meanings is itself a procedure which has a good deal in common with the more interesting forms of 'deconstruction', so called.[1]

Fundamentally, the inscrutable or tendentious poem calls into question the possibility of defining the text *qua* poem when, by definition, definition attempts to 'bring to light' that which in and of the poem remains obscure. Paradoxically, modernism's destruction of the rational positing of essence results from the obsession with its own essence. To attempt to name poetry is *in essence* a philosophical question. But if the essence of poetry is to speak of a dialogue between *dichten* and *denken* we have to begin from certain preconceptions about what positions 'poetry' and 'thought' take up in relation to one another. If poetry is that which differs from its (philosophical) commentary – from what usually turns out to be a version of 'rational thought' or a 'law of genre' – it can never be articulated by the voice of philosophy, or by any juridical voice, psychological, ideological, or literary-critical, which tries to get at the generic truth disclosed by its curiously mute Saying. Poetry, therefore, can only 'come to light' in the luminousness of proximity by one's thinking (it) in (its) difference from philosophy. This does not mean that poetry achieves an inverse or negative status in terms of something 'lost' to itself as the negative experience of a transcendent, full meaning; instead, it takes place as pure negativity, the meaning of negativity. Nor does it merely represent the downside of philosophical enquiry even though it 'calls' from a negative space; in (its) resistance to any semantic totalisation, the 'poetic' text may show up the limits to philosophical appropriation. Philosophy discovers its 'own' limit and negation in the Thing-in-itself, which it attempts to define as something existing within and yet beyond the poetic space as a transcendent object. Always secondary to the systematic, legitimating discourses of a culture, poetry nevertheless usurps the law by proving that all systems leak. But this *scriptible* text is not thereby an essence, which has as its property the non-appropriable. It only has this being in its otherness to philosophy and the law in general. The modernist text comes into its meaning-fullness by dint of its meaning-lessness: it can only be described as poetry if by that term we mean the resistance of language to the metaphoricity of Being. but we are never in the position to present the content of this formal property of language as such.

The heterogeneity of the modernist text would appear to possess a radical obscurity which refuses access to the presentation of a mark or trait, resisting all philosophical articulations including those which defer to a pastoral enclave of poetic origination.[2] 'Obscurity', therefore, does not name an absence at the heart of the text, for it already re-marks the text as the presence of an absence. In other words, the text is always present in its withdrawal, but this does not imply that by a dialectical procedure it presents itself as pure presence or withdrawal. The positing of an absence, however, sets up a distance between language and meaning which enacts the negative relationship between the text and the literary (and philo-sophical) qualities with which it has come to be imbued. The error of the avant-garde has been to presume that the political effect of this negativity is self-evident, with the paradoxical result that more and more critical space is taken up with attempts to explain its performance.[3]

This argument for the contingency of poetic knowledge revises the tradition of Heideggerian inquiry into poetic Saying, for which the poetic utterance 'speaks' Being and conceives it in an appropriable 'letting-be' of language. Heideggerian de-struction rejects psychological readings and the subjective basis of interpretation in favour of a process of 'enactment'. As Timothy Clark explains, 'The "meaning" to be *enacted* in relation to *Dichtung* is neither a matter of self-representation nor the cratylic illusion of onomatopoeia or other aspects of the subjective experience of reading. The "meaning" is no more than the *enactment*; reference, as it were, with-out a referent.'[4] For Heidegger, poetry is the prime example of the act of thinking which brings the object-world into presentation. Poetic language is the language of an originary thinking that is free from the representa-tionalism of rational inquiry. Because it speaks to, rather than through, con-sciousness, poetic thinking is the ethical capability to simultaneously let-be and bring-forth with regard to Being. However, when not approximating the 'emptiness' of this ontological gathering in rhapsodic terms such as 'the pure delight of the beckoning stillness',[5] Heidegger's own late discussions of Hölderlin, Trakl and Rilke cannot avoid ontic designations which betray his aestheticist ideology. The Saying of Hölderlin's poetry, for example, always points nostalgically and mythically to a time before rational philos-ophy and science exploited the natural world, re-presenting it as a 'stand-ing reserve'. 'The Rhine' in Hölderlin's poem preserves the river by bringing it forth and letting it be, while the hydroelectric plant dams and uses it up. Whether or not one agrees with Heidegger's environmental pol-itics, there can be no doubt that his explanation is also an interpretation, and an interpretation based on presuppositions about Hölderlin's worth as a great national poet and about the Rhine as a great national symbol. The rhetoric of ontology sublimates the nostalgia for nationalist identity.[6]

In spite of its refusal of a subjective basis, Heidegger's 'dialogue' between poetry and thought remains rooted in a romantic philosophy of the aesthetic which privileges art as a non-rational form of knowledge. Andrew Bowie's commentary on the philosophy of Manfred Frank shows how a romantic aesthetic of subjective unity can fit in with a Heideggerian view of enactment. For Frank, art provides a way of *knowing* the world beyond the referential and representational constraints of rational under-standing because it allows things to 'come to light' (truth as *aletheia*) instead of merely reproducing them (truth as *adequatio*). By keeping an unknowable absolute, or infinity, as its interpretative horizon, romantic aesthetics preserves a gulf between meaning and intuition which sanctions an inexhaustibility of interpretation itself. Because rational understanding and its cognates (corresponding to 'representation') are static, having no way of transforming human existence, the absolute is posited as the horizon of imagination, that creative and interpretative act which reveals truth in the form of a temporal disclosure. This revealing is also a withdrawal, as the infinite interpretation to which the acts of imagination give rise cannot be analysed by the understanding. According to Frank, it is precisely this fragmentation of the *ratio* which creates a sense of subjective unity 'without which contradiction and difference could not be shown as such'; it is a 'unity of ourselves as self-conscious beings, which we cannot conceptually explain, but without which such fundamental experiences as loss, difference, temporality, ignorance become inexplicable.'[7] The work of art forms the privileged locus of this opening, precisely because it is the space of imagination, and therefore of the *free subjectivity* through which imagination works. Thus, Frank provides an account of encompassing subjectivity by way of a traditional reading of the romantic project filtered through Heidegger's notion of *aletheia*. But this account remains virtually as static as the philosophy of adequation it claims to overthrow, for it reproduces the historically contingent autonomy of the art-object, which presupposes the opposition between finite and infinite realms corresponding to 'science' and the 'spirit of man'. Under this structure, subjectivity itself is always selfconscious, self-determining and therefore outside ideology. This position is belied by the fact that it is predicated, through the work of art, by an always already-withdrawn absolute which somehow, ineffably, manages to be a 'unity', the Kantian 'transcendental unity of apperception', which makes the rules. The work of art, too, becomes a unity in itself; therefore, even the fragmentary appearance of the modernist text must be predisposed towards this unity, because it is unified by its very fragmentation, the fact that it cannot be determined by the understanding. It follows that every work of art testifies to the same unity, the same intuition, the same state of being. The moment art appears to diverge from this philosophical programme, its fragmentation becomes 'absolute' but read in terms of cultural decline. Bowie comes close to acknowledging this (although he evades the real problem by becoming part of the symptom, writing of the 'deep malaise' of the contemporary): 'Frank himself rarely uses contemporary art as an example. The gap between what his philosophy says about the significance of art and what contemporary art seems to mean in present-day society is considerable and cannot be ignored.'[8] We are left with the vague idea that it is the fragment' – which points to a foreseeable unity in the mind of the empirical subject, and that 'modern' art has nothing to offer but a fragmentation without return, the fragment of a fragment. Such a distinction can be made in the first instance only by imbuing the work of art with an original, a priori meaning not arising from the work of art itself. The alleged unity comes from a structural *retrait* within the discourse of romantic aesthetics: the fragmentary nature of the artwork is determined by its proximity to self-reflexion, in that, in the case of the poem, the text thematises the relationship between fragmentation and unity. But once the genre is succeeded (or displaced) by another, which does not come under the aegis of such a thematic, or which confounds thematising altogether, there is always *too little or too much* fragmentation. Instead of a relationship between meaning and intuition, we have a (non)relationship between meaning and the signifier. This is why, for Paul de Man, the problem of translation stands for the condition of the text in general:

> What we have here is an initial fragmentation; any work is totally fragmented in relation to this *reine Sprach* [the pure or sacred language], with which it has nothing in common, and every translation is totally fragmented in relation to the original. The translation is the fragment of a fragment, is breaking the fragment – so the vessel keeps breaking, constantly – and never reconstitutes it; there was no vessel in the first place, or we have no knowledge of this vessel, or no awareness, or no access to it, so for all intents and purposes there has never been one.[9]

Prynne's essays, reviews and letters show that he combines a belief in the values of negativity and obscurity with a highly luminous idea of their meaning: experiencing language as something totally distanced and other becomes a way to regain proximity. But, if there is an emphasis on the *enactment* of this encounter with alterity, it is quickly enveloped by massive thematising statements as to the homely nature of that *proximity*, whether in terms of an occult heaven or of a cosmology of universal love:

> We have to go to the exactness and completeness of poetry to tell us what such a condition of home would be like. And if you want it in its largest sense, you have to go to the largest distance from it in order to come right back round to take it in at one sweep.
>
> In fact there are only two things in the universe which are simple, and one of them is the universe taken as a whole: and the other is its language, because its language is its capacity for love.[10]

These claims sit uneasily with the remarks on German modernism Prynne made in 1963, which take British Poetry to task for having 'never surrendered the primary metaphor of fracture as spatial, with an antecedent zonal consciousness secure against internal splintering'. Until, that is, we see that he is contrasting the Tennysonian 'pattern of coherent feeling', and Imagistic 'spatial consciousness' with the visionary condition of European modernism (even if that condition might lend itself to 'visions of final breakdown').[11] Prynne's subsequent writings attempt to reaffirm a visionary and *heimlich* meaning to language's 'distance' in the face of the *unheimlich* nature attributed to it. To this extent, his poetic is as far removed from Heidegger's thought as it is close to it. In stating that 'poetically man dwells on this earth', Heidegger is 'asking himself what is the condition of being that makes it possible for man to be at home on the earth.'[12] But for Heidegger, poetic dwelling has more in common with the not-at-home than with the homeliness idealised by Prynne. In *Being and Time*, 'Uncanniness [*Unheimlichkeit*] is the basic form of Being-in-the-world, even though in an everyday way it has been covered up.'[13] Heidegger's notion of the 'call of Being' is crucial for understanding this 'anxious' not-at-home condition, and helps articulate the relationship of *Dichtung* with Being and alterity, because the call is in effect a 'doubling' of the self in that 'the caller is *Dasein* in its uncanniness: primordial, thrown Being-in-the-world as the "not-at-home" – the bare 'that-it-is' in the "nothing of the world . . . it is something like an *alien* voice.'[14] As a constituent of *Dasein*, the call attests to anxiety. As we have seen, Heidegger's thought includes elements of nostalgia and the wish for transcendent unity. In *Being and Time* they are subject to a form of radical questioning through the *Unheimliche*, and only later reasserted. As Avital Ronell writes, 'how does the experience of fascination and originary disappropriation [in *Being and Time*] turn itself into an experience of appropriation and individuation? Heidegger gives no answers to these questions.'[15]

We have already seen how Frank and Bowie 'appropriate and individuate' Heideggerian truth. One of Prynne's most sophisticated commentators, Michael Grant, makes a comparable move to subjectivise the poetics of *Dasein*. Here, though, the 'subjective' is hypostatised into an 'encompassing' notion of Saying which supposedly transcends the ego. Grant's version of the modernist text is self-effacing at the very moment it testifies to a projected self, concentrating almost exclusively on versions of the open 'question' forged by an inscrutable aesthetic:

> Prynne's poetry aims at effecting a disappearance of the ego in an encompassing subjectivity that communicates without intermediary with the essence. Thus, the poem conceives of itself as a 'model question', a question both to and of the model that turns the subject, the reader, and opens him to his own access to being.[16]

Grant refers to the 'model question' posed by 'L'Extase de M. Poher', the poem's 'multifarious idioms . . . designated by a single sign, "rubbish"'.[17] The poem's refusal of lyric clarity is its way of getting rid of the Cartesian ego, but its obscurity is merely a 'disguise' for a deeper level of conscious-ness brought about by its multiplication of possible subject-positions. In other words, because the text does not *impose* a delimited subject-position on the reader, it opens the reader's response (a 'clearing') to a proliferation of linguistic 'enactments', none of which can be termed identificatory as such. The access to 'being' proposed on the strength of this learning treats these heterogeneous enactments as secondary to a 'whole' ('encompass-ing') experience that underlies them. This is the only way in which such a loss of subjectivity can be reinscribed as an 'essence' that is of the order of the self rather than of the ego. For Grant, the term 'subject' would appear to be synonymous with the 'self', and he forges a mystical concept of identity in which, as pure being, the 'deep' subject coincides with itself.[18]

There is, however, no reason to suppose that the 'communicational' structure of the poem works in this way. The more the reader subscribes to a metaphor of depth informing the poem, the more he or she becomes removed from its language. The text turns into a purely self-reflexive pro-cedure, not in terms of the poem's 'own' self-referentiality but by reflecting the reading subject's anxiety about interpretation. Attempts to 'get through' to this meaning end by judging the limits of the reader's own heuristic efforts and makes 'criticism posthumous or tautological'.[19] Grant's descrip-tion is not predicated on the idea of access to a single meaning or matrix signified by the text, but instead proposes a moment of *Dasein* brought into being by the text's radical deferment of an ego-position sanctioned by the interpretative act. Nevertheless, the illusion of depth occurs by assigning a metaphysic of unity and totality to what the text posits. If the ego-position is continuous with the category of the signified (that is, of a priori representation), the modernist text resists this by confronting the reader with a 'chain of signifiers' which never arrives at any destination within the poem itself.[20] But the openly symbolic nature of this chain is belied by the *Gestalt* signified by an 'encompassing subjectivity'. Were the chain to be truly indeterminate, it could only represent a subject that would be the deferral of the presentation of a self. Lacan's point that 'the signifier represents a subject for another signifier' is critically relevant here:

> suppose that in the desert you find a stone covered with hieroglyphics. You do not doubt for a moment that, behind them, there was a subject who wrote them. But it is an error to believe that each signifier is addressed to you – this is proved by the fact that you cannot understand any of it. On the other hand you define them as signifiers, by the fact that you are sure that each of these signifiers is related to each of the others.[21]

Although Lacanian theory is 'psycho-analytic' in that it is centred on the problem of the subject, it nevertheless points the way to a psychoanalytic reading that is not subject-centred. A traditional Freudian view would preempt the question of *encounter* between the critic and the modernist text by assuming that it has already taken place, and that the place is inhabited by the residua of the artist's personality, the artist's 'influences', and the artist's motivations. Lacan talks of the psyche as an inscrutable text offered up for (and resisting) translation and interpretation; the analysand's discourse requires translating and interpreting, as if it were spoken in an other language. The poem, too, is composed of 'foreign' elements in its allusions to and borrowings-from other languages and literatures, as well as in its philological commutations, its parapraxes, ellipses, overdeterminations and figural 'detours'. But the poem is not cryptic, like a crossword, nor is it encrypted with pathological significance like the analysand's discourse: it does not embody (as figure, in the sense of *Gestalt*) the psyche of the poet in any form.[22] Literary interpretaions that resort to biographical material and psychobiographies are the most obvious examples of subject-centred criticism, but certain types of 'immanent' literary criticism are more tellingly haunted by the traces of the subject, for example the 'New Criticism', which retains the idea of the author in a textually subliminal and central 'meaning'.[23] The modernist poem resists these approaches as well as traditional psychoanalytic interpretation because in lacking the subject of an 'encounter', it lacks a 'case history' or a representative context from which might be drawn the pathological clues to its meaning. The self-centred, anecdotal poem is clearly distinct from the modernist text in that it gives the effect of a subjective 'real' by presenting the reader with the figure of a 'human' subject in the form of the lyric ego. The 'naive' novel, in contrast, might possess no aura of a genuine personality 'behind' the text, but in its dialogic coherence it does present subjective fictions, which may be articulated in the terms of their own poetic world. A 'fiction' can only be read as such because it takes its references from the realm of the 'non-fictional'. Both of these forms, the anecdotal poem and the realist novel, seem immediately representable through the figure of the author 'behind' them or through the figuration of 'real' subjects. But the modernist poem suspends, or brackets, the poles of fiction and non-fiction and presents language as an object qua substance; its 'space' is unique in its concentration on resistance in/of the phenomenology of language, and this makes reading impossible for those who divide the world into reified categories of fiction and reality. This does not mean, however, that the modernist text appears magically without a subject, as it might seem from my critique of Grant's encompassing subjectivity. Rather, it stands in relation to the truth of the subject by enacting the *disappearance* of subjectivity.

In its difference, poetry as art 'comes to light'; like a piece of sculpture before a civic assembly, it is 'unveiled'. In this sense, as Heidegger explains, it appears in relation to truth (αληθEια):

Λογοσ lays that which is present before and down into presencing . . .
Because the Λογοσ lets lie before us what lies before as such, it discloses
[unveils] what is present in its presencing. But disclosure is ΑληθΕια.
This and Λογοσ are the Same. ΑΕγΕιν lets αληθΕια, the unconcealed as
such, lie before us . . . All disclosure releases what is present from concealment. Disclosure needs concealment. The 'Α − Ληθ ξια rests in Λη θη,
drawing from it and laying before us whatever remains deposited in Λη θη.
Λογοσ is in itself and at the same time a revealing and concealing. It is
ΑληθΕια.[24]

Commenting on Lacan's interest in this passage, Mikkel Borch-Jacobsen
remarks that he co-opts Heidegger's epistemology into a phenomenology
of desire, and therefore of the subject: 'the "lying" subject speaks the
"truth" of his desire, to the extent that this desire, in its pure nullity,
appears only by disappearing, and so on.'[25] Lacan reads Heidegger through
Kojève, and as one of Borch-Jacobsen's footnotes acknowledge, this is
something Jacques Derrida draws on in his critique of 'truth' in Lacan, that
Lacan 'resituates *Dasein* in the subject'.[26] The epistemological implication
is relevant to the discussion of the modernist text: a cogent analysis of the
cogito, the humanist subject, the metaphysics of presence – all of those
categories called into question by psychoanalysis – must proceed from a
position which is radically heterogeneous to the subject *in the illusion of
its self-identity*. Not in order to deny the subject's existence, but so that the
subject (even in its most abstract forms, e.g. the Phallus in Lacan) is not
mistaken for the ground of its being. This is why for Heidegger *Dichtung*
means nothing, but is the Saying of Being. It stands in relation to Being
and not to beings.

There is, therefore, nothing expressed or 'projected' by the modernist
poem. Any encompassing subjectivity proposed on its behalf comes into
being through this 'opening', which is to say that indeterminacy is imbued
with what I will call a *determined opening*. The notion of an encompassing
subjectivity, in the form of the opening of what is 'let be', is another way of
refusing any determinate identity, which is to say that it expects to open
onto a transcendent subjectivity in the form of a sublimated self-identity.
The opening is always also a closing. If the notion of encompassing subjectivity exists without preconception or determinancy, why bother with it
at all *except* to confirm belief in some transcendent or 'post-positional' self-
identity sanctioned by the 'aesthetic experience'? Without the iterable,
differentiating context that makes the text *legible* (in this case, what we will
come to call 'poetry'), there can be no Saying as such. This does not mean
that a poem becomes 'readable' in the sense of its containing discernible
thematic elements; it is not a matter of interpretation, but of the conditions
for any degree of legibility, including the ability to remark that *Dichtung* is

the Saying of Being in the first place. As Timothy Clark writes, 'there is no *Dichtung* in the sense required by Heidegger, only its effect or illusion within a machine of textuality . . . Nothing takes place but the stage itself. Moreover this (non) taking place remains a necessary element in any text. Nothing is *there* to be read except *readability* itself, which is tantamount to *unreadability*.'[27]

The 'outside' or 'beyond' of interpretation is therefore nothing origi-nary, but is a metaphysical account of a 'mark'. By denying the existence of iterability in an attempt to turn to the mark itself would be, phenome-nologically speaking, to happen upon a hieroglyphic script, inscribed by no one, written in no language. In poetics, the desire to apprehend the mark 'itself' is already motivated by something other than philosophical indifference, for it demands that the mark be *significant* in its own in-difference, justified by its *de facto* presence. To wish to account for poetry by way of its originality is to treat it as a philosophical sublimation of the desire for another meaning, the *Gestalt* that ushers in the inviolably human. The liberal humanist perspective in literary criticism represents this desire to shore up the western tradition of 'typifying' what is thought to represent the discretely human, in the form of simultaneously creating and prohibiting difference. The point of origin is the moment of original differentiation of human types and the type of the human. Humanism seeks paradoxically to affirm this original differentiation and to treat it as a transcendent, pure difference, the utopia where difference exists indif-ferently. This translates into the metaphysic of Unity, which effects to can-cel difference under the sign of identity as if identity didn't entail difference as a structural necessity. The origin is always seen as a homely identity from which 'man' has fallen and to which 'he' may return. in the unity of its *Gestalt* (and its *Geschlecht*), art becomes synonymous with the theological concept of redemption where it offers access to an Adamic realm freed from the constraints of desire and political institutions.[28] But redemption cannot be called upon except as a 'hopeful' condition; it is not a *telos*, because poetry's indeterminacy and obscurity, without which it would sink to the level of common signification, cannot actually name the path of redemption except by way of the re-mark. 'In itself', the poetic text enacts an ideal annulment of difference by erasing its own presence. But this withdrawal from position, which is actually the position of an ideal identity, works precisely to inaugurate poetic identity above and beyond the radical heterogeneity of the modernist text. This is why a poet's work can still be identified as a *corpus* in spite of its semantic dis-persal. I am not talking here simply about the collection of a set of texts under the name of their author, or *merely* about perceivable stylistic traits that link poem to poem, but about the purpose behind recognising the authorial trait as such. Derrida writes of Heidegger's need to homogenise textual disparity in this way. Trakl's poetry can only enact its Saying by way of an unsaid unity:

> Gedicht . . . is, in its place, what gathers together all the Dichtungen (the poems) of a poet. This gathering together is not that of a complete corpus, of the oeuvres completes, but a unique source that is not presented in any part of any poem. This gathering is the site of origin, the place from which and toward which the poems come and go according to a 'rhythm'. Not elsewhere, into some other thing, and yet not to be confused with the poems insofar as they say (sagen) something, Gedicht is 'unspoken (ungesprochene)'. What Heidegger wants to indicate, to announce rather than show, is the unique site (Ort) of this Gedicht. That is why Heidegger presents his text as an Erörterung, that is to say, according to the reawakened literalness of the word, a situation that localises the unique site or the proper place of Gedicht from which the poems of Trakl sing.[29]

The fundamental question of the modernist poem has to do with the significance ascribed to semantic dispersal, the values attached to 'meaning' and 'non-meaning' in and of the text. The psychoanalytic model I have discussed above is important here because it underlines the necessity of thinking about the text in terms of an encounter, even where the text does not add up to a specific subject-position. Lacan's example of the hieroglyphic inscription is an instance of this: the 'encounter' occurs between the marked stone and a reader who cannot read it. The psychoanalytic approach here centres on the relationship of a subject with the field of the (imaginary or symbolic) object within the 'gaze' of which he or she takes up a position. Here, we are dealing with the gaze in its most resistant, material form, as something *shown* yet not thematised by the text. It is not simply that the text 'looks' at me, soliciting a response through its very inscrutability, but that, as Lacan points out in his example of the imitation eyes on mothwings, the gaze is distinguished from the physical attribute of sight, for it is the *showing object* that arrests the attention of the subject and not an empirical other who is observing the subject.[30]

Thus far, we are still within the realm of a phenomenology of vision centred on the image. Yet, in spite of his emphasis on the phenomenology of seeing, Lacan is theorising the relation of the subject to the Other in a more fundamental way. This is why he prefaces the discussion of the Gaze with remarks on the dreamwork. The essential component of the Gaze is that it shows itself as something to be seen, rather than being an eye that looks and is in turn looked-at; in this way it is like the dream, which *indicates* its subject-matter through the images it presents, and by way of ghostly speech, in that the dream signifies by way of language as much, if not more, than by pictures. Indeed, considering that the dream is always reported through the medium of speech, and that its significance derives as much from the process of secondary revision as from any original content it might have had, the Gaze might just as easily be understood as a Call, as for example when in a dream related by Freud, a father's guilt is aroused over the death of his son (and over his subsequent lack of vigilance in allowing the coffin containing the body to catch fire while he sleeps in the next room) when the boy calls to him reproachfully, 'Father, don't you see I'm burning?'[31] The look is one thing (the dead child 'looks just as if he is asleep'), the voice is another: 'Desire manifests itself in the dream by the loss expressed in an image at the most cruel point of the object.'[32] The poem's reality, too, is of the order of a gaze that does not see; its uncanniness arises from the fact that it does not see, that it 'calls' from another place, and 'stages' a vision in the realm of the imaginary. That which is staged by the dream is significant, too, in that what is seen becomes more insistent once the eyes are closed, whereas the ear is an organ that cannot be closed. In the subconscious world of the dream, 'something' calls to the subject, 'something slips, passes, is transmitted, from stage to stage, and is always to some degree eluded in it – that is what we call the gaze.'[33]

In making this analogy between the modernist poem and the dream, and stressing the importance of the linguistic dimension of the image, I am not trying to reinvest the poem with the mimetic elements of phantasy, which are a major component of the dreamwork. Rather, I stress those aspects of the dream that reveal it as the locus of an unpresentable other: what is staged here is the strange contingency of that 'object' which is elided from the field of representation. This is what delivers the dream into the suspense of that which Lacan calls the Real, that left-over which takes the place of the representation.[34] In analysis, this point at which interpretation 'drops-out' becomes decisive in locating the position of the subject, in that the subject answers the call of the real.[35] The poem, on the other hand, is distinct from the dream in that it is nothing except the suspense of the real, the real as theory. Prynne's 'hieroglyphic' text is situated in the field of the Other, whatever that 'other' turns out to be. This apprehension of the Other might be regarded as a version of the poetics of mysticism; Michel de Certeau notes that 'Mysticism presupposed the internal perception by an ego of its exteriority'[36] But whereas the mystic takes this ek-stasis as a sign of the sacred, the analyst views the positing of sacred value as a way of filling the void exposed by the primitive experience of homelessness with the phantasy of a perfected and controlling other. Vincent Descombes has suggested that the fragmented forms of modern art have come to be rationalised as 'the mystic itinerary of the individuation of self within the world.'[37] The reading subject sees (interprets) him or herself from the position of the Other (ultimately as the *objet a*, as that which is lacking in the Other, the lack of adequation, perception, unity, knowledge), in a movement akin to the metaphor of 'seeing oneself see oneself', and this strange doubling marks the moment of the uncanny. The 'gaze' of the modernist text, and specifically the most inscrutable poems in *Brass*, represents a phenomenology of strangeness. In the Freudian text, as well as in Heidegger's ontology of being, this corresponds to the structure of the uncanny, the *Unheimliche*.

In 'The Bee Target On His Shoulder', the increasingly bizarre pile-up of idiomatic phrases, unplaceable designations, bogus quotations and thetic demonstratives lacking any clear external reference allows for little contextual reappropriation, nor does it allow for any ultimately unifying explanation of its content, unless we pass off the whole problem by treating the text as an instance of authorial stream-of-consciousness. Similarly, the entire poem might be categorised as 'dreamlike', in the sense of its being made up of the 'day's residues'. But if this rubbish bears any relation to the dream, it needs to be theorised as more than the mere notion of half-thoughts drifting through the mind of the poet, firstly because this would be to reinstate the idea of the poem as a formal mimesis of the poet's perceptions comprising the subject of the text, and secondly because the poem's scholarly evasions are too strategic to allow for such an unproblematic reading. As I argued earlier, the constantly shifting idioms of the text bracket the space of representation so that it is expropriated by the frames on which it depends. It *is* possible to detect 'themes' running through the poem, but even here the attempt to extract significance from them is based on the fallow ground of excluding many other elements of the text. And maybe that is the point; for example, the 'father' who is 'struck / in the plain', and whose 'wavy boots glow / as he matches / the headboard', later 'pokes / about for the gay snuff of Algiers', then 'pauses' on the 'bonny bank' of a blue tablet on the wall of a shop commemorating 'ATV Channel Nine', 'to empty / his boots of seedlings and filthy change' (148–50). Later still, his daughter 'traces / the path' of his 'boots / on the lawn', a tragi-comic event that places us ('we') into a relationship with death: 'little / sister we sob merrily & settle down / by the newest grave' (150–1). Indeed, the whole chain of reference seems to deal with love of (or arising from) loss, the emptied boots traced on the lawn. Changing his horses in mid-stream, Prynne alters the syntagm of proverbial utterances so that the evocation of fragmentation moves from the trope of violence to love, viz. the father: 'Together we love him limb from / limb, walking in the moonlight' (149). This love is costly, 'like rime'; translated into the negative posturing of the *Symbolistes*, it must be sustained 'in *le silence des nuits, l'horreur des cimetières*' (150). All of which can be construed as thematising the inevitable loss of meaning that occurs in interpreting the text itself. Absurdity and paradox must be accepted if readers are to affirm anything of the traditional, pastoral attributes of the lyric:

> Water the
> ground with song, aria
> with cloud, *that's* his
> aunt with the brown teapot jammed
> into edible, macerated crumpet. So you
> shrilled unwittingly in the 3rd chorus.

('The Bee Target On His Shoulder', 148)

Thus, in a sudden fit of wistful versifying, the 'newest grave' transports us to a bathetically mellifluous elegy:

> fresh
> earth as the clay to see with,
> standing by the head,
> making the song with shadows set
> over the reed-bed.

('The Bee Target On His Shoulder', 151)

'Loss' becomes the text itself, the temporality on which it is found: 'That's / what they're for, seasons and for days and years in / the circle of teeth by the cosy fire' (151). If narrative lines can be made out against the crackle of ventriloquised utterances, their 'matrix' signifies the lack of a matrix, and the theoretical aporia of that lack, which is erected as an interpretative (w)hole at the moment it is thematised as loss.[38] Any attempt to rationalise this core of meaning fails because the moment of 'recognition' immediately becomes the recognition that meaning has been found only at the expense of the greater part of the text, so that the greater part is what remains, and remains as the noise, or the rubbish, the *objet a* which now constitutes both the text and the reading subject (the 'subject of the text'). As Borch-Jacobsen writes,

> The *objet a* thus has the remarkable property of furnishing an image of the subject, *insofar as he is lacking in that image*: a marvellous broken mirror, muddy and opaque, in which the subject can see himself as he is not and with which he can identify himself in his absence of identity: a marvellous Medusa-head, marvellous *aletheia* of the subject.[39]

The theory proceeds from the experience of seeing 'my own image in the mirror, gazing at me with strange anxiety-producing *unheimlich* eyes, which do not belong to me'.[40]

I have already identified the importance of the *Unheimliche* for this discussion through Heidegger's notion of the 'call of Being', which places it firmly in the realm of the experience of anxiety and entails a structural 'doubling' of the subject. This 'doubleness' means that the self has subjective identity as a self through the experience of itself as something other, in that the call 'comes *from* me and yet *from beyond me and over me*'.[41] The call is not an other self calling from the public space of the lifeworld – that is why Heidegger describes it in a way that is baffling in terms of wordly phenomena, for the call is silent: '"It" calls, even though it gives the concernfully curious ear nothing to hear which might be passed along in further retelling and talked about in public'[42] – rather, it has its origin in the 'nothing' of the *Dasein*, which precedes the self and in-forms the self as subject to Being.[43] This is why the call places one into relation with death and to 'care' or anxiety, the death, that is, which represents the world in priority to the subject as something not-at-home to the self. When Freud apprehends the philological peculiarity of the word *Heimlich* in his 1919 essay '*Das Unheimliche*', he anticipates Heidegger's notion of the *Dasein*, albeit in a way Heidegger might not have recognised. How is it, Freud asks, that *Heimlich* can mean both that which is 'homely', 'friendly', 'familiar', 'cosy', even 'holy', and also contains the senses of its apparent opposite, *Unheimlich*, that which is 'uncomfortable', 'secretive', 'strange'?

> In general we are reminded that the word '*heimlich*' is not unambiguous, but belongs to two sets of ideas, which, without being contradictory, are yet very different: on the one hand it means what is familiar and agreeable, and on the other, what is concealed and kept out of sight . . . we notice that Schelling says something which throws quite a new light on the concept of the *Unheimlich*, for which we were certainly not prepared. According to him, everything is *unheimlich* that ought to have remained secret and hidden but has come to light.[44]

The *Heimlich* crosses over into the *Unheimlich* because of its figural and 'economic' (οικονϖμια, of the home and the household) instability, just as the concept of the home as property involves the element of privacy, concealing it from the gaze of strangers. That which is 'proper' must be concealed in order for it to remain property. The term extends to the 'private parts' of the human body, and gets occulted by having a similar sense in the discourse of mysticism, in that it is a form of knowledge which can be approached only through what is obscure, divine and figurative.[45] Freud links this 'double meaning' to the psychopathology of narcissism and repression, something which ought to have remained hidden but comes to light in analysis, when he writes of the uncanny experience of the self's 'doubling': in the form of the 'immortal soul', the double 'originally' took the form of an insurance against the destruction of he ego, but the exaltational side of this 'primary narcissism' inevitably gave way to a darker side in which 'the "double" reverses its aspect. From having been an assurance against immortality, it becomes the uncanny harbinger of death.'[46] When religion (in the 'primitive' form of primary narcissism) fails to maintain its allure over the spiritual realm it has called into being, secular manifestations of the occulted body take over, producing the familiar 'fictions' of uncanny experience: doppelgangers, shadows, disturbing coincidences, *déjà vu*, repetition. Far from disappearing with the passing of primary narcissism, the double, as 'other' (Heidegger's 'nothing'), gets repressed and becomes a call:

> A special agancy is formed there, which is able to stand over the against the rest of the ego, which has the function of observing and criticising the self and of exercising a censorship within the mind, and which we become aware of as our 'conscience'.[47]

Returning to Heidegger, we can see that what has been posited as the self is not 'itself' existentially original, but has its being in the field of the Other (not an other consciousness, but the alterity of an outside-self). This is why (the) one can never be returned home to the 'property' of any self-identity without having already been evicted by the repressive 'un' of the *un-heimlich*. Drawing on an essay by Borch-Jacobsen, Avital Ronell gives a succinct articulation of this part of *Being and Time*:

> Being-evicted (das *Nicht-zuhause-sein, Being-not-at-home*), ought to be understood in an existential-ontological manner as the most original phenomenon. This, notes Borch-Jacobsen, is your habitation in the world, this your *unheimlich* familiarity prior to any opposition of the 'subject' and 'object', of 'self' and 'other', of *chez-soi* and 'the alien', of the 'familiar' and the 'secret' (this resembles, he adds, the motif of Freud's *Unheimliche*), where the anguish of the 'strangely familiar' emerges on the ground of an initial indistinction of a narcissistic character between the self, or 'ego', and 'the external world', the 'ego' and 'other'. The more dreadfully disquieting thing is not the other or an alien; it is, rather, yourself in oldest familiarity with the other – for example, it could be the Double in which you recognise yourself outside of yourself (and which announces to you your death by dispossessing you of your own life, thus your own death.)[48]

That which seems familiar is already haunted by the unfamiliar. The uncanny does not inscribe a relationship with the modernist poem merely because it reflects the reader's anxiety at finding unexplainable gaps in the text, prompted by the readerly 'refusal to admit the insignificance of certain characteristics' which, according to Hélène Cixous, betrays Freud's own '*resistance* to castration and its effectuality'.[49] The uncanny points to that which *returns* in the reading and its commentary, because the 'dead' space of the unexplainable text, like death 'itself', always gets re-marked.

In the matter of radical loss in *Brass*, the resistance of the text ensures that the reader confronts the recurrence of his or her own loss in attempting to find poetic unity. In this sense, the text produces a deathly effect, that of the Gaze, which seems to recognise us, but which we cannot recognise. But the moment the poet re-presents that loss, for example in 'L'Extase de M. Poher' as the presence of an essential 'Rubbish' of 'mere political rhapsody' (161), and which has come to signify the ground beneath our feet of a certain 'Heideggerian' limit or horizon (death as that which sanctions the single Self), he mimes this same re-mark, the effect of an unspeakable loss which comes again. Just as in the poem 'Thoughts on the Esterházy Court Uniform' the thematisation of loss betrays a residual belief in a sacred, redemptive gain that seeks to verify the transcendent, cosmic home at the moment it has been questioned.[50] Prynne's treatment of 'home' in this poem is far more complex than his description in the Olson lecture:

> And yet home is easily our
> idea of it, the music of decent and proper
> order, it's this we must leave in some quite
> specific place if we are not to carry it
> everywhere with us.
>
> ('Thoughts on the Esterházy Court Uniform', 98)

As Cixous writes, 'If all which has been lost returns, as Freud illustrated it in the *Traumdeutung*, nothing is ever lost if everything is replaceable, nothing has even disappeared and nothing is ever sufficiently dead; the relationship of presence to absence is in itself an immense system of "death", a fabric riddled by the real and a phantomisation of the present.'[51]

Clearly, the uncanny in Prynne's work has little in common with its traditional status as an effect of unease or terror in gothic fiction and the ghost story. The uncanny in *Brass* arises from the uneasy relationship of the reader with a poem that will not give up its 'inner' significance, reflecting instead the encounter of the reading subject with heuristic anxiety. The very notion of the encounter has a skewed, tendentious significance, linked as it is to the 'spirituality' of the self and its being as a revenant (i.e. one who returns from the dead; one who returns to a place). Heidegger's later writings substitute for the uncanny the restitutive term 'strange' (*fremd*), gleaned from Trakl's poem '*Frühling der Seele*'. 'By strange,' Heidegger writes, 'we usually understand something that is not familiar, does not appeal to us – something that is rather a burden and an unease.'[52] However, the etymology of the word really means 'forward to somewhere else, underway toward . . ., onward to the encounter with what is kept in store for it. the strange goes forth, ahead. But it does not roam aimlessly, without any kind of determination. The strange element goes in search toward the site where it may stay in its wandering. Almost unknown to itself, the "strange" is already following the call that calls it on the way into its own.'[53]

In the Trakl essay, the Call is not longer heard in its uncanniness – 'strange', but no longer uncanny. We can take this to mean that Heidegger is suppressing (repressing?) his earlier theory, and/or believes that he has moved beyond it. In any case, this new order of strangeness has been sanctioned by a return to etymological origin; that which has remained synchronically hidden has now 'come to light'. The strange now occupies a site, which, like the silent place of *Gedicht*, has called it to itself, 'into its own'. Its character is still defined by the cognates of the uncanny in *Being and Time*. As we have seen that Freud, too, arrived at his elaboration of this concept by way of the philological method, how can we accept one etymological thesis rather than the other? To a great extent, the question is bogus because, as Cixous has shown, the interpretation of strangeness attempts to repress the very strangeness it gives rise to. In the late essays of Heidegger, the soul is invited to follow a path (*unterwegs*) towards a home which is always already unfamiliar and alien. No rhetoric of 'primitive' destining will resolve this.

The terms of being-on-the-way, encounter and the uncanny all prepare us for Paul Celan's meditation on poetry in his address 'The Meridian', and for Prynne's elegy for Celan 'Es Lebe der König'. If *Brass* has had relatively more critical attention than other books by Prynne, this poem (and its relation to Celan's work) has been given pride of place in that criticism, most likely because it has the allure of combining ease and difficulty of interpretation in a clearly identifiable context with extreme textual tendentiousness. David Trotter has written extensively on *Brass* and the role of this poem in it, and Geoffrey Ward has devoted an essay to the links between Prynne and Celan. However, although these two critics agree that Prynne's poetic is, like Celan's, based on a technique of estrangement, they offer quite different interpretations of its significance. Trotter argues in moral tones that Prynne's technique effects a Celanian 'humanising absurdity', which returns us to our proper, 'human' selves, whereas Ward is more circumspect, suggesting that Prynne's and Celan's poetry of 'human encounter' is always subject to the symbolic order of language, so that 'What constitutes home and what estrangement seem to move like a Möbius strip'.[54] Both readings maintain humanist notions of the subject, but Ward is far more attentive to shifts in response to what constitutes 'human' and 'nonhuman' categories in both Prynne and Celan. Ward does not reduce all questions of the relationship between aesthetics, the subject, and the State to the moral decisions of a private self as Trotter tends to do, and he is aware that if Celan talks of the poetic 'counter-word' as being a 'homage to the majesty of the absurd which bespeaks the presence of human beings', he also says that poetry is 'an eternalisation [*Unendlichsprechung*] of nothing but mortality, and in vain'.[55] Paradoxically, it is as if this 'in vain' were to provide the negative ground from which the 'human' is bespoken. Celan himself is unclear about what he saw as the paradoxical, *heimlich/unheimlich* intention of poetry: 'This means going beyond the human, stepping into a realm which is turned toward the human, but uncanny – the realm where the monkey, the automatons and with them . . . oh, art, too, seem to be at home.'[56] When automatons seem to be at home, the 'human' is estranged, and yet Celan is constantly seeking a human home, a pathway back to 'our' selves;

> Is it on such paths that poems take us when we think of them? And are these paths only detours, detours from your to you? But they are, among how many others, the paths on which language becomes voice. They are encounters, paths from a voice to a listening You, natural paths, outlines for existence perhaps, for projecting ourselves into the search for ourselves . . . A kind of homecoming.[57]

These tentative sentences already mime a homecoming: the 'natural' paths, which allow language to issue from the subject as 'voice', provide the ground beneath our feet on which we become ourselves even as we search for ourselves, *because* of that search. But Celan's equivocation, and his nostalgia for a way back to a true *Heimat*, contains none of the rarefied, mandarin pronouncements of Prynne's essay on the subject, 'A Pedantic Note'. Prynne hopes to shore up an 'English condition' that has been suborned by what he regards as an Olsonian pejorocracy of linguistic misuse. Furthermore, his idealised nostalgia takes the form of a demand for a return to some archaic, pastoral identity that will 'traverse the field without moral debate or transcendent abstraction'.[58] In other words, a State of being so literally and properly in place that it silences all political, ethical and metaphysical questions (and, therefore, all dissent).

Celan's sense of home, on the other hand, is nostalgic because it comes from the experience of one who has been dispossessed of family, culture and country, as well as exiled from his native language (or 'mother-tongue'), by the Nazi Fatherland.[59] Celan's tentative explorations of the theme of home carry the weight of a great hope yet constantly yield to negative expression ('mortality . . . in vain'). His poetic texts attempt to take this negativity as far as it will go within the figural language of modernism. But there is always a tension in his writing between this voiding of a language and an identity that will return to itself untainted by appropriation and oppression, and the mystical affiliations of the Heideggerian return to being. There would be no tension if we accepted that Heidegger's 'question' of being simply represents a critique of *being-for-myself* over *being-is*. In this case, Celan's 'speechlessness' would mark an attempt to affirm a radical withdrawal from what Heidegger regards as the tradition of nihilism from Hegel to Nietzsche. But Heidegger's representation of the question of being in terms of a project of cultural renewal, in which being comes to support German nationalistic ascendancy, means that he continues to subordinate difference to identity.[60] Celan's work may be said to counter the self-originating and aggressive stance of being-for-myself (or for the State) with a 'being for a dispossessed community', but in 'The Meridian' this constantly runs the risk of being converted into the abstracted terms of being as a mysticism centred on a singular 'one', exemplified by the humanist transcendence invoked by the 'counter-word'.

Both Trotter and Ward concentrate on Celan's notion of the 'counter-word', that 'terrifying silence' which 'takes . . . breath and words away', because Celan's example of a counter-word gives Prynne the title of the central poem in *Brass*: 'Es Lebe der König'.[61] Drawing on the final scene of Büchner's play *Danton's Death*, in which Lucille, wife of Danton's friend Camille Desmoulins, condemns herself by crying 'Long live the king!' to a passing patrol of Citizens, Celan insists that the counter-word represents a 'poetic' act of defiance. It is not that Lucille merely reverts to support for the Ancien Régime in disgust at the Terror, she declaims the futility and absurdity of a political condition in which no allegiance, either to monarchy or revolution, has any human significance. 'Long live the king!' puts her own life on the line and is therefore a speech-act of commitment *in extremis*:

> It is a word against the grain, the word which cuts the 'string', which does not bow to the 'bystanders and old warhorses of history'. It is an act of freedom. It is a step.
>
> . . . Allow me, who grew up on the writings of Peter Kropotkin and Gustav Landauer, to insist: this is not homage to any monarchy, to any yesterday worth preserving.
>
> It is homage to the majesty of the absurd which bespeaks the presence of human beings.[62]

Just as in the re-renaming of Leningrad as St Petersburg, when there is no clear way forward the fact of oppression brings about 'revolution', or in other words a turning 'back towards' the only homeland that offers itself as an alternative, even if it is already estranged. Rather than simply reinstating the symbols of Tzarism as a return to the 'good old days', the symbolic archive is plundered for that which is most outrageous to the regime, the very thing the regime wished to obliterate from memory. Like Osip Mandelstam, Celan wrote in 'response' to the experience of State terrorism and genocide, and from this experience it must have been evident that Nazism and Stalinism represented manifestations of a similar oppression.

Prynne's writing, on the other hand, has no such insistence, and its commitments (in his more didactic texts, at any rate) stem from the rather less noble contraries of idealism and spleen. From 'L'Extase de M. Poher' we might gather that Prynne's counter-word is the 'rubbish' we have seen determining the more resistant texts in *Brass*. In place of the 'bystanders and old warhorses of history', we have 'the hands of the town / clerk, the army stuffing its drum' (161). Here, the 'model question' set up by the counter-word inaugurates an inquiry concerning the last vestiges of human beings, the status of their waste. But Prynne's tone of moral hectoring in this poem means that the counter-word has less to do with the extreme act of which Celan writes than with the inheritance of Baudelairean distaste for the *petit bourgeoisie*. Just as in 'The Ideal Star-Fighter' (with its undertones of Wyndham Lewis's polemical drivel), where Prynne can write 'we have already induced / moral mutation in the species' (165). 'L'Extase' has 'formal derangement of the species' (160). That 'rubbish' is considered to be the 'ultimate sexual point of the whole place turned / into a model question' (161) implies a strong link between 'species' and the 'sexual', so that the poem commits itself to *Geschlecht* in a way that is a far cry from the radical voiding of the term in Celan's '*Radix Matrix*':

Wer,
wer wars, jenes
Geschlecht, jenes gemordete, jenes
schwarz in den Himmel stehende:
Rute und Hode –?

(Wurzel.
Wurzel Abrahams. Wurzel Jesse. Niemandes
Wurzel – o
unser.)

Who,
who was it, that
lineage, the murdered, that looms
black into the sky:
rod and bulb –?

(Root.
Abraham's root. Jesse's root. No one's
root – O
ours.)[63]

As Werner Hamacher writes of this poem, 'The language of the poem is *die Sekunde des Geschlechtes*, in which it – cut, murdered – no longer communicates and mediates itself with, but im-parts that which is cut along with it in its nothingness. it is itself the stigma of castration, and in its historical, its most unacceptable form, the stigma of the murder of European Jewry in the extermination camps of the Nazi regime.'[64] If, as Philippe Lacoue-Labarthe argues, Auschwitz is the 'useless residue (*le déchet*) of the Western idea of art, that is to say, of *techne*',[65] then Prynne's 'most intricate presence' of rubbish, coupled with his suggestion that 'any other rubbish is mere political rhapsody' (161), at the very least reveals a level of abjection, or of spleen, which Adorno characterised as expressing 'the desire to compensate for the lack of authority and evidence inherent in a merely mediated and derived knowledge of what is most immediate – real suffering'.[66] The real political character of art is anything but rhapsodic; as Celan's poetry reveals, the political is not to be found in the poem as the simple representation of a position, but in that which is left unsaid but inscribed nonetheless as repression and as ideology.

And yet, in 'The Meridian', Celan's belief in a poetic movement through the uncanny – objectified in the Medusa-head, the puppets, ape-forms, and automata of art – towards the human, the *heimlich*, represents the limited, extremely personal form taken by his political vision. 'The Meridian' itself forms an uneasy, frustrated response to Heidegger's analyses of the uncanny in *Being and Time* and the 1953 Trakl essay, as well as to the silence maintained by Heidegger on the issue of the Shoah. When Celan calls poetry *'einsam und unterwegs'* ('lonely and on the way', *en route*), he clearly alludes to Heidegger's pastoral lore of the path, the way (not the 'road') to language and being.[67] The poem is be-coming, intending towards another, and 'everything and everybody is a figure [*Gestalt*] of this other toward which it is heading.'[68] Language, however, instead of being the destination to which the path is on the way, is more like a vehicle carrying poetic material towards perception: 'The poem becomes . . . the poem of a person who still perceives [*Wahrnehmenden*], still turns towards phenomena [*Erscheinenden*, those appearances], addressing and questioning them. The poem becomes conversation – often desparate conversation.'[69] And, like Prynne's 'model question', the poem takes us towards a clearing, to 'an "open" question "without resolution", a question which points towards open, empty, free spaces – we have ventured far out.'[70] I have argued earlier in this chapter that such an openness could only escape determination – determined even in its indeterminacy – when it becomes completely emptied of all metaphysical content, including the notion of a percipient subject. Only the word 'empty' in Celan's account keeps it from being identified with the positivity of Heidegger's 'open'. It would be the mark of otherness, of death, itself. But as it comes under the structure of the re-mark, alterity can never appear in any pure sense. The uncanny is not the *knowledge* of death and otherness, but the un-knowing relation to them in the apprehension that death returns. Death may be the point of utter negativity, nevertheless, it is not (itself) in that void.[71] Celan's later poems strive for a negative effect which counters the apotheosis of romantic-modernist language in an inversion of inversion, an effect which cancels-out any immanence that might still be assigned to the Holocaust (including the notion of 'holocaust') by the German tradition.[72] In this sense, its 'poetry' remains depthlessly uncanny, refusing to endorse the 'humanism' that has become the very ground of exclusion and terror. 'The Meridian', though, hangs on to the *heimlich*, humanising idea of 'free spaces'. Like Prynne, Celan does not think that poetry achieves this openness ('The absolute poem – no, it certainly does not, cannot exist'[73], he regards it as a hope for 'a u-topian light',[74] Read through the logic of the counter-word, this utopia, the no-place, would appear to be more strange than reassuring, but Celan does not here talk of the 'counter-light' or the '*Lichtdung*' he introduces elsewhere,[75] and the claims about the *unheimlich* nature of the utopian are contradicted by a retreat from the double: 'Art (this includes Medusa's head, the mechanism, the automaton), art, the uncanny strangeness which is so hard to differentiate and perhaps is only *one* after all – art lives on.'[75]

In spite of its vanity and mortality, it seems, the poem represents a 'kind of homecoming' ('*Eine Art Heimkehr*').[77] Celan and Prynne again touch circles in this emphasis on the (non) politics of the singular (for Prynne, the politics for one man, 'the / folds of our intimate surface' (12)). Although Andrew Ross is somewhat dismissive of the counter-word in his discussion of Prynne and Celan, I think he is partly correct to say that 'Celan's use of language . . . makes for an *individual discourse*; it is only *one*, highly idiosyncratic, language among others. For all its politically charged power it does not, however, offer a discourse *of* or *about* individuality which we are going to be able to find socially useful.'[78] The sociological tone is beside the point, for Celan's work is to a great extent a writing in defiance of 'utility' in its most dangerously instrumental form. It would have been difficult for Celan to have identified with what 'we' find useful because his entire mode of expression starts out from the oppressor's tongue (the German language in which he wrote), and the necessity of subverting its rationale. His discourse is *one*, but not necessarily *individual*. It is certainly *lonely*, and this can be said to translate Heidegger's publicly voided condition of *Dasein* – except that the Self vis-à-vis *Dasein* is already *two*; it is only taken as one in the phantasy of the properly and indivisibly *heimlich*. Where the distinction between the self and the public (Heidegger's '*das Man*') becomes reified into a private phantasy of the percipient subject versus the masses, we return to the politics of Poundian modernism.

Geoffrey Ward's essay describes the ways 'Es Lebe der König' and other poems in *Brass* (most notably 'Royal Fern') employ a Celanian language at the micro level: a constellation of recurring nouns, 'snow', 'water', 'sky', 'key', 'window', 'day', 'path', 'seed', 'night', 'dream', 'star', 'words which are at hand in their familiarity, signs of the far-away in their calmly non-human associations . . . are not at all pointers to a simplified or an avidly poeticised world, but are *condensations* in poetry of human encounter: with the world outside the single self or species, through the verbal order outside which no encounter may be thinkable, but which is itself encountered as other, and yet into which we are born.'[79] In 'Royal Fern', for example, we find

> By the beads you sleep, laden with scrip.
> How can you love me in dream,
> always walking from field to field,
> You sleep on, seeded by snowy drift.

('Royal Fern", 158)

and, later in the same poem,

> Still the snow hums, fetching my life:
> the pain to come, still the key
> takes cover in the chamois case.
> The key is the edge of our day.

('Royal Fern", 158)

In 'Es Lebe der König',

> Fire and honey oozes from cracks in the earth;
> the cloud eases up the Richter scale. Sky divides
> as the flag once more becomes technical, the print
> divides also: starlight becomes negative. If you
> are born to peaks in the wire, purple layers in the
> glass format, re-enter the small house with
> animals too delicate and cruel. Their throats fur
> with human warmth, we too are numbered like
> prints in the new snow

('Es Lebe der König', 168)

The sky, the snow, the house, and the water recur throughout as a pattern. It is possible, as Ward contends, that they cohere around the reference-point of Celan's suicidal act of throwing himself into the Seine. The poem speaks of 'the landing-stage' where 'We stand / just long enough to see you, // we hear your / fearful groan and choose not to think of it' (168). But the poem cannot be read as providing a documentary narrative of the event; rather, it checks any posited empathy arising from the semblance of reference to an actual event by estranging the reader from pathos. At a superficial level, this is achieved by provoking the desire for a context in which the vague reference to an event and the nodal points, or 'key words', of the text will come together, giving access to a symbolically meaningful account of reality. The poem's title, and its dedication, identify that there is a recognisable context, unlike other poems in the collection such as 'Viva Ken', 'The Five Hindrances', and 'The Bee Target On His Shoulder', which are purely tendentious. But the discovery of Celan's biography provides only the most tentative purchase on the text, so that we have to read the poem at a level more specific to its actual 'saying': if the poem describes Celan's death, why is the landing-stage at the edge of a 'pool' with 'cropper sides, evaporating by the grassy slopes' (168); why does the mention of the pool follow from 'the small house', which 'the beloved enters', and which then 'becomes technical'? The house has already been re-entered 'with / animals too delicate and cruel', and which have throats that 'fur with human warmth'. Even so, the moment the reader begins to connect these items, the attempt becomes futile. There is an information overload based on the positing of reference outside the space of the poem: so many definite articles and demonstratives pointing to reality, so many images and conceivable permutations of images. As in Prynne's earlier work, the ambiguities and disconnections of syntax provide the most insurmountable obstacle to understanding, but here Prynne is much more ruthless in his attack on semantic coherence. And yet 'Es Lebe der König' is not utterly intractable, for it combines contextual 'clues' with a connotative basis actualised at the level of an intertext. That is to say, the language of Celan's own poetry provides the real point of entry into the poem. Compare the above quotations from 'Royal Fern' and 'Es Lebe' with Celan's *Mit Wechselndem Schlüssel* ('With a Variable Key'):

> With a variable key
> you unlock the house in which
> drifts the snow of that left unspoken.
> Always what key you choose
> depends on the blood that spurts
> from your eye or your mouth or your ear.
>
> You vary the key, you vary the word
> that is free to drift with the flakes.
> What snowball will form round the word
> depends on the wind that rebuffs you.[80]

The key, speech, appears to have the freedom of the non-human. Like the configurations of ice in *The White Stones*, Celan's snowflakes possess an emotive, inhuman quality, for they are both frozen and random. Snowflakes drift through the air, but fall and compress into 'drifts'; although their airborne freedom is identified with words, when they eventually drift together and harden into snowballs, they compact around the chosen word. Numerous keys, or words, unlock the house, which permits the snow 'of that left unspoken' to enter, and it is as if this initial act of free choice, in choosing the key (there is clearly not *one* key that will fit the lock), quickly 'freezes' into the un(re)cognisable, *unheimlich*, substance of something unspeakable. 'Choice' has already been determined by a violent event (indexed by the spurting blood) which precedes the act of speech. But the ensuing iciness does not simply provide a negative analogue for the unspeakable, for if the snowball seals off and isolates the word, it also protects and 'insulates' it from the rebuffing wind on which it depends. Celan intimates a condition of language that is both open and closed to experience, free from representation and yet determined by the need to represent. Like the snowball, it is both that which is to hand for being and that which freezes sense on touch. This freezing or closing-off of meaning forms both the mark of pain and a protection against it. A step beyond the human, it is close to what Trotter has to say about the spirit of anti-pathos in Celan and Prynne: 'When accosted by real cries, the poems of *Brass* do thrill themselves to ice, do turn a Medusa-head on the pathos of poet and reader alike.'[81] Pain has turned the threshold to stone.

'Es Lebe der König', like Prynne's more recent work, such as *Word Order* (1989), registers pain and distress in anonymously private and public terms, and invokes pathos largely in order to 'freeze' it: the 'plum', which 'exudes its / fanatic resin and is at once forced in' (168) is later 'a nick of pain, is so and is also / certainly loved' (169). The indication of pain baffles, because it is associated with an object that appears to be meaningless in terms of the experience of pain. The fruit is 'fanatic', and leads to 'exotic motive' (168). The word 'plum' also signifies the 'best of something', the 'plum choice', and the poem both maintains and subverts this nuance by equating desire with distress: if the 'nick of pain' that the plum is is 'certainly loved', the poem has prepared for it with the exhortation 'Give us this love of murder and / sacred boredom' (169). The initial question, what love of murder?, finds no answer in the poem and so gives way to interpretation at the formal level of the utterance, which plays on the Lord's Prayer ('Give us this day, our daily bread') to challenge pathos.[82] Choosing not to think of 'your / fearful groan', 'we' are forced to have choice overridden by irrational, uncontrollable factors, 'the most worthless / accident', 'a patchwork of / revenge' (the line-break forcing emphasis or 'stress' on these words). As Ward writes, referring to the recurrence of the word 'chance' in *Word Order* but linking this to 'Es Lebe', 'Chance hovers ambiguously, pointing to the triumph of the random, a world without meaning, and to the possibility of a hidden order underpinning our ceaseless collisions and accidents.'[83] If there is ambiguity here, it is not that of having to choose between the conditions of chaos and order, but the duplicity of the uncanny inherence of both in the semi-random effects of the text. In a brief discussion of 'With a Variable Key', Katherine Washburn notes that 'The poem is a house or *techne*'.[84] Likewise, in 'Es Lebe', 'The house becomes technical' (168); 'Give us this love of murder and / sacred boredom, you walk in the shade of / the technical house' (169). These lines may refer to Heidegger's description of *Dichtung* as the 'House of Being' and as *techne*, which is, he claims, 'a bringing forth of beings in that it *brings forth* present beings as such being *out of* concealedness, and specifically *into* the unconcealedness of their appearance'.[85] Thus, Prynne's word 'shade' is crucially ambiguous in relation to *techne* in that it suggests both cool relief from 'the sky now hot with its glare, turning / russet and madder' (168) and the realm of the shades, the shadowy otherworld of death. If Celan was driven to *Dichtung* as the only medium through which to 'say' the unspeakable, he nevertheless found in it only the subversion of 'bringing forth . . . into . . . unconcealedness' and the annihilation of Heideggerian *techne*. In Celan's early poetry, 'death is a master from Germany'; for Celan, *dichtung* must think through the meaning of being always in the faceless face of the master who would reduce beings to ash.[86] In Prynne's work, however, the abstractions of 'chance' and 'order' have taken over from these racial and political pressures, and the formal appropriation of Celan's tropes attests to what Ward calls the 'universal malady' of human suffering. Like the heuristic problem of meaning in Prynne's poem, the sense or senselessness of violence would appear to be a matter of discovery, but discovery always underpinned by the loss of meaning which is death 'itself'. In his 1963 discussion of modernism in German poetry, Prynne describes Celan's formal procedures:

> Celan has published four volumes in the last fifteen years, and the tendency has been towards an increasingly rigorous and lapidary abstraction: Yvan Goll's dream world informed by a Mallarméan geometry of the spirit. The full text of his "Totesfuge" is included in this anthology [Hamburger and Middleton's *Modern German Poetry, 1910–1960*], and this well illustrates his early dactylic eloquence; but the prismatic sparcity of his later manner is inadequacy represented . . . Here Celan adopts Mallarmé's primary stratagem of purity, to set off the images that evolve from his thinly-populated poetic universe. His "Kreuzmetapher", or combination of terms from different levels of discourse and abstraction, deploys a curious sense of imaginative dimensions almost empty of content; as Heselhaus observes, his phenomena are less significant than the relations that obtain between them.[87]

In his elegy, seven years later, Prynne draws attention to that 'stratagem of purity' by reiterating images of 'whiteness':

> Take it away and set up
> the table ready for the white honey, choking the
> white cloth spread openly for the most worthless
> accident. The whiteness is a patchwork of
> revenge too, open the window and white fleecy
> clouds sail over the azure.
>
> ('Es Lebe der König'. 169)

Unlike the spacings of Mallarmé's poetry, there is nothing pure about these 'blanks'; they turn from being moments of 'pure space' (retaining, for Mallarmé, the symbolisation of purity), to trope menace and violence. The strangely definite recurrence of the whites in Prynne are an extension of ordinary usage, for 'white' already has both positive and negative connotations in familiar expressions such as 'white noise', 'white heat', 'white riot'. In *Wound Response* (1974), Prynne will write of 'white murmur' ('Treatment in the Field', 214) and 'white rate' ('upon his lips curious white flakes, like thin snow . . . to set damage control at the same white rate' ('Of Movement Towards a Natural Place', 221). In Celan's poetic world, milk can become black (as in *'Todesfuge'*: 'Black milk of daybreak we drink you at night'), and other symbols of sustenance, such as honey, also turn towards danger.[88] Yet Prynne's response to the figuration of danger and the violent event remains at the level of formal abstraction. Perhaps this is the only possible elegiac response to the non-encounter with Celan's death? Lacking any real knowledge of the event itself, stunned into estrangement, the poem turns its Medusa-head on the scene.

The formal effect of the Medusa-head in *Brass* alternates between the voiding of figuration in the modernist project and its reinscription into thematic interests, where the mediation on pain sanctions an ethic based on what Prynne believes to be the literal, objective and physical response to experience that is the 'just' order of being itself. In a published letter to the poet and novelist Douglas Oliver, Prynne declares his hostility to what he sees as a debased morality arising from the pathos of modern life. Sentimentality has a pathological motive in that it tries to cancel out the existence of pain and violence. But his elision only makes the subject more sensitive and fearful of the physical fact of pain. This is why, when Prynne produces a poetic of anti-pathos, of the Medusa-head, he insists that pain must be loved: 'This is ethic certainty, which makes the pain real and thus the love absolute.'[89] Otherwise,

> the image of suffered love is
> scaled off, shattered to a granulated pathos
> like the dotted pigments of cygnus
>
> ('The Ideal Star-Fighter', 165)

The objectivism of the modernist text resists 'mimetic sentimentalism' by presenting the reader with a worked surface which discloses nothing but anti-pathetic loss. Only by losing the comfort and reassurance of subject-position provided by the naturalistic poem will the reader get a shot at genuine experience. Prynne doesn't want his poems to be '"human" like a friendly dog' so that they can shore up the mood of empirical disillusion common to postwar British writing.[90] Against this prevailing mood, he looks to the pathology of extreme experience as something that has the potential to 'move right out of range' of what in *Kitchen Poems* he had called 'those sickening and / greasy sureties' (17–18), and in 'A New Tax on the Counter-Earth' 'the greasy rope-trick' (171) of debased morality and the cash-in culture that underpins it. The physical fact of pain is a 'wound' in the subject's self-image, thus, 'The ethic vector is violent and discontinuous, developing schizophrenia of the body-percept and the embedding of will within larger spiritual bodies, but also revealing absolute moments of truth.'[91] The overdetermined, schizoid poetic text allows access to a form of knowledge which, in disorientating the *heimlich* sense of selfhood, somehow discloses a hidden order of reality composed of 'larger spiritual bodies'. Again we see that Prynne determines the effect of the *unheimlich* by appealing to what he describes in the 1971 lecture on Olson as the cosmic order of love.

The Medusa-head, then, may entail frozen forms, absurdity, and even psychosis. But Prynne believes that its 'chaos' may be the only access to a higher order of being. Like the shaman's 'madness', individual consciousness is presented as necessarily dispersed, and mystically associative in that the schizoid 'dissociation of sensibility' is one who, by 'civilised' standards, fails to separate his own identity from other identities, and constantly confuses 'fact' and 'fantasy', desire and rational expectations: the schizophrenic is always making new connections between prescribed categories, and so has the ability to break through the existing order. Prynne's work suggests that the method behind radically dissociative modernist texts is based on a strategic appropriation of such states of being. As far as one can discern it, his project is reminiscent of Eliot's to the extent that it seeks to replace 'false' associations of sensibility with real or true associations, but by embracing 'violent and discontinuous' poetic forms embedded in the non-rational, it goes under the tantra of a (dis)association which would have confounded Eliot himself.[92] The Project is 'singular', but also duplicitous; the 'real' it apprehends appears as a universal, mystical order which coheres beyond the immediate space of the poem. Prynne alludes to the Medusa-head in his letter, linking it to the discussion of pain:

How interesting it is to see, if one reads *In One Side and Out the Other* [by John James, Andrew Crozier and Tom Phillips] or *Printed Circuit* [Crozier] or *Brass* or *Oppoetique* [Oliver's *Oppo Hectic*], that the Anglo team have their teeth really sunk into pain, great physical gouts of it, as opposed to the water-colour joys of the American art gallery nympholepts. Your novel [Oliver's *The Harmless Building*] confirms this; its elegance is much too vorticist for the pre-sexual phenomenology preferred in l'Amerique du Nord. Only Frank O'Hara had that pail of serpents always in view.[93]

Prynne refers to O'Hara's poem 'In Memory of My Feelings', which subjects pathos of confessing hysteria and vulnerability to a hardened detachment:

> My transparent selves
> flail about like vipers in a pail, writhing and hissing
> without panic, with a certain justice of response
> and presently the aquiline serpent comes to resemble the Medusa.[94]

Prynne's increasing use of language derived from the physical sciences reveals a growing disenchantment over the gap between what he sees as the visionary state of the transcendental Real and the perception of physical response as a 'wounding' of moral ideals. Pain, and the imperative that it be loved, is now regarded as a transcendent experience. The 'larger spiritual bodies . . . revealing absolute moments of truth' look less and less pertinent as a hidden order informing poetic meaning, and Prynne searches for a new *Gestalt* based on an ethic of physical response. But, far from standing as the literal condition of the Real itself, the 'transcendent concretion' that is the 'love of pain' is pitted against desire and self-deception, re-marks the fragmented text with the threat of symbolic castration: 'together we love him limb from / limb' ('The Bee Target On His Shoulder', 149). As radical loss, fragmentation both elicits and annuls desire, replacing it with a chastening flagellation of the spirit, self-denial masquerading as truth. The 'subject' of fragmentation is one whose response to loss is penitential. Prynne's work remains in the tradition of high modernist art for which fragmentation and negativity are expected to guarantee an aesthetic based on the sacred autonomy of the self, even when that self has been reduced to the 'facts' of somatic response. The distinctly male shade returning from the re-presentation of loss is an effect of mourning, exile, and fracture, signs of the wounded body as *objet a*. The *unheimlich* text, with all its cognates in the fragmentary realm of the dream, the tendentiously obscure poem, and the Medusa-head of art, finds its Real not in the form of the mystical absolution of the masculine self, but in the subject's attempts to fulfil the desire of the Other by cancelling desire in the self. The paradox of 'singular' and 'double' presences is one informed by the structure of the autonomous self, which finds its identity by repressing its being-for an other. In *Brass*, we discover that 'marvellous Medusa-head, marvellous aletheia of the subject' described by Borch-Jacobsen, 'The *objet a* of phantasy' which 'portrays the subject *on the verge (au bord*; literally, "on the rim") of disappearing, suspended (and thus "propping up" his desire) *on the verge* of castration'.[95] Or, as Prynne's poetic of the 'counter-self' puts it, 'Only at the rim does the day tremble and shine' ('Of Movement Towards a Natural Place', 221.)

Notes

1 Wheale, 'J. H. Prynne', 773–4.
2 Jacques Derrida discusses Mallarmé's relation to the 'marking' and 're-marking' of poetry in 'The Double Session' in *Dissemination*, and the 're-trait' in 'The *Retrait* of Metaphor', *enclitic*, 2:2 (fall 1978), pp. 5–33. In 'the Double Session', Derrida shows that non-meaning is as important a consideration in modernist poetry as meaning or interpretation. In his discussion of Benjamin's 'The Task of the Translator', Paul de Man makes a similar point in his theory that translation 'desacralises' the notion of an original text by revealing the lack of adequation between the material signifier and what it is thought to signify (its 'signified'). For de Man, the translator's attempt to carry over a postulated core of meaning from one language to another, with its inevitable misappropriations, discloses the nonadequation between the will to mean and figuration in a native, 'original' language as well as in a translation. Translation 'relates to what in the original belongs to language and not to meaning.' (*The Resistance to Theory* (Manchester: Manchester University Press, 1986), 84.) It is the condition of language in general to turn away from the idea of meaning embodied in perception (which, in Saussurean terms, is the notion of a signified preceding the signifier, and therefore able to stand without it). Therefore, language is never 'at home' to intention and cognition; nor, in its alterity to the subject of perception, is it mystical in the proleptic, messianic sense, for precisely the same reason: there can be no 'pure language' (what Benjamin calls *reine Sprach*, the pre or sacred language), because language is irreducibly non-semantic and non-phenomenal. In de Man's reading of Benjamin, poetic language 'consists in the rigorous separation and the acting out of the separation of the sacred from the poetic . . . It is within this negative knowledge of its relation to the language of the sacred that poetic language initiates. It is, if you want, a necessarily nihilistic moment that is necessary in any understanding of history.' (*The Resistance to Theory*, 92.) In this case, the modernist text would present itself as a translation without an original, like Benjamin's fragments that cannot be reconstituted as a fragmented totality, because its parts do not refer to what Michael Riffaterre calls a 'matrix' (*Semiotics of Poetry* (Ithaca: Indiana University Press, 1978), which would be an implicit, core meaning. In that it seems to be upholding the now familiar view of literature as being 'non-referential' or 'self-referential', de Man's theory would appear to be in line with Riffaterre's. But, as Cynthia Chase has shown, de Man is actually criticising the still-representational idea of the 'determinate negation of entities' by showing that it is based on the 'indeterminable negativity of materiality and figure' ('Translating Romanticism: Literary Theory as the Criticism of Aesthetics in the Work of Paul de Man', *Textual Practice*, 4:3 (winter 1990), p. 355). This means that the text cannot be recuperated (determined) as literature by setting it apart from 'ordinary', referential language.

3 See for example Steve McCaffery's essay 'Language Writing: From Productive to Libidinal Economy', which describes the 'tactility' of poetic texts that explode sentences out from their phonematic components. The text is reduced to a field of 'marks or gestures rather than semantic exchange objects' so that it registers in terms of a pre-linguistic drive which is 'the surplus-value of meaning itself.' (*North of Intention*, 155.) That is, it is an *excess* of meaning, which has no utilitarian value, and it is therefore, McCaffery claims, of a primary and subversive libidinal order, rather like the Lacanian 'Thing'.

McCaffery mistakes the Lacanian 'symptom' for a positivist version of desire and supposes *jouissance* to transcend the ideological underpinnings of capital (how can its 'surplus-value' be *opposed* to economic production?). Moreover, he assumes that the text can be in the position of the material signifier as a pure 'mark or gesture' beyond meaning (that is, as language) and yet represent 'the surplus-value of meaning itself' (the double genitive refuses to allow 'surplus' to exceed meaning altogether). In this way, a hermeneutic centring on the problem of cognition is passed off as a poetics of libido, with the result that the 'objectivist' indetermination of the text is imbued with the subjective trappings of desire.

4 Timothy Clark, 'French Heidegger and an English Poet: Charles Tomlinson's "Poem" and the Status of Heideggerian *Dichtung*', *Man and World: An International Philosophical Review*, Vol. 20 (1987), p. 309.

5 Martin Heidegger, 'A Dialogue on Language', in *On the Way to Language*. Trans. Peter D. Hertz (San Francisco: Harper and Row, 1975), 45.

6 Martin Heidegger, *The Question Concerning Technology and Other Essays*. Trans. William Lovett (New York: Harper and Row, 1977), 16. See Allan Megill, *Prophets of Extremity: Nietzsche, Heidegger, Foucault, Derrida* (Berkeley: University of California Press, 1985), esp. 167–75; Jacques Derrida, '*Geschlecht* II: Heidegger's Hand', in John Sallis, ed., *Deconstruction and Philosophy: The Texts of Jacques Derrida* (Chicago: University of Chicago Press, 1987).

7 Manfred Frank, *Einführung in die Frühromantische Ästhetik*, 340, quoted in Andrew Bowie, 'Revealing the Truth of Art', *Radical Philosophy*, 58 (summer 1991), p. 24.

8 Bowie, 'Revealing the Truth of Art', p. 24.

9 de Man, *The Resistance to Theory*, 91.

10 Prynne, 'On *Maximus IV, V, & VI*' (no page number).

11 Prynne, '"Modernism" in German Poetry', *The Cambridge Review*, 9 March 1963, p. 333. Earlier, Prynne has written that the '"accent on the physical object of feeling" in the Imagist programme was of course almost from the start a mythic requirement; but even so, the organisation of imagistic components was indeed primarily spatial rather than visionary' (p. 332).

12 Prynne, 'On *Maximus IV, V, & VI*'.

13 Heidegger, *Being and Time*, 322.

14 Heidegger, *Being and Time*, 321. '"It" calls, against our expectations and even against our will' (320). Drawing on this passage, Avital Ronell suggests that the call is an irruption of the Lacanian Real (*The Telephone Book*, 30–1). See Slovoj Žižek's argument, in *The Sublime Object of Ideology* (London: Verso, 1989), that the Real marks, in its positivity, nothing but the embodiment of pure negativity (170 ff.), and the 'subject is the "answer" of this Real' (173): 'this original void, this lack of symbolic structure, is the subject, the subject of the signifier' (175).

15 Ronell, *The Telephone Book*, 58. See Alphonso Lingis's introduction to Emmanuel Levinas, *Collected Philosophical Papers* (Dordrecht: Martinus Nijhoff, 1987), xi–xii. Heidegger's later texts 'identify the existing as not at home in the world as the

existentiel form of alienation characteristic of the metaphysical epoch. Thus Heidegger reinterprets the sacred or the ideal in such a way to constitute a primal
dimension of coming to be at home here, via building and dwelling'.

16 Michael Grant, 'J. H. Prynne', *The Dictionary of Literary Biography*, Vol. 40: *Poets of
Great Britain and Ireland since 1960*. Part II (Detroit: Bruccoli Clark, 1985), 451–2.

17 Grant, 'J. H. Prynne', 451.

18 When commuted to the essential quality of a 'deep' self, Heidegger's subject
becomes the proper subject of proper objects. For this to occur, the language of the
poem would have to disappear in favour of the aether of 'communication'. This
would be a bizarre conclusion to draw from a text that 'says itself' as nothing but the
array of language and writing. For a self to appear that is anything more than uncertain and divided, language must disappear. See Jacques Lacan, 'From Love to the
Libido', in *The Four Fundamental Concepts of Psychoanalysis*. Trans. Alan Sheridan
(New York: Norton, 1978) and Mikkel Borch-Jacobsen on the relationship between
identity and appropriation in *The Freudian Subject*. Trans. Catherine Porter (Stanford: Stanford University Press, 1988), 26: 'We shall have to reconsider the idea that
desire has a connection, however minor, with an *object* (even if the object is always
already lacking, because it is articulated by way of a verbal demand), and at the same
time we shall have to reconsider the idea of a *subject* of desire (even if it is the subject of original representation, language and repression, always already inadequate
to itself)'.

19 Rod Mengham, 'A Lifelong Transfusion: *The Oval Window* of J. H. Prynne', *The
Grosseteste Review*, Vol. 15 (1983–84), p. 209. Mengham undermines the formalist
view of the self-reflexive text, which endows certain traits in the language of literary
texts with metalinguistic truth. But as Rainer Nägele has pointed out, 'there is often
a confusion between self-referential and self-reflective: the self-referential linguistic
act is not necessarily self-reflective, nor is self-reflective discourse more self-referential than any other. A poem that presents and stages certain devices and operations
of language does not necessarily "know" or talk *about* them; and self-reflective texts
that talk about themselves are often the blindest toward their own performance as
linguistic acts.' (*Reading After Freud: Essays On Goethe, Hölderlin, Habermas, Nietzsche, Brecht, Celan, and Freud* (New York: Columbia University Press, 1987), 165.)
However, in avoiding this critical fallacy, Mengham falls foul of the problem of 'external reflection', as Žižek calls it, which manufactures a way out of the problem of the
overdetermined text by transposing 'the "essence", the "true meaning" of a text into
the unattainable beyond, making of it a transcendent "Thing-in-itself". 'All that is
accessible to us, finite subjects, are distorted reflections, partial aspects deformed by
our subjective perspective; the Truth-in-itself, the true meaning of the text, is lost for
ever.' (*The Sublime Object of Ideology*, 212.)

20 Literary critics have tended to use this idea of the signifier indiscriminately, equating
the 'free play of the signifier' with the condition of fictionality or the aesthetic, completely missing the point that 'fiction' or 'the aesthetic' has now *become the signified*.
For Saussure, signifier and signified exist in relation to one another like the recto and
verso sides of a leaf of paper (Ferdinand de Saussure, *Course in General Linguistics*.
Ed. Charles Bally and Albert Sechehaye with the collaboration of Albert Riedlinger.
Trans. and annotated by Roy Harris. (London: Duckworth, 1983), 111). Derrida's
emphasis on the signifier in *Of Grammatology* and elsewhere represents initially a
critique of the metaphysics of the relationship between sound and thought, and substance and form, in Saussure's theory. Cut loose, the signifier might inaugurate a new
world of pure sound, but the moment one hears that world of sound as *value* (for

instance as something closer to the self, in an ontology based on respiration) it comes into the ear's view as something signified.

Furthermore, by displacing the static availability of the signified and the referent (the 'concepts' of which, in spite of Saussure's claims in the *Course*, tend to collapse into each other), one does not void referentiality; as Derrida writes in his essay 'Devant la loi', the 'text retains an essential rapport to the play of framing and the paradoxical logic of boundaries, which somehow upsets the "normal" system of reference, while *revealing* an essential structure of referentiality. This obscure revelation of referentiality no more refers than the eventness of the event is an event . . . What differs from one work to the other [in the case of Kafka's parable 'Before the Law' and *The Trial*, in which the parable reappears] if it is not content, is also not *form* (the signifying expression, the phenomena of language or rhetoric) but the movements of framing and referentiality.' ('devant la loi', in Alan Udoff, ed., *Kafka and the Contemporary Critical Performance* (Bloomington: Indiana University Press, 1987), 146.)

21 Lacan, *The Four Fundamental Concepts of Psychoanalysis*, 198–9. For an important clarification of this section of *The Four Fundamental Concepts*, see Mikkel Borch-Jacobsen, *Lacan: The Absolute Master*. Trans. Douglas Brick (Stanford: Stanford University Press, 1991), 185ff. 'If the signifier, as Lacan says, "represents a subject", and "not a signified", it is not because the subject is distinguished from the traditional "fixed" signified: the subject is now the *elusive* signified of all signifiers, what they all represent in his absence; but he is none the less their signified, to which their references refer' (187). Thus, Lacan is far from denying reference, but in substituting the 'subject' for the 'signified', he undermines the static, empiricist notion of reference, which appears in Saussure as the confusion between the categories of the signified and the referent. For Lacan, language does not represent a subject for another subject, it represents the subject *for another signifier*: the subject is in language and language is in the subject.

22 In the case of Freud's *History of an Infantile Neurosis*, the analysand's discourse was in fact composed of several different languages, which signified in their own conglomerate language, 'a compendium of rhymes, puns, silent distortions, and secret verbal contortions' (Translator's Introduction to Nicholas Abraham and Maria Torok, *The Wolf Man's Magic Word: A Cryptonymy*. Trans. Nicholas Rand. Foreword by Jacques Derrida (Minneapolis: University of Minnesota Press, 1986), lvii). This fragmentary poetic, needless to say, can only be determined in relation to the personality of the Wolf Man 'himself', or, in the sophisticated analysis of Abraham and Torok, through knowledge of the context of the Wolf Man's trauma provided by the narratives that inform and support his discourse.

23 See W. K. Wimsatt and Monroe Beardsley, 'The Intentional Fallacy', in *The Verbal Icon: Studies in the Meaning of Poetry* (New York: Noonday Press, 1954).

24 Martin Heidegger, 'Logos (Heraclitus, Fragment B 50)' in *Early Greek Thinking: The Dawn of Western Philosophy*. Trans. David Farrell Krell and Frank A. Capuzzi. San Francisco: Harper and Row, 1984), 70–1. Translation modified in Borch-Jacobsen, *Lacan*, 106.

25 Borch-Jacobsen, *Lacan*, 107.

26 Derrida, *The Post Card: From Socrates to Freud and Beyond*. Trans. with an introduction and additional notes by Alan Bass (Chicago: University of Chicago Press, 1987), 470; Borch-Jacobsen, *Lacan*, 258–9.

27 Clark, 'French Heidegger and an English Poet', p. 324.

28 See Leo Bersani, *The Culture of Redemption* (Cambridge, MA: Harvard University Press, 1991).

29 Derrida, '*Geschlecht* II: Heidegger's Hand', 190. Heidegger begins his 1953 essay on Trakl by pointing out that by the word 'discussion' (*Erörterung*) he means the 'proper place or site of something' and the 'heeding' of that site (*On the Way to Language*, 159).

30 Lacan, *The Four Fundamental Concepts*, 73–4ff. See also Roger Caillois, 'Mimicry and Legendary Psychasthenia', trans. John Shepley, in Annette Michelson, Rosalind Krauss, Douglas Crimp and Joan Copjec, eds, *October: The First Decade, 1976–1986* (Cambridge, MA, The MIT Press, 1987).

31 Sigmund Freud, *The Interpretation of Dreams*. Trans. James Strachey. Ed. James Strachey and Alan Tyson. Present vol. ed. Angela Richards. The Pelican Freud Library, Vol. 4 (Harmondsworth: Penguin, 1978), 652–3; Lacan, *The Four Fundamental Concepts*, 57–60.

32 Lacan, *The Four Fundamental Concepts*, 59.

33 Lacan, *The Four Fundamental Concepts*, 73. By emphasising senses and categories other than that of sight, I am aiming a show the textual nature of what is still being put forward by Lacan as a phenomenology (even while his text confounds phenomenology). It is as something that can be *seen* that Lacan justifies his concept of the phallus as the master-signifier (discussed by Borch-Jacobsen in *Lacan*, 216–17ff), the priority of which has been questioned by Derrida in '*Le facteur de la verité*: 'In this sense castration-truth is the opposite of fragmentation, the very antidote for fragmentation: that which is missing from its place has in castration a fixed, central place, freed from all substitution' (*The Post Card*, 441).

The dream, like the poem, often testifies to the experience (or positing) of synasthesia, the conflation of one sense with another, which is consonant with an imaginational staging.

34 Lacan, *The Four Fundamental Concepts*, 59–60. This is Lacan's version of what Freud termed the 'naval' of the dream: 'There is often a passage in even the most thoroughly interpreted dream which has to be left obscure; this is because we become aware during the work of interpretation that at that point there is a tangle of dream-thoughts which cannot be unravelled and which moreover adds nothing to our knowledge of the content of the dream.' (Quoted in Borch-Jacobsen, *The Freudian Subject*, 24.)

35 As Žižek argues, 'the Real is not a transcendent positive entity, persisting somewhere beyond the symbolic order like a hard kernel inaccessible to it, some kind of Kantian "Thing-in-itself" – in itself it is nothing at all, just a void, an emptiness in a symbolic structure marking some central impossibility. It is in this sense that the enigmatic Lacanian phrase defining the subject as an "answer of the Real" is to be understood: we can inscribe, encircle the void place of the subject through the failure of his symbolisation, because the subject is nothing but the failure point of the process of his symbolic representation.' (Žižek, *The Sublime Object of Ideology*, 173.) Therefore, 'this original void, this lack of symbolic structure, *is* the subject, the subject of the signifier' (175).

36 Michel de Certeau, *Heterologies: Discourse on the Other*. Trans. Brian Massumi (Manchester: Manchester University Press, 1986), 166.

37 Vincent Descombes, *Proust: Philosophie du Roman* (Paris: Les Editions de Minuit, 1983), 320.

38 See Riffaterre, *Semiotics of Poetry*, esp. Chapter One. In a discussion of Gautier's poem '*In Deserto*', Riffaterre writes that the matrix 'is a hierarchy of representations imposed upon the reader, despite his personal preferences, by the greater or lesser expansion of the matrix's components, an orientation imposed upon the reader despite his linguistic habits, a bouncing from reference to reference that keeps on

pushing the meaning over to a text not present in the linearity, to a paragram or hypogram . . . The significance is shaped like a doughnut, the hole being either the matrix of the hypogram or the hypogram as matrix' (12–13). 'The Bee Target On His Shoulder' is more like the inner rim of this doughnut.

The word 'matrix', of course, also stands for 'mother', which would facilitate the extension of this discussion into a Kleinian reading of loss, as Angela Moorjani has done with Hoffmann's 'The Sandman' in *The Aesthetics of Loss and Lessness*.

39 Borch-Jacobsen, *Lacan*, 252.

40 Borch-Jacobsen, *Lacan*, 252.

41 Heidegger, *Being and Time*, 320, but quoted here from Avital Ronell's fuller translation in *The Telephone Book*, 33.

42 Heidegger, *Being and Time*, 322.

43 Heidegger, *Being and Time*, 321–2: 'What could be more alien to the "they", lost in the manifold 'world' of its concern, than the Self which has been individualised down to itself in uncanniness and been thrown into the "nothing".' The statement should not be confused with a solipsism arising from the Cartesian positing of a self-sufficient subjectivity, but an attempt to account for the emergence of selfhood in its potentiality-for-Being.

44 Sigmund Freud, '*Das Unheimliche*', in *Art and Literature*. Trans. James Strachey. Present vol. ed. Albert Dickson. The Pelican Freud Library, Vol. 14 (Harmondsworth: Penguin, 1985), 345.

45 Freud, '*Das Unheimliche*', 346–7.

46 Freud, '*Das Unheimliche*', 357.

47 Freud, '*Das Unheimliche*', 357.

48 Ronell, *The Telephone Book*, 69.

49 Hélène Cixous, 'Fiction and Its Phantoms: A Reading of Freud's *Das Unheimliche* (The "Uncanny")', in *New Literary History*, 7:3 (spring 1976), p. 536; p. 535. Cixous criticises the Lacanian reliance on the phallus as arbiter of meaning in readings such as Samuel Weber's 'The Sideshow, or: Remarks on a Canny Moment', *Modern Language Notes*, Vol. 88, No. 6, (1973), pp. 1102–33. But Weber, too, emphasises the 'recurrence and repetition of castration' as the uncanny effect, for 'repetition consists not in the re-presentation of the identical but rather in the indefinite, incessant and often violent displacement of marks and traces never entirely reducible to a signified significance', a point which bears on the tension between perception and language that we have 'seen' recurring throughout Prynne's work; if 'Uncanny is a certain indecidability which affects and infects representations, motifs, themes and situations', it implies a second moment or movement, namely the defence against this crisis of perception and phenomenality, a defence which is ambivalent and which expresses itself in . . . compulsive curiosity' (p. 1132).

50 Cf. Andrew Ross's remarks about *Brass* in 'The Oxygen of Publicity', *Poetics Journal*, No. 6 (1986), p. 67: 'From *Brass* (1971) onward, something like an ethics of speech – a "politics of melody" – makes its appearance in English writing again, but *as if it were a novelty* – and this is not nothing after eight hundred years of usage. Much of Prynne's writing since then seems to get by on lyrical lip-service . . . But the lines almost always tighten their hold on the logic of events . . . or else come around to reviewing the terms of their social contract.'

51 Cixous, 'Fiction and its Phantoms', p. 543.

52 Heidegger, *On the Way to Language*, 162–3.

53 Heidegger, *On the Way to Language*, 163.

54 David Trotter, 'A Reading of Prynne's *Brass*', *P. N. Review*, Vol. 5, No. 2 (1977), p. 51

(and see his discussion in *The Making of the Reader*, 218–30); Geoffrey Ward, 'Nothing but Mortality: Prynne and Celan', in Antony Easthope and John O. Thompson, eds, *Contemporary Poetry Meets Modern Theory* (London: Harvester Wheatsheaf, 1991), 143.

55 Paul Celan, 'Der Meridian' in *Gesammelte Werke in Fünfe Banden*. (Ed. Beda Alleman and Stefan Richert with the assistance of Rudolf Bücher. Vol. 3 (Frankfurt am Main: Suhrkamp, 1983), 190; 200. 'The Meridian', in *Collected Prose*. Trans. Rosmarie Waldrop (Manchester: Carcanet Press, 1986), 40; 52. Ward, 'Nothing But Mortality', 150. Trotter, too, emphasises this *Unendlichsprechung* in Prynne's work, but he always reins it in to an argument for the grounding of a moral self, a selfhood that is conceived as self-sufficient and therefore at home to itself.

56 Celan, *Collected Prose*, 42–3.

57 Celan, *Collected Prose*, 53.

58 Prynne, 'A Pedantic Note in Two Parts', p. 351. Note here Prynne's own slip into moralism in the less tendentious poems in *Brass* ('The Ideal Star-Fighter' and 'A New Tax on the Counter-Earth'), and Trotter's analysis of them (in 'A Reading of Prynne's *Brass*', and *The Making of the Reader*). These poems speak of 'moral mutation in the species' (165) where 'The moral drive isn't / quick enough, the greasy rope-trick / has made payment an edge of rhetoric; / the conviction of merely being / right, that has / marched into the patter of balance' (171). While they continue the indignant argument against technocracy begun in *Kitchen Poems*, they imply an ethical order in which intellect, imagination (realised through the negative aspects of the dreamstate) and the pure response to physical conditions of being, such as pain, constitute a form of 'goodness' which may redeem humanity from the false sentiments of imposed morality, where the 'horizon is lit / with the rightness of wayward sentiment, cash / as a principle of nature' (172).

59 'Celan (b. 1920) drowned himself in the Seine in 1970. However much his suicide was the culmination of private despair, it may also have been determined by the Final Solution that shadowed both his poetry and historical lifetime. Celan was Romanian by birth: both his parents were deported and perished in the death-camps. Exiled in Paris from 1948 until his death, "a Jew with an unpronounceable name" (Celan being an anagrammatisation of Anczel, the "cz" sound being unavailable in French) the poet was, in Benjamin Hollander's words, "forced to occupy his estrangement deeply".' (Ward, 'Nothing But Mortality', 140. See Benjamin Hollander, ed., *Translating Tradition: Paul Celan in France* (Issues 8/9 of the San Francisco journal *Acts: A Journal of New Writing*, 1988.) See also Michael Hamburger's introduction to his edition of *Poems of Paul Celan* (London: Anvil Press, 1988); Jerry Glenn, *Paul Celan* (New York: Twayne Publishers, 1973); Amy D. Colin, ed., *Argumentum e Silentio: International Paul Celan Symposium* (Berlin: Walter de Gruyter, 1987). Amy Colin's own study, *Paul Celan: Holograms of Darkness* (Bloomington: Indiana University Press, 1991) gives a very detailed account of the poet's cultural background and the pressures his Bukovinian community faced from both Fascist and Stalinist regimes, as does John Felstiner's superb *Paul Celan: Poet, Survivor, Jew* (New Haven: Yale University Press, 1995).

60 Vincent Descombes has written that the primary influence of Heidegger's thinking on French philosophy was that, through his work on Nietzsche, the 'logic of identity is countered with a "thinking based upon difference".' This entails a critique of phenomenology, which does not escape 'the irruption of the self into the equation of *being* with *being for myself* . . . Where Parmenides said, "being is", modern philosophy proclaims that "being is for myself".' (*Modern French Philosophy*. Trans. I. Scott-Fox and J. M. Harding (Cambridge: Cambridge University Press, 1980), 75–6.) In

contending that Heidegger no more escapes this condition than those before him, I am disagreeing with Philippe Lacoue-Labarthe's ultimate defence of the 'thinker of Todtnauberg' in *Heidegger, Art, and Politics: The Fiction of the Political*. Trans. Chris Turner (Oxford: Basil Blackwell, 1990). Although Lacoue-Labarthe insists that the thinking of being, which radically questions the ideology of racial self-origination, e.g. the Nazi myth, should not be reduced to Heidegger's political errors, he neglects the mysticising, aestheticising representations of Being that are everywhere apparent in Heidegger's work, the ideological underpinnings of which show that the pastoral innocence of being is itself a dangerous myth. At the end of his book, Lacoue-Labarthe can seriously ask the question: 'Was the silence – the safeguarding of Germany – worth the risk for thought itself, of a (confessionless) confession of complicity with crime?' (117). 'It is this question,' he continues, 'which, "for a thousand years" . . . the thinker's thinking leaves open. The ultimate paradox is that it is preserved, as memorial, in a poem by a Jewish poet [Celan], which is entitled . . . *Todtnauberg*' (117). If Celan has written in memory of Heidegger, it certainly wasn't because he wished to safeguard the German nation.

61 Lacoue-Labarthe, *Heidegger, Art, and Politics*, 47. *Dichtung* itself becomes an '*Atemwende*', a 'turning back of breath', the title of Celan's 1967 collection of poems (*Gesammelte Werke*, Vol. 3, 195). In 1973, Anthony Barnett published Prynne's 'Es Lebe der König' separately, sandwiched between Rosmarie Waldrop's translations of Celan's 'Conversation in the Mountains' and Edmond Jabes's 'Answer To A Letter'. (*The Literally Supplement*, Writings, I. London: Nothing Doing (Formerly in London), 1973.)

62 Celan, *Collected Prose*, 40.

63 *Poems of Paul Celan*, 186–7.

64 Hamacher, 'The Second of Inversion', p. 297.

65 Lacoue-Labarthe, *Heidegger, Art, and Politics*, 46.

66 Theodor W. Adorno, *Prisms*. Trans. Samuel and Shierry Weber (London: Neville Spearman, 1967), 89.

67 Celan, *Gesammelte Werke*, Vol. 3, 198; *Collected Prose*, 49.

68 Celan, *Collected Prose*, 49.

69 Celan, *Collected Prose*, 50; *Gesammelte Werke*, 198.

70 Celan, *Collected Prose*, 50.

71 Cf. Cixous, 'Fiction and Its Phantoms', p. 548: 'So, of the *Unheimliche* (and its double, fiction) we can only say that it never completely disappears . . . that it "represents" that which in solitude, silence, and darkness will (never) be presented to you. Neither real nor fictitious, "fiction" is a secretion of death, an anticipation of nonrepresentation, a doll, a hybrid body composed of language and silence that, in the movement which turns it and which it turns, invents doubles, and death.'

72 On this 'inversion of inversion' see Hamacher, 'The Second of Inversion', p. 285ff. In *Heidegger, Art, and Politics*, Lacoue-Labarthe calls the organic conception of politics and aesthetics (and the merging of the two) 'immanentism', a term that he feels could replace 'totalitarianism'. He writes: 'The infinitisation or absolutisation of the subject, which is at the heart of the metaphysics of the Moderns, here finds its strictly operational outcome: the community creating, the community at work creates and works itself, so to speak, thereby accomplishing the subjective process *par excellence*, the process of self-formation and self-production. This is why that process finds its truth in a "fusion of the community" (in festival or war) or in the ecstatic identification with a Leader who in no way represents any form of transcendence, but incarnates, in immanent fashion, the immanentism of a community' (70). For a critique of the name

'Holocaust', see Emil L. Fackenheim, 'The Holocaust: A Summing up after Two Decades of Reflection', in Colin, *Argumentum e Silentio*. Fackenheim argues that the word 'Shoah', meaning 'total destruction', is a more suitable term to describe the persecution of the Jews than the term 'Holocaust', with its implicit notion of a 'burnt sacrifice'.

73 Celan, *Collected Prose*, 51.

74 Celan, *Collected Prose*, 51.

75 For example in this poem from *Schneepart* (1971): 'IN SAURIAN / skins, I bed you, you / have the falling sickness, down / on the sills, / the gable- / holes / bury us with the dung of light.' (Paul Celan, *Last Poems*. Trans. Katherine Washburn and Margaret Guillemin (San Francisco: North Point Press, 1986), 109. Even for readers and translators of the most 'textual' of poetry, the idea of reaching Perception (the light at the end of the tunnel) remains paramount; as Katherine Washburn writes in her illuminating introduction, 'One learns indeed to puzzle out, over many readings, the personal, historical, and literary data, the strands of associations, obsessions, and illusions which fuse in a single poem, and to be content, finally, with a sympathetic unknowing – the state of readership in which some genuine perception may at last become possible' (xiii).

76 Celan, *Collected Prose*, 52; *Gesammelte Werke*, Vol. 3, 200.

77 Celan, *Collected Prose*, 53; *Gesammelte Werke*, Vol. 3, 201.

78 Ross, 'The Oxygen of Publicity', pp. 64–5. Earlier in the same essay, Ross has written that the counter-word legitimises 'the maverick spirit of a vocabulary of humanism which tries to go beyond those interpretive strangleholds of Left and Right, revolution and reaction.'

79 Ward, 'Nothing but Mortality', 142–3.

80 *Poems of Paul Celan*, 89.

81 Trotter, *The Making of the Reader*, 220.

82 The poem is subtly intertextual in that it alludes to the rhetoric of prayer Celan uses frequently in his work. A prime example would be the poem 'Tenebrae' (from *Sprachgitter*) which, as Ward shows, produces a radical sense of unease by making the imagery of the Communion refer to the Shoah: 'Does the poem imply that the *individuality* of suffering as the pathway to redemption, so fundamental to Christianity, is now entirely consumed, devoured, in the genocidal flame of the Holocaust? Could these voices beyond the grave articulate a *revenge* on the God whose face was turned away while the furnaces burned? A hovering shadow of irony is not to be excluded from the ambiguities of "Tenebrae". In sum, one might want to say that by inscribing speech from beyond the human realm, by including possible reference to Jewry in the Holocaust but conveyed in the German language of the oppressor, the poem exerts a biting revenge on the master-order into which any poetic utterance is born, substituting its own tenebrous realm, *unheimlich* home.' ('Nothing but Mortality', 145.) This perhaps explains Prynne's use of the word 'revenge' in his poem, although one could only understand it as such as an evocation of Celan's language applied to the singularity of violence in Celan's case, not as a comment on the Nazi genocide.

83 Ward, 'Nothing but Mortality', 149.

84 Washburn, Introduction to Celan, *Last Poems*, p. xiii.

85 Heidegger, 'The Origin of the Work of Art', in *Poetry, Language, Thought*. Trans. Albert Hofstadter (New York: Harper and Row, 1975), 59.

86 Celan, 'Todesfuge' ('Death Fugue') in *Poems of Paul Celan*, 60–3. Celan's perplexed relationship with 'the poet of Todtnauberg' proceeds, like that of Derrida, from

the 'opening' of a certain ambiguity or duplicity in Heidegger's writing, where the 'flaming of spirit' is also 'spirit in flames'. As Derrida writes, 'this duplicity affects all the thinking up to and including that of ash [*le cendre*], that whiteness of ash which belongs to destiny consumed and consuming, to the conflagration of the flame which burns itself up.' (*Of Spirit*, 97.)

87 Prynne, '"Modernism" in German Poetry', p. 337.

88 'White' has both negative and positive connotations in Celan's poetry. For example, in '*Heimkehr*' ('Homecoming'), 'White, stacked into distance. / Above it, endless, / the sleigh-track of the lost.' (*Poems of Paul Celan*, 108–9.) Whereas, in a very late text, beginning 'THE POLES', the bleakness of the snowdrift creates some degree of succour: 'I lose you to you, that / is my snowy comfort, // say that Jerusalem *is*, // say it, as though I were this / your whiteness, / as though you / were mine' (344–5). The most overtly Celanian poem in *Brass* is 'Royal Fern', which contains echoes of many of Celan's texts, including 'With a Variable Key'': 'Still the snow hums, fetching my life: / the pain to come, still the key / takes cover in the chamois case. / The Key is the edge of our day'. (158). Even the title goes by way of Celanian parapraxis, working as a kind of cryptonym of 'Es Lebe der König': the Flowering or Royal Fern, *Osmunda Regalis*, seems to have little significance for the text which follows it, until we consider that Celan's poetic (exemplified by the 'royal' counter-word) is based on the practice of estrangement, or *Ferne* in German. Again, the poem may draw something from Shakespeare: 'we have the receipt of fern-seed, we walk invisible' (*King Henry IV*, Part 1, II.i.95). Cf. the poem 'Lupin Seed' (173); the lupin is one of 'the herbs and flowers of night' which 'banish the growth of night' (Frances Yates, *Giordano Bruno and the Hermetic Tradition*, 193).

89 Prynne, 'From a Letter to Douglas Oliver'' (9, 10, 11 January 1972), *The Grosseteste Review*, Vol. 6, Nos. 1–4 (1973), p. 153.

90 Prynne, 'From a Letter to Douglas Oliver', p. 153.

91 Prynne, 'From a Letter to Douglas Oliver', p. 152.

92 Pound was largely responsible for making *The Waste Land* the modernist exemplar it has become. See Eliot, *The Waste Land: A Facsimile and Transcript of the Original Drafts*. Ed. Valerie Eliot (London: Faber & Faber, 1972); Peter Ackroyd, *T. S. Eliot* (London: Hamish Hamilton, 1984), 116–19: 'the "nineteen pages" which Pound praised were the result of his own "Caesarian Operation" . . . Where Eliot was untrustful or uncertain of what he had done, wishing to clarify it with other material, Pound found its very resistance to interpretation . . . to be the key to its power' (117).

93 Prynne, 'From a Letter to Douglas Oliver', pp. 153–4.

94 *The Collected Poems of Frank O'Hara*. Ed. Donald Allen, with an introduction by John Ashbery (Berkeley: University of California Press, 1995), 253. David Trotter reads the Medusa-head in O'Hara's poem through 'The Meridian', although he doesn't discuss Celan's essay until much later in the book. He most likely took the initial idea from Prynne's letter. (*The Making of the Reader*, 160ff.)

95 Borch-Jacobsen, *Lacan*, 234.

BIBLIOGRAPHY

Aarsleff, Hans, *From Locke to Saussure: Essays on the Study of Language and Intellectual History*. Minneapolis: University of Minnesota Press, 1982.

Abraham, Nicholas, and Torok, Maria, *The Wolf Man's Magic Word: A Cryptonomy*. Trans. Nicholas Rand. Foreword by Jacques Derrida. Minneapolis: University of Minnesota Press, 1986.

Ackroyd, Peter, 'Legislators of Language', review of Andrew Crozier and Tim Longville, eds, *A Various Art* (Manchester: Carcanet, 1987), *The Times*, Thursday, 3 December 1987.

——, *T S Eliot*. London: Hamish Hamilton, 1984.

Adorno, Theodor W., *Prisms*. Trans. Samuel and Shierry Weber. London: Neville Spearman, 1967.

——, 'Enleitung zu Benjamins "Schriften"', in *Gesammelte Schriften 11: Noten zur Literatur*. Ed. Gretel Adorno and Rolf Tiedemann (Frankfurt am Main: Suhrkamp, 1974).

Allbright, W. F., and Lambdin, T. O., 'The Evidence of Language.' Fascicle 54 of the revised *Cambridge Ancient History*. Cambridge: Cambridge University Press, 1966.

Allnutt, Gillian, D'Aguiar, Fred, Edwards, Ken, and Mottram, Eric, eds, *The New British Poetry*. London: Paladin, 1988.

Altieri, Charles, *Self and Sensibility in Contemporary American Poetry*. Cambridge: Cambridge University Press, 1984.

Anderson, David, ed., *Pound's Cavalcanti: An Edition of the Translations, Notes, and Essays*. Princeton: Princeton University Press, 1983.

Ardizzone, Maria Luisa, *Guido Cavalcanti: The Other Middle Ages*. Toronto: Toronto University Press, 2002.

Armitage, Simon, and Crawford, Robert, *The Penguin Book of Poetry from Britain and Ireland Since 1945*. London: Penguin, 1998.

Barnaby, Karin, and d'Acierno, Pellegrino, eds, *C. G. Jung and the Humanities: Toward a Hermeneutics of Culture*. London: Routledge, 1990.

Barrett, John H., and Yonge, C. M., *Collins Pocket Guide to the Sea Shore*. London: Collins, 1958.

Barthes, Roland, *Image – Music – Text*. Essays selected and translated by Stephen Heath. London: Fontana, 1982.

Benjamin, Walter, *Charles Baudelaire: A Lyric Poet in the Era of High Capitalism*. Trans. Harry Zohn. London: Verso, 1985.

——, *The Correspondence of Walter Benjamin 1910–1940*. Ed. and annotated by Gershom Scholem and Theodor W. Adorno. Trans. Manfred R. Jacobson and Evelyn M. Jacobson. Chicago: Chicago University Press, 1994.

Bernstein, Michael, *The Tale of the Tribe: Ezra Pound and the Modern Verse Epic*. Princeton: Princeton University Press, 1980.

Bersani, Leo, *The Culture of Redemption*. Cambridge, MA, Harvard University Press, 1991.

Blavatsky, Helena Petrovna, *The Secret Doctrine*. Pasadena: Theosophical Universe Press, 1970.

Bone, Elizabeth, ed., *Ritual Human Sacrifice in MesoAmerica: A Conference at Dumbarton Oaks, October 13th and 14th, 1979*. Washington, DC: Dumbarton Oaks Research Library, 1984.

Borch-Jacobsen, Mikkel, *Lacan: The Absolute Master*. Trans. Douglas Brick. Stanford: Stanford University Press, 1991.

——, *The Freudian Subject*. Trans. Catherine Porter. Stanford: Stanford University Press, 1988.

Bourdieu, Pierre, *Outline of a Theory of Practice*. Trans. R. Nice. Cambridge: Cambridge University Press, 1977.

Bové, Paul A., ed., *Early Postmodernism: Foundational Essays*. Durham, NC: Duke University Press, 1995.

Bowie, Andrew, 'Revealing the Truth of Art', *Radical Philosophy*, 58 (summer 1991), pp. 20–4

Bradbury, Malcolm, and McFarlane, James, eds, *Modernism: 1890–1930*. Harmondsworth: Penguin, 1976.

Butterick, George, *A Guide to* The Maximus Poems *of Charles Olson*. Berkeley: University of California Press, 1980.

Byrd, Don, *Olson's Maximus Poems*. Urbana: University of Illinois Press, 1980.

Caillois, Roger, 'Mimicry and Legendary Psychasthenia', trans. John Shepley, in Annette Michelson, Rosalind Krauss, Douglas Crimp and Joan Copjec, eds, *October: The First Decade, 1976–1986*. Cambridge, MA: The MIT Press, 1987.

Caldwell, Roger, 'The flight back to where we are', review of J. H. Prynne, *Poems*, *The Times Literary Supplement*, 23 April 1999, p. 27.

Campbell, Joseph, ed., *The Mystic Vision: Papers from the Eranos Yearbooks*, Vol. 6. London: Routledge and Kegan Paul, 1969.

Casillo, Robert, *The Genealogy of Demons: Anti-Semitism, Fascism, and the Myths of Ezra Pound*. Chicago: Northwestern University Press, 1988.

Cavalcanti, Guido, *Rime*. Ed. Marcello Ciccuto. Milan: Rizzoli Editore, 1978.

——, *The Complete Poems*. Trans. Marc Cirigliano. New York: Italica Press, 1992.

Celan, Paul, *Gesammelte Werke in Fünfe Banden*. Ed. Beda Alleman and Stefan Richert with the assistance of Rudolf Bücher. Vol. 3. Frankfurt am Main: Suhrkamp, 1983.

——, *Collected Prose*. Trans. Rosmarie Waldrop. Manchester: Carcanet Press, 1986.

——, *Last Poems*. Trans. Katherine Washburn and Margaret Guillemin. San Francisco: North Point Press, 1986.

——, *Poems of Paul Celan*. Trans. Michael Hamburger. London: Anvil Press, 1988.

Chase, Cynthia, 'Translating Romanticism: Literary Theory as the Criticism of Aesthetics in the Work of Paul de Man', *Textual Practice*, 4:3 (winter 1990), pp. 349–75.

Christensen, Paul, *Charles Olson: Call Him Ishmael*. Austin: University of Texas Press, 1979.

Cixous, Hélène, 'Fiction and Its Phantoms: A Reading of Freud's *Das Unheimliche* (The "Uncanny")', *New Literary History*, 7:3 (spring 1976), pp. 525–48.

Clark, Timothy, 'French Heidegger and an English Poet: Charles Tomlinson's "Poem" and the Status of Heideggerian *Dichtung*', *Man and World: An International Philosophical Review*, Vol. 20 (1987), pp. 305–26.

Clark, Tom, *Charles Olson: The Allegory of a Poet's Life*. New York: Norton, 1991.

Coe, Michael D., *The Maya*. Harmondsworth: Penguin, 1971.

Colin, Amy D., ed., *Argumentum e Silentio: International Paul Celan Symposium*. Berlin: Walter de Gruyter, 1987.

——, *Paul Celan: Holograms of Darkness*. Bloomington: Indiana University Press, 1991.

Cook, Albert Stamborough, ed., *The Old English* Elene, Phoenix, *and* Physiologus. Hew Haven: Yale University Press, 1919.

Creeley, Robert, *The Collected Poems of Robert Creeley 1945–1975*. Berkeley: University of California Press, 1982.

Davenport, Guy, *The Geography of the Imagination: Forty Essays*. San Francisco: North Point Press, 1981.

Davie, Donald, *Thomas Hardy and British Poetry*. London: Routledge and Kegan Paul, 1973.

——, *The Poet in the Imaginary Museum: Essays of Two Decades*. Ed. Barry Alpert. Manchester: Carcanet, 1977.

——, *Studies in Ezra Pound*. Manchester: Carcanet, 1991.

de Certeau, Michel, *Heterologies: Discourse on the Other*. Trans. Brian Massumi. Manchester: Manchester University Press, 1986.

Deleuze, Gilles, and Guattari, Félix, *Anti-Oedipus: Capitalism and Schizophrenia*. Trans. Robert Hurley, Mark Seem and Helen R. Lane. Preface by Michel Foucault. New York: Viking, 1983.

de Man, Paul, *The Resistance to Theory*. Manchester: Manchester University Press, 1986.

Derrida, Jacques, 'Limited Inc. abc . . .', *Glyph* 2 (1977), pp. 162–254.

——, 'The *Retrait* of Metaphor', *Enclitic*, 2:2 (fall 1978), pp. 5–33.

——, *Writing and Difference*. Trans., with an introduction and additional notes, by Alan Bass. London: Routledge and Kegan Paul, 1978.

——, *Dissemination*. Trans. Barbara Johnson. Chicago: Chicago University Press, 1981.

——, *Of Grammatology*. Trans. Gayatry Chakravorty Spivak. Baltimore: Johns Hopkins University Press, 1984.

——, 'Devant la loi', in Alan Udoff, ed., *Kafka and the Contemporary Critical*

Performance. Bloomington: Indiana University Press, 1987.

——, 'Geschlecht II: Heidegger's Hand', in John Sallis, ed., *Deconstruction and Philosophy: The Texts of Jacques Derrida*. Chicago: University of Chicago Press, 1987.

——, *Of Spirit: Heidegger and the Question*. Trans. Geoff Bennington and Rachel Bowlby. Chicago: University of Chicago Press, 1987.

——, *The Post Card: From Socrates to Freud and Beyond*. Trans. with an introduction and additional notes by Alan Bass. Chicago: University of Chicago Press, 1987.

——, *Spectres of Marx: The State of the Debt, the Work of Mourning, and the New International*. Trans. Peggy Kamuf. London: Routledge, 1994.

Descombes, Vincent, *Modern French Philosophy*. Trans. L. Scott-Fox and J. M. Harding. Cambridge: Cambridge University Press, 1980.

——, *Proust: Philosophie du roman*. Paris: Les Editions de Minuit, 1983.

Diggins, John P., *The Bond of Savagery: Thorstein Veblen and Modern Social Theory*. Brighton: Harvester Press, 1978.

Dodds, E. R., *The Greeks and the Irrational*. Berkeley: University of California Press, 1951.

Dorn, Ed, *Views*. Ed. Donald Allen. San Francisco: Four Seasons Foundation, 1980.

Duncan, Robert, *The Opening of the Field*. New York: Grove Press, 1960.

——, *The Truth and Life of Myth: An Essay in Essential Autobiography*. Freemont, MI: The Sumac Press, 1968.

Durant, Alan, *Ezra Pound, Identity in Crisis: A Fundamental Reassessment of the Poet and His Work*. Brighton: Harvester Press, 1981.

Eliade, Mircea, *Shamanism: Archaic Techniques of Ecstasy*. Trans. Willard R. Trask. Princeton University Press, 1972.

——, *Occultism, Witchcraft, and Cultural Fashions*. Chicago: University of Chicago Press, 1976.

——, *The Myth of the Eternal Return: Cosmos and History*. Trans. Willard R. Trask. London: Arkana, 1989.

Ellingham, Lewis, and Killian, Kevin, *Poet Be Like God: Jack Spicer and the San Francisco Renaissance*. Hanover: Wesleyan University Press / University Press of New England, 1998.

Eliot, T. S., *Selected Poems*. London: Faber & Faber, 1961.

——, *Four Quarters*. London: Faber & Faber, 1964.

——, *The Waste Land: A Facsimile and Transcript of the Original Drafts*. Ed. Valerie Eliot. London: Faber & Faber, 1972.

——, *Selected Prose of T. S. Eliot*. Ed. Frank Kermode. London: Faber & Faber, 1975.

Felstiner, John, *Paul Celan: Poet, Survivor, Jew*. New Haven: Yale University Press, 1995.

Fenollosa, Ernest, *The Chinese Written Character as a Medium for Poetry*. Ed. Ezra Pound. San Francisco: City Lights Books, 1964.

Finley, M. I., *The Ancient Greeks*. Harmondsworth: Penguin Books, 1996.

Fóti, Veronique M., *Heidegger and the Poets: Poiesis / Sophia / Techne*. New Jersey: Humanities Press, 1992.

Foucault, Michel, *The Order of Things: An Archaeology of the Human Sciences*. London: Tavistock, 1974.

French, Peter, *John Dee: The World of an Elizabethan Magus*. London: Ark, 1984.

Freud, Sigmund, *The Interpretation of Dreams*. Trans. James Strachey. Ed. James Strachey and Alan Tyson. Present vol. ed. Angela Richards. The Pelican Freud Library, Vol. 4. Harmondswoth: Penguin, 1978.

——, *'Das Unheimliche'*, in *Art and Literature*. Trans. James Strachey. Present vol. ed. Albert Dickson. The Pelican Freud Library, Vol. 14. Harmondsworth: Penguin, 1985.

Gasché, Rodolphe, *The Tain of the Mirror: Derrida and the Philosophy of Reflection*. Cambridge, MA, Harvard University Press, 1986.

Geiringer, Karl (in collaboration with Irene Geiringer), *Haydn: A Creative Life in Music*. Berkeley: University of California Press, 1983.

Geyer-Ryan, Helga, *Fables of Desire: Studies in the Ethics of Art and Gender*. Cambridge and Oxford: Polity Press / Blackwell, 1994.

Gilson, Etienne, *History of Christian Philosophy in the Middle Ages*. London: Sheed and Ward, 1955.

Glenn, Jerry, *Paul Celan*. New York: Twayne Publishers, 1973.

Glover, Michael, 'Not a recluse in the pub', review of J. H. Prynne, *Poems*, *The Independent on Sunday*, 22 August 1999, p. 13.

Gourmont, Remy de, *The Natural Philosophy of Love*. Trans. Ezra Pound. New York: Rarity Press, 1991.

Grant, Michael, 'J. H. Prynne', in *The Dictionary of Literary Biography*, Vol. 40: *Poets of Great Britain and Ireland since 1960*. Part II. Detroit: Bruccoli Clark, 1985.

Graves, Robert, *The Greek Myths: Volume One*. London: Penguin Books, 1960.

Gregor, James A., *Phoenix: Fascism in Our Time*. New Brunswick: Transaction Publishers, 1999.

Gunn, Thom, *Selected Poems 1950–1975*. London: Faber & Faber, 1979.

Hamacher, Werner, 'The Second of Inversion: Movements of a Figure through Celan's Poetry', *Yale French studies*, No. 69: *The Lesson of Paul de Man*, pp. 276–311.

Harrison, Jane, *Themis: A Study of the Social Origins of Greek Religion*. London: Merlin Press, 1963.

Heidegger, Martin, *Being and Time*. Trans. John MacQuarrie and Edward Robinson. Oxford: Basil Blackwell, 1962.

——, *On the Way to Language*. Trans. Peter D. Hertz. San Francisco: Harper and Row, 1975.

——, *Poetry, Language, Thought*. Trans. Albert Hofstadter. New York: Harper and Row, 1975.

——, *The Question Concerning Technology and Other Essays*. Trans. William Lovett. New York: Harper and Row, 1977.

——, *The Basic Problems of Phenomenology*. Trans. Alfred Hofstadter. Bloomington: Indiana University Press, 1982.

——, *Early Greek Thinking: The Dawn of Western Philosophy*. Trans. David Farrell Krell and Frank A. Capuzzi. San Francisco: Harper and Row, 1984.

Henriksen, Line, 'Chiaroscuro: Canto 36 and *Donna mi prega*', *Paideuma*, Vol. 29,

No. 3 (winter 2000), pp. 33–57.

Henry, P. L., *The Early English and Celtic Lyric*. London: Allen and Unwin, 1966.

Herodotus. A New and Literal Version from the text of Baehr, with a Geographical and General Index, by Henry Cary. London: G. Bohn, 1854.

Hesse, Eva, ed., *New Approaches to Ezra Pound: A Co-ordinated Investigation of Pound's Poetry and Ideas*. London: Faber & Faber, 19969.

Hesse, Hermann, *Demian*. Trans. W. J. Strachan. London: Granada, 1979.

Hobsbawm, Eric, *Age of Extremes: The Short Twentieth Century 1914–1991*. London: Michael Joseph, 1994.

—— and Ranger, Terence, eds, *The Invention of Tradition*. Cambridge: Cambridge University Press, 1983.

Hollander, Benjamin, ed., *Translating Tradition: Paul Celan in France. Acts: A Journal of New Writing*, Nos. 8/9 (1988).

Homberger, Eric, ed., *Ezra Pound: The Critical Heritage*. London: Routledge, 1972.

Hopkins, G. S., 'Indo-European *deiwos and Related Words, *Language Dissertations Published by the Linguistic Society of America* (Supplement to *Language*), XII (1932).

Jahn, Janheinz, *Leo Frobenius: The Demonic Child*. Austin: University of Texas African and Afro-American Studies and Research Centre, 1974.

Jameson, Fredric, *Postmodernism, or, The Cultural Logic of Capitalism*. Durham: University of North Carolina Press, 1991.

Jones, Rowland, *The Circles of Gomer*. A Scolar Press Facsimile. Menston: The Scolar Press, 1970.

Jones, Tobias, *The Dark Heart of Italy: Travels Through Time and Space Across Italy*. London: Faber & Faber, 2003.

Joris, Pierre, and Buck, Paul, eds, *Matières d'Angleterre: anthologie bilingue de la nouvelle poésie anglaise*. Amiens: Trois Cailloux (Maison de la Culture d'Amiens), 1984.

Jung, C. G., *The Psychology of the Unconscious: The Evolution of Thought*. Trans. Beatrice M. Hinkle. London: Kegan Paul, Trench, Trubner and Co., 1933.

——, *A Study of the Transformations and Symbolism of the Libido. A Contribution to the History of Symbols of Transformation: An Analysis of the Prelude to a Case of Schizophrenia*. Vol. 5 of *The Collected Works of C. G. Jung*. Trans. R. F. C. Hull. London: Routledge and Kegan Paul, 1956.

——, *Alchemical Studies*. Vol. 13 of *The Collected Works of C. G. Jung*. Trans. R. F. C. Hull. London: Routledge and Kegan Paul, 1968.

——, *The Spirit in Man, Art, and Literature*. Vol. 15 of *The Collected Works of C. G. Jung*. Trans. R. F. C. Hull. Princeton: Princeton University Press, 1972.

—— and Kerényi, C., *Essays on a Science of Mythology: The Myth of the Divine Child and the Mysteries of Eleusis*. Trans. R. F. C. Hull. Princeton: Princeton University Press, 1969.

Kenner, Hugh, *The Pound Era*. Berkeley: University of California Press, 1971.

King, Angela, and Clifford, Susan, eds, *The River's Voice: An Anthology of Poetry*. Dartington: Green Books, 2000.

King, W. B. R., 'The Pleistocene Epoch in England', *The Quarterly Journal of the*

Geographical Society, CXI (1955), pp. 187–208.

Lacan, Jacques, *The Four Fundamental Concepts of Psychoanalysis*. Trans. Alan Sheridan. New York: Norton, 1978.

——, *The Seminar of Jacques Lacan. Book I: Freud's Papers on Technique 1953–1956*. Ed. Jacques-Alain Miller. Trans. with notes by John Forrester. Cambridge: Cambridge University Press, 1988.

Lachman, Gary, *Turn Off Your Mind: The Mystic Sixties and the Dark Side of the Age of Aquarius*. London: Sidgwick and Jackson, 2001.

Lacoue-Labarthe, Philippe, *Heidegger, Art, and Politics: The Fiction of the Political*. Trans. Chris Turner. Oxford: Basil Blackwell, 1990.

—— and Nancy, Jean-Luc, 'The Nazi Myth', *Critical Inquiry*, 16 (winter 1990), pp. 291–312.

Larrington, Carolyne, ed., *The Feminist Companion to Mythology*. London: Pandora Press, 1992.

Lawrence, D. H., *Birds, Beasts and Flowers*. London: Martin Secker, 1931.

Lawson, Andrew, 'Basil Bunting and English Modernism', *Sagetrieb*, Vol. 9:1/2 (spring and fall, 1990), pp. 95–119.

Levenson, Michael, ed., *The Cambridge Companion to Modernism*. Cambridge: Cambridge University Press, 1999.

Levinas, Emmanuel, *Collected Philosophical Papers*. Dordrecht: Martinus Nijhoff, 1987.

Lewis, I. M., *Ecstatic Religion: An Anthropological Study of Spirit Possession and Shamanism*. Harmondsworth: Penguin, 1971.

Lewis, Wyndham, *Wyndham Lewis on Art: Collected Writings 1913–1956*. Ed. Walter Michel and C. J. Fox. London: Thames and Hudson, 1969.

Longenbach, James, *Modernist Poetics of History: Pound, Eliot, and the Sense of the Past*. Princeton: Princeton University Press, 1987.

——, *Stone Cottage: Pound, Yeats, and Modernism*. New York: Oxford University Press, 1988.

Luck, George, *Arcana Mundi: Magic and the Occult in the Greek and Roman Worlds*. UK: Crucible, 1987.

Lukacs, Georg, *The Destruction of Reason*. Trans. Peter Palmer. London: The Merlin Press, 1980.

Makin, Peter, *Provence and Pound*. Berkeley: University of California Press, 1978.

——, *Pound's Cantos*. London: George Allen and Unwin, 1985.

Marriott, D. S., 'Contemporary British Poetry and Resistance: Reading J. H. Prynne', *Parataxis: Modernism and Modern Writing*, 8/9 (1996), pp. 159–74.

Marx, Karl, *Grundrisse: Foundations of the Critique of Political Economy*. Trans. Martin Nicolaus. Harmondsworth: Penguin, 1973.

Maud, Ralph, *Charles Olson's Reading: A Biography*. Carbondale: Southern Illinois University Press, 1996.

McCaffery, Steve, *North of Intention: Critical Writings 1973–1986*. New York and Toronto: Roof Nightwood Editions, 1986.

McEvoy, James, *The Philosophy of Robert Grosseteste*. Oxford: Clarendon Press, 1982.

McGann, Jerome J., *The Romantic Ideology: A Critical Investigation*. Chicago: University of Chicago Press, 1983.

McGauley, Tom, 'Prynne's Simon Fraser Lecture', in *Minutes of the Charles Olson Society*, No. 28 (April 1999), p. 3.

McKeon, Richard, trans., *Selections from Medieval Philosophers, Vol. II: Roger Bacon to William of Ockham*. New York: Scribner's, 1930.

Megill, Allan, *Prophets of Extremity: Nietzsche, Heidegger, Foucault, Derrida*. Berkeley: University of California Press, 1985.

Mellors, Anthony, 'Toy of Thought: Prynne and the Dialectics of Reading', *Salt* 11: In the Mix: International Regionalism and Hypermodernism 1 (1999), pp. 55–68.

—— and Smith, Robert, eds, *Poets on the Verge. Angelaki: Journal of the Theoretical Humanities*, Vol. 5, No. 1 (April 2000).

Mengham, Rod, 'A Lifelong Transfusion: *The Oval Window* of J. H. Prynne', *The Grosseteste Review*, Vol. 15 (1983–84), pp. 205–9.

Merrill, *The Poetry of Charles Olson*. Newark: University of Delaware Press, 1982.

Miller, James E., Jr, *The American Quest for a Supreme Fiction*. Cambridge: Cambridge University Press, 1979.

Miller, J. Hillis, *Topographies*. Stanford: Stanford University Press, 1995.

Miller, Tyrus, *Late Modernism: Politics, Fiction, and the Arts Between the World Wars*. Berkeley: University of California Press, 1999.

Moorjani, Angela, *The Aesthetics of Loss and Lessness*. London: Macmillan, 1992.

Mylonas, George E., *Eleusis and the Eleusinian Mysteries*. Princeton: Princeton University Press. 1961.

Nägele, Rainer, *Reading After Freud: Essays on Goethe, Hölderlin, Habermas, Nietzsche, Brecht, Celan, and Freud*. New York: Columbia University Press, 1987.

Nicholls, Peter, *Ezra Pound: Politics, Economics, and Writing*. London: Macmillan, 1984.

——, *Modernisms: A Literary Guide*. London: Macmillan, 1995.

Noll, Richard, *The Jung Cult: Origins of a Charismatic Movement*. London: Fontana, 1996.

O'Hara, Frank, *The Collected Poems of Frank O'Hara*. Ed. Donald Allen, with an introduction by John Ashbery. Berkeley: University of California Press, 1995.

Olson, Charles, *Call Me Ishmael* (New York: Grove Press, 1947), 11.

——, *Projective Verse*. New York: Totem Press, 1959.

——, *The Distances* New York: Grove Press, 1960.

——, *The Maximus Poems*. London: Cape Goliard Press, 1960.

——, *Human Universe and Other Essays*. Ed. Donald Allen. New York: Grove Press, 1967.

——, *Mayan Letters*. London: Jonathan Cape, 1968.

——, *The Maximus Poems IV, V, VI*. London: Cape Goliard Press, 1968.

——, *Additional Prose: A Bibliography on America, Proprioception, and Other Notes and Essays*. Ed. George Butterick. Bolinas: Four Seasons Foundation, 1974.

——, *Muthologos: The Collected Lectures and Interviews*. Ed. George Butterick. 2 Vols. Bolinas: Four Seasons Foundation, 1978.

——, *The Collected Poems of Charles Olson*. Ed. George Butterick. Berkeley: University of California Press, 1987.

——, *Collected Prose*. Ed. Donald Allen and Benjamin Friedlander. Berkeley: University of California Press, 1997.

Parke, H. W., and Wormell, D. E. W., *The Delphic Oracle*. Oxford: Oxford University Press, 1956.

[Parody of J. H. Prynne, *Down Where Changed*], *Quarto*, No. 9, August 1980, p. 1.

Pater, Walter, *Marius the Epicurean: His Sensations and Ideas*. London: Macmillan, 1927.

Paul, Sherman, *Olson's Push: Origin, Black Mountain, and Recent American Poetry*. Baton Rouge: Louisiana State University Press, 1978.

Perloff, Marjorie, *The Dance of the Intellect: Studies in the Poetry of the Pound Tradition*. Cambridge: Cambridge University Press, 1987.

Phillips, E. D., 'The Legend of Aristeas: Fact and Fancy in Early Greek Notions of East Russia, Siberia, and Inner Asia', *Artibus Asiae*, XVIII, 2 (1955), pp. 161–77.

Plotinus, *The Enneads*. Trans. Stephen MacKenna. London: Faber & Faber, 1956.

Poetry Otherwise: Shaping a Language for the New Millennium. Flyer for a summer school at Emerson College, Sussex, 16–22 July 2000.

Pound, Ezra, 'Pastiche. The Regional', in *The New Age*, Vol. XXV, No. 17 (21 August 1919), p. 284.

——, *The Selected Letters of Ezra Pound 1907–1941*. Ed. D. D. Paige. London: Faber & Faber, 1950.

——, *The Spirit of Romance*. New York: New Directions, 1952.

——, *ABC of Reading*. London: Faber & Faber, 1961.

——, *The Cantos of Ezra Pound*. London: Faber & Faber, 1964.

——, *Guide to Kulchur*. New York: New Directions, 1968.

——, *Literary Essays of Ezra Pound*. Ed. T. S. Eliot. London: Faber & Faber, 1968.

——, *Gaudier-Brzeska: A Memoir*. New York: New Directions, 1970.

——, *Jefferson and/or Mussolini*. New York: Liveright, 1970.

——, *Selected Prose: 1909–1965*. Ed. with an Introduction by William Cookson. New York: New Directions, 1973.

——, *Collected Early Poems*. London: Faber & Faber, 1977.

——, *Selected Poems 1908–1959*. London: Faber & Faber, 1977.

——, *Ezra Pound and Dorothy Shakespeare: Their Letters 1909–1914*. Ed. Omar Pound and A. Walton Litz. New York: New Directions, 1984.

Prynne, J. H., '"Modernism" in German Poetry', *The Cambridge Review*, 9 March 1963, pp. 331–7.

——, 'A Pedantic Note in Two Parts', in *The English Intelligencer*, Series 2, Part I (1966/67), pp. 346–51.

——, *Day Light Songs*. Pampisford: R. Books, 1968.

——, 'Review of *Maximus IV, V, VI*', *The Park*, Nos. 4/5 (1969), pp. 65–7.

——, *The White Stones*. Lincoln: Grosseteste Press, 1969.

——, *Fire Lizard*. Barnet: Blacksuede Boot Press, 1970.

——, *A Night Square*. London: Albion Village Press, 1971.

——, 'On *Maximus IV, V, & VI*: A Lecture Given at Simon Fraser University on July 27th, 1971.' Transcribed by Tom McGauley, in *Serious Iron* (Iron 12), 1971, unnumbered pages.

——, *Into the Day*. Cambridge: privately printed, 1972.

——, 'Es Lebe der König', in *The Literally Supplement*, Writings, I. London: Nothing Doing (Formerly in London), 1973.

——, 'From a Letter to Douglas Oliver', in *The Grosseteste Review*, Vol. 6, Nos. 1–4 (1973), pp. 152–4.

——, *Wound Response*. Cambridge: Street Editions, 1974.

——, *Vernal Aspects*, in *The Grosseteste Review*, Vol. 10, 1–4 (summer 1977), pp. 37–40.

——, *Poems*. Edinburgh and London: Agneau 2, 1982.

——, 'A Letter to Andrew Duncan', *The Grosseteste Review*, Vol. 15 (1983–84), pp. 100–18.

——, 'English Poetry and Emphatical Language', *Proceedings of the British Academy*, Vol. LXXIV (1988), pp. 135–69.

——, *Poems*. Fremantle, Western Australia, and Newcastle-upon-Tyne: Fremantle Arts Centre Press / Bloodaxe, 1999.

Rabaté, Jean-Michel, *Language, Sexuality, and Ideology in Ezra Pound's* Cantos. London: Macmillan, 1986.

Rainey, Lawrence, *Institutions of Modernism: Literary Elites and Public Culture*. New Haven: Yale University Press, 1998.

Redman, Tim, *Ezra Pound and Italian Fascism*. Cambridge: Cambridge University Press, 1991.

Reeve, N. H., and Kerridge, Richard, *Nearly Too Much: The Poetry of J. H. Prynne*. Liverpool: Liverpool University Press, 1995.

Renfrew, Colin, *Archaeology and Language: The Puzzle of Indo-European Origins*. London: Jonathan Cape, 1987.

Riddel, Joseph, 'Decentring the Image: The "Project" of "American" Poetics?', in Josué V. Harari, ed., *Textual Strategies: Perspectives in Poststructuralist Criticism*. London: Methuen, 1980.

Riffaterre, Michael, *Semiotics of Poetry*. Ithaca: Indiana University Press, 1978.

Riley, Denise, 'A Set of Seven', *fragmente: a magazine of contemporary poetics*, 4 (autumn/winter 1991), pp. 14–17.

Roberts, Julian, *Walter Benjamin*. London: Macmillan, 1982.

Ronell, Avital, *The Telephone Book: Technology, Schizophrenia, Electric Speech*. Lincoln and London: University of Nebraska Press, 1989.

Ross, Andrew, *The Failure of Modernism: Symptoms of American Poetry*. New York: Columbia University Press, 1986.

——, 'The Oxygen of Publicity', *Poetics Journal*, No. 6 (1986), pp. 62–71.

Rothenberg, Jerome, and Rothenberg, Diane, *Symposium of the Whole: A Range of Discourse Towards an Ethnopoetics*. Berkeley: University of California Press, 1983.

—— and Joris, Pierre, *Poems for the Millennium: The University of California Press Book of Modern and Postmodern Poetry. Vol. 2: From Postwar to Millennium*. Berkeley: University of California Press, 1998.

Said, Edward, 'The World, the Text, and the Critic', in Josué V. Harari, ed., *Textual Strategies: Perspectives in Poststructuralist Criticism*. London: Methuen, 1980.

——, *Orientalism*. London: Penguin, 1985.

Sauer, C. O., *Land and Life: A Selection from the Writings of Carl Ortwin Sauer*. Berkey: University of California Press, 1983.

Saussure, Ferdinand de, *Course in General Linguistics*. Ed. Charles Bally and Alber Sechehaye with the collaboration of Albert Riedlinger. Trans. and annotated by Roy Harris. London: Duckworth, 1983.

Selerie, Gavin, *To Let Words Swim into the Soul: An Anniversary Tribute to the Art of Charles Olson*. London: 1980.

Shaw, J. E., *Cavalcanti's Theory of Love: The Canzone d'Amore and Other Related Problems*. Toronto: University of Toronto Press, 1949.

Sidney, [Sir Philip], *A Defence of Poetry*. Ed. Jan van Dorsten. Oxford: Oxford University Press, 1986.

Sieburth, Richard, *Instigations: Ezra Pound and Remy de Gourmont*. Cambridge, MA; Harvard University Press, 1978.

Simpson, David, *Romanticism, Nationalism, and the Revolt Against Theory*. Chicago: University of Chicago Press, 1993.

Sinclair, Iain, *The Shamanism of Intent: Some Flights of Redemption*. Uppingham, Rutland: Goldmark, 1991.

—— ed., *Conductors of Chaos*. London: Paladin, 1996.

Smith, Neil, *Uneven development: Nature, capital, and the Production of Space*. Oxford: Basil Blackwell, 1984.

Smith, Paul, *Pound Revised*. London: Croom Helm, 1983.

Spicer, Jack, *The House that Jack Built: The Collected Lectures of Jack Spicer*. Ed. Peter Gizzi. Hanover: Wesleyan University Press / University Press of New England, 1998.

Spiegelberg, Harbert, *The Phenomenological Movement: An Historical Introduction*. The Hague: Martinus Nijhoff, 1969.

Surette, Leon, *A Light from Eleusis: A Study of the Cantos of Ezra Pound*. Oxford: Clarendon Press, 1979.

——, *The Birth of Modernism: Ezra Pound, T. S. Eliot, W. B. Yeats, and the Occult*. Montreal: McGill-Queen's University Press, 1993.

Swinburne, Algernon Charles, *Poems and Ballads and Atalanta in Calydon*. Ed. Kenneth Hayes. London: Penguin, 2001.

Sword, Helen, *Ghostwriting Modernism*. Ithaca: Cornell University Press, 2002.

Taussig, Michael, *Shamanism, Colonialism, and the Wild Man: A Study in Terror and Healing*. Chicago: University of Chicago Press, 1987.

Taylor, Richard, and Melchior, Claus, eds, *Ezra Pound and Europe*. Amsterdam: Rodopi, 1993.

Tennyson, Alfred Lord, *The Poems of Tennyson*. Ed. Christopher Ricks. London: Longman's, 1969.

Terrell, Carroll F., *A Companion to* The Cantos *of Ezra Pound*. Berkeley: University of California Press, 1993.

Tomlinson, Charles, 'Experience into Music: The Poetry of Basil Bunting', *Agenda*, Vol. 4, Nos. 5–6 (1966), pp. 11–16.

Torrey, E. Fuller, *The Roots of Treason: Ezra Pound and the Secrets of St Elizabeth's*. London: Sidgwick and Jackson, 1984.

Trotter, David, 'A Reading of Prynne's *Brass*', in *P. N. Review*, Vol. 5, No. 2 (1977), p. 51.

——, *The Making of the Reader: Language and Subjectivity in Modern American, English and Irish Poetry*. London: Macmillan, 1986.

Tryphonopoulos, Demetres P., *the Celestial Tradition: A Study of Ezra Pound's* Cantos. Waterloo: Wilfrid Laurier University Press, 1992.

Turner, Victor, *The Ritual Process*. Harmondsworth: Penguin, 1974.

van der Post, Laurens, *Jung and the Story of Our Time*. Harmondsworth: Penguin, 1978.

Veblen, Thorstein, *Absentee Ownership and Business Enterprise in Recent Times: The Case of America*. New York: Augustus M. Kelley, 1964.

Vickers, Brian, ed., *Occult and Scientific Mentalities in the Renaissance*. Cambridge: Cambridge University Press, 1984.

Vickery, John B., *The Literary Impact of* The Golden Bough. Princeton: Princeton University Press, 1973.

von Hallberg, Robert, *Charles Olson: The Scholar's Art*. Cambridge, MA: Harvard University Press, 1978.

Wallis, Brian, ed., *Art after Modernism: Rethinking Representation*, New York: New Museum of Contemporary Art, 1984.

Ward, Geoffrey, 'Nothing But Mortality: Prynne and Celan', in Antony Easthope and John O. Thompson, eds, *Contemporary Poetry Meets Modern Theory*. London: Harvester Wheatsheaf, 1991.

Weber, Samuel, 'The Sideshow, or: Remarks on a Canny Moment', *Modern Language Notes*, Vol. 88, No. 6 (1973), pp. 1102–33.

West, M. I., *The Orphic Poems*. Oxford: Clarendon Press, 1983.

Wheale, Nigel, 'J. H. Prynne', in James Vinson and d. Kirkpatrick, *Contemporary Poets*. London: St James Press, 1985, 679–80.

Whorf, Benjamin Lee, *Language, Thought, and Reality: Selected Writings of Benjamin Lee Whorf*. Ed. with an introduction by John B. Carroll. Cambridge, MA, MIT Press, 1971.

Wilde, Alan, *Horizons of Assent: Modernism, Postmodernism, and the Ironic Imagination*. Baltimore: Johns Hopkins University Press, 1981.

Wimsatt, W. K., and Beardsley, Monroe, *The Verbal Icon: Studies in the Meaning of Poetry*. New York: Noonday Press, 1954.

Wordsworth, William, Letter to John Wilson, 7 June 1807, in *The Letters of William and Dorothy Wordsworth*, Vol. I: The Early Years 1787–1895. Arr. and ed. by Ernest de Selincourt, revised by Chester L. Shaver. Oxford: Clarendon Press, 1967.

Wright, Elizabeth, *Psychoanalytic Criticism: Theory in Practice*. London: Methuen, 1984.

Yates, Frances A., *Giordano Bruno and the Hermetic Tradition*. London: Routledge and Kegan Paul, 1964.

Yeats, W. B., *Collected Poems*. London: Macmillan, 1950.

Young, Neil, and Crazy Horse, *Zuma*. Warner Brothers Records, 1975.

Žižek, Slavoj, *The Sublime Object of Ideology*. London: Verso, 1989.

INDEX

Note: 'n.' after a page reference indicates the number of a note on that page.